Teaching Sociology Successfully

Teaching Sociology Successfully is a comprehensive guide to teaching and learning sociology confidently and successfully. Carefully combining insightful anecdotes and practical ideas with key theoretical concepts on planning, learning styles and assessment, this book is an essential tool for both new and experienced teachers of sociology. Each chapter focuses on a particular aspect of the teaching and learning process – from preparing to teach the subject for the first time to measuring student progress over time – in an approachable yet rigorous way.

This practical guide will help you to:

- improve your knowledge of specifications and syllabuses at GCSE and AS/A Level;
- provide the best pedagogic approaches for teaching sociology;
- think about learning styles, skills and capacities in relation to teaching sociology;
- gain practical ideas and activities for improving student's argumentation, evaluation and essay writing skills;
- apply strategies for teaching abstract sociological theories and concepts;
- make the teaching of research methods engaging and interesting;
- deal with practical issues such as planning and assessing learning;
- encourage students' independent learning and revision;
- connect ICT, social networking websites and the mass media to further students' sociological knowledge;
- tackle the thorny issues of politics and controversial topics.

Drawing on the author's own experiences, *Teaching Sociology Successfully* helps readers to identify, unpack and negotiate challenges common to those teaching sociology. Complete with a variety of pedagogical resources, it provides tasks and further reading to support CPD and reflective practice. This book will be an invaluable tool for students on PGCE social science training courses, as well as School Direct candidates and undergraduates studying BEds in similar fields.

Andrew B. Jones is Assistant Head Teacher for CPD and Professional Mentoring at The Reach Free School, Hertfordshire, UK. Previously he was Head of Religious Education and Sociology, and Lead Practitioner for Teaching and Learning at Goffs School, Hertfordshire. He has also been a Specialist Leader of Education with the West Hertfordshire Teaching Schools Partnership, a Teacher Advisor ⎓⎓⎓⎓ has written for the *Guardian* and *Huffington Post* on various ⎓⎓⎓ ion.

TEACHING SOCIOLOGY SUCCESSFULLY

A Practical Guide to Planning and Delivering Outstanding Lessons

Andrew B. Jones

Routledge
Taylor & Francis Group

LONDON AND NEW YORK

First published 2017
by Routledge
2 Park Square, Milton Park, Abingdon, Oxon OX14 4RN

and by Routledge
711 Third Avenue, New York, NY 10017

Routledge is an imprint of the Taylor & Francis Group, an informa business

British Library Cataloguing in Publication Data
A catalogue record for this book is available from the British Library

Library of Congress Cataloging in Publication Data
Names: Jones, Andrew B., author.
Title: Teaching sociology successfully : a practical guide to planning and
delivering outstanding lessons / Andrew B. Jones.
Description: 1 Edition. | New York : Routledge, 2017.
Identifiers: LCCN 2016050176| ISBN 9781138190009 (hardback) | ISBN
9781138190016 (pbk.) | ISBN 9781315641317 (ebook)
Subjects: LCSH: Social sciences–Study and teaching.
Classification: LCC H62 .J596 2017 | DDC 301.071–dc23
LC record available at https://lccn.loc.gov/2016050176

ISBN: 978-1-138-19000-9 (hbk)
ISBN: 978-1-138-19001-6 (pbk)
ISBN: 978-1-315-64131-7 (ebk)

Typeset in News Gothic
by Saxon Graphics Ltd, Derby

In memory of Joan Doris Jones

Contents

Figures

Tables

Tasks

Acknowledgements

I am first and foremost indebted to Dr. Denise Jackson whose comments on my initial drafts and advice on sociology has been invaluable. I would also like to acknowledge Dr. Alex Grainger, Tom Cahill, Daniel Chichester-Miles, Nigel Appleyard, Ben Pearce and various colleagues at Goffs School who read and commented upon drafts of this book. Additionally, I would like to thank Pam Hook and Geraldine Stone for reading my text on SOLO taxonomy and giving me permission to reproduce the SOLO taxonomy symbols. Similarly, I am thankful to Ross Morrison McGill (a.k.a @TeacherToolkit) for his advice on, and permission to use, his 5-minute lesson plan template. I am also grateful to Clare Ashworth for inviting me to write this book and Sarah Tuckwell and Christopher Byrne for their advice on writing it. In addition to the people named, there are so many people that I have briefly corresponded with to check things and I appreciate their time and responses. I should also acknowledge the wonderful students at Goffs School who have been unwitting guinea pigs over the last 5 years as I experimented with various learning activities in class. Lastly, I would like to thank Kunyee and Anand for letting me get on and write in the evenings.

I would also like to acknowledge WJEC for granting me permission to use the mark scheme reprinted in Chapter 10 (Figure 10.2). Also, the Office of National Statistics (ONS) charts in Chapter 8 are reprinted under the Open Government Licence v3.0 (see Figures 8.1 and 8.2).

1 Why teach sociology?

'Philosophers have only interpreted the world, in various ways; the point is to change it.'

Karl Marx, Theses on Feuerbach: Thesis 11 (1845)

'I get Karl Marx. I think I'm a Marxist. Russell Brand is a Marxist, isn't he? I read his book called *Revolution* and he agreed with all this.'

Molly – a Year 12 Sociology student

This chapter includes:

- Teaching sociology in schools and colleges: the mammoth, but rewarding challenge facing teachers.
- The purpose of teaching sociology: towards a *modus operandi*, including:
  - The importance of specialist skills;
  - The importance of social solidarity;
  - Why school is a mini-society preparing tomorrow's citizens.
- Scope of this book: an outline of each chapter that follows this introduction.

Teaching sociology in schools and colleges

Teaching sociology is a brave thing to do. It is a huge subject that covers, amongst other things, identity, culture, families, education, healthcare, social class, stratification, politics and crime. In fact, like many subjects, the vast array of topic areas can be mind-boggling at first and where to start can seem like standing at an entrance to a gigantic and foreboding maze. However, finding your way around this maze will be one of the most rewarding things you ever do as sociology is an absolutely fascinating subject. In fact, sociology uncovers the human world that both you and your students inhabit. It seeks to explain our relationships at home with family, amongst friends at school and even with each other in the classroom as well as examining the social norms and shared values that shape those relationships. Moreover, sociology not only explores society's origins, development, organisation and institutions, but also unpacks, evaluates and considers possible solutions to society's problems; these problems may include gender inequality, knife crime and unhealthy lifestyles, for example. As the sociologist Anthony Giddens (1987) has pointed out, social research conducted by trained sociologists in government agencies, universities and interest groups has had an enormous influence on the running of modern society, especially as their findings will often be presented to policy makers making decisions that affect us all (p. 5).

Of course, in addition to explaining how society works, sociology also seeks to evaluate competing claims on how society is ordered. One of the ironies of teaching sociology is that we are entertaining the pessimistic notion that students have been born into a world of stratified social structures, powerful institutions and dominant ideologies where their opinions do not count whilst at the same time arguing optimistically that they can work hard and climb a meritocratic ladder to achieve a higher status in life. We are also teaching, on the one hand, that a student's gender impacts on everything from their choices of General Certificate of Secondary Education (GCSE) and Advanced Subsidiary Level and Advanced Level (AS/A Level) subjects to their future earning power, whilst also suggesting, on the other hand, that these differences allow society to function in a more cohesive way. This subject of arguments and counter-arguments may seem confusing and baffling to ourselves, let alone our students. It does, nonetheless, represent the uncertain terrain of the social and political world that our students will have to make sense of at some stage in their lives and we should, therefore, give them every chance of making sense of it as possible. If taught successfully, sociology's importance cannot be underestimated – it can teach students the world and, hopefully, motivate them to be interested and engaged with it.

The purpose of teaching sociology: towards a '*modus operandi*'

Despite establishing the importance of sociology in itself, it remains to be said how sociology can be applied as an academic subject in schools and colleges, especially simplifying what it hopes to achieve. Perhaps it is now time to start learning from the sociologists themselves. Helpfully, it was one of the founding fathers of sociology, the French sociologist Emile Durkheim (1956), who said that education has two main functions, namely: to teach 'specialist skills' and to teach 'social solidarity'. He also said that schools are mini-societies that socialise children in preparation for adulthood. Although I do not claim to be a 'functionalist' (this is the theoretical school that Durkheim is associated with), I would argue that sociology in schools and colleges can in some ways fulfil these purposes.[1]

Firstly, the *specialist skills* that students develop through studying sociology will enable them to explain different opinions and positions on how society should be studied, interpreted and ordered. In turn, this allows students to evaluate the strengths and weaknesses of these arguments before assessing their impact on ourselves and others. These skills will then equip students with the critical thinking skills needed to see whether particular sociological perspectives are applicable to the world they know. Moreover, these skills can also be used to assess whether sociological perspectives can be used to formulate potential social policies. Therefore, it is self-evident that these specialist skills are not only useful for careers in public life, public office or academia, but will also facilitate better argumentation, articulation and debating skills that will be applicable in a whole host of other curriculum subjects.

Secondly, another aspect of sociology is looking at how we as well as other people live, behave and are affected by political decisions – this can create a sense of common purpose or shared values. Subsequently, students may be compelled to participate in public life through a realisation of *social solidarity* with others. Although social solidarity is a functionalist concept, alternative theories can come into play here. For instance, social action theory encourages students to practice *erklärendes Verstehen*, or 'empathetic understanding', towards others by putting themselves in 'their shoes' (Walker, 2013). Here, students can explore how other people feel about issues such as child poverty, violent crime and family diversity and this can lead to a more insightful understanding of why people may have different views. As a consequence, students may empathise with others and feel more concerned for their welfare and well-being. They may see that other social groups that are uncommon to them share many of their norms, values and goals in life.

And lastly, our students occasionally fall out, disagree and have arguments with each other and it is only by sitting them down and exploring their differences that they can be reconciled through dialogue and understanding. This last point mirrors the social world of adults that the students are moving into. We adults disagree on everything from the role of prisons to the right level of immigration, but we also need to have a dialogue with each other if we are to reconcile these differences. In this sense, the social world of our students share some of the conflicting characteristics of our adult world. Thus, Durkheim believed that schools act as microcosms of the real world in that they are *mini-societies* in which students learn to disagree, make up and move on together. Furthermore, by teaching students sociology, we are arguably giving them the experience and skills to better understand the wider society they are about to enter. The differing perspectives taught, discussed and debated in sociology will relate to the conflicting views found at all levels of social life; from opinions on gay marriage to views on welfare spending. These disagreements can often be controversial and become quite heated, but by better understanding each other's perspectives on these issues, we are more likely to come up with practical solutions to common social issues.

Therefore, the *modus operandi* of this book is to build up your knowledge, skills and confidence as a sociology teacher in order to deliver a subject that will give students the specialist skills of explanation and evaluation, a view of the world that will motivate them to be part of it and, at the very least, the knowledge that the social world of adults can be just as exciting, fulfilling and, if honest, as complicated as the teenage world they currently inhabit.

Scope of this book

This book consists of 13 chapters. They cover a host of ideas that are needed to both teach sociology successfully and to be an outstanding practitioner. The first 5 chapters are mostly focused on improving your knowledge of the typical sociology syllabus as well as the best pedagogic approaches to teaching the subject. Chapters 7 to 13, however, deal with more practical issues, such as planning and assessment. A brief outline is given below.

Chapter 2 gives an overview of the current state of sociology in schools in England and Wales. It includes a look at the way sociology is assessed at key stages 4 and 5 as well as what most specifications/syllabuses at GCSE and AS/A Level include. Chapter 3 looks at sociological pedagogies and examines whether we can apply sociological perspectives to our teaching, especially reflectively. It looks at functionalism, critical pedagogy (Marxism), social action theories, feminism and postmodernism. Following on from this, Chapters 4 and 5 look at common ideas in education, especially in terms of learning styles and teaching styles and assesses how these can be of use in the sociology classroom.

Chapters 6, 7 and 8 look at teaching sociological skills, theories and research methods respectively. Chapter 6 considers practical teaching ideas that can be used throughout lessons to help teach skills such as argumentation and evaluation as well as test students' knowledge of key words. The chapter also includes plenty of activities that you can use in your own classroom. Chapter 7 uses additional theoretical and practical ideas, such as concept mapping and SOLO taxonomy, to demonstrate how best to teach complicated concepts and theories whereas Chapter 8 focuses on making the rather dry subject of research methods more active and fun.

Chapters 9 and 10 outline effective planning and assessment ideas for teaching sociology successfully. A lot of the ideas are tried and tested in other subjects, but in these chapters we look at their practical application to sociology.

Chapters 11 and 12 consider practical ways in which to get students engaged with sociology and learning away from the classroom. Chapter 11, for example, centres on nurturing students' independent learning skills and then moves on to revision tips. Chapter 12 then looks at how you can harness ICT, social networking websites and the mass media to further your students' sociological knowledge.

Lastly, Chapter 13 discusses the thorny issue of politics in sociology. This can be a difficult area in school as many sociological perspectives underpin political ideologies and students may ask for your opinions. Not only does this unduly influence your students, but it can raise questions concerning the political bias of teachers. The chapter also covers how to cover controversial issues, especially as most of the sociological syllabuses on offer include sensitive issues, such as divorce and 'family breakdown'. Chapter 13 is followed by a few 'last words' summing up the importance of the subject.

Please note that I have occasionally used *italics* to denote keywords. Generally, this is on the first time of using them in parts of the text where they are being specifically discussed; otherwise they are not italicised. I have also used italics for book titles, unit/scheme of work titles and words taken from languages other than English. They are sometimes used to add emphasis, too.

Further reading

Abercrombie, N. (2004). *Sociology: A short introduction.* **Cambridge: Polity.**
Abercrombie's introduction centres on the sociology of everyday life and does not expect the reader to be well versed in sociological vocabulary, concepts and theories. It is a largely jargon free primer on key sociological issues.

Fevre, R. & Bancroft, A. (2010). *Dead white men and other important people.* **Basingstoke: Palgrave Macmillan.**
This introduction to sociology is based on the experiences of an undergraduate studying the subject in the first year of her sociology degree. It covers key ideas and perspectives, but is written as a novel.

Giddens, A. & Sutton, P. W. (2012). *Sociology* **(7th ed.). Cambridge: Polity.**
This is an excellent reference book on the key themes and perspectives found in sociology, which includes examples of key studies and research methods. This is a textbook aimed at undergraduates and AS/A Level students, but is a helpful reference for any teacher of sociology.

Berger, P. L. (1999). *Invitation to sociology.* **New York: Anchor Books.**

Mills, C. Wright (1959). *The sociological imagination.* **New York: Oxford University Press.**

Bauman, Z. & May, T. (2001). *Thinking sociologically* **(2nd ed.). Oxford: Blackwell.**

All three of these books are recommended as good introductions to sociology. Anyone really interested in fully comprehending the subject may choose to read them in addition to those books suggested above. *The Sociological Imagination* in discussed in depth in Chapter 3.

Note

1   For a contemporary look at the relevance of Durkheim's concept of 'specialist skills', see Young, M. and Miller, J. (2015), *Curriculum and the specialization of knowledge: Studies in the sociology of education*, London: Routledge.

Bibliography

Abercrombie, N. (2004). *Sociology: A short introduction*. Cambridge: Polity.

Bauman, Z. & May, T. (2001). *Thinking sociologically* (2nd ed.). Oxford: Blackwell.

Berger, P. L. (1999). *Invitation to sociology*. New York: Anchor Books.

Durkheim, E. (1956). *Education and sociology*. New York: Free Press.

Fevre, R. & Bancroft, A. (2010). *Dead white men and other important people*. Basingstoke: Palgrave Macmillan.

Giddens, A. (1987). *Social theory and modern sociology*. Cambridge: Cambridge University Press.

Giddens, A. & Sutton, P. W. (2012). *Sociology* (7th ed.). Cambridge: Polity.

Marx, K. (1845). *Theses on Feuerbach*. Retrieved May 28, 2015, from https://www.marxists.org/archive/marx/works/1845/theses/index.htm

Walker, H. J. (2013). *A mile in my shoes: A prolegomenon for an empathetic sociology*. (Electronic Thesis and Dissertation Repository, Paper 1292). Retrieved from http://ir.lib.uwo.ca/etd/1292/

Mills, C. Wright (1959). *The sociological imagination*. New York: Oxford University Press.

Young, M. & Miller, J. (2015). *Curriculum and the specialization of knowledge: Studies in the sociology of education*. London: Routledge.

2 Sociology in schools

This chapter includes:

- What does sociology at GCSE and AS/A Level look like? Including:
  - a discussion on assessment objectives at both GCSE and AS/A Level;
  - the importance of knowledge and understanding;
  - the essential skills of selection, interpretation and application;
  - and the significance of analysis and evaluation skills.
- What are the common themes at GCSE?
- What are the common themes at AS and A Level?
- Some advice on choosing a syllabus.

As stated in the introduction, sociology looks at society's origins, development, organisation and institutions in order to gain an insight into its workings as well as consider and evaluate possible solutions to its problems. Of course, the breadth and range of sociological topics is immense, but in schools and colleges the subject has to be narrowed down in order to fit it into the wider curriculum and to complete courses within the key stages. Therefore, in this chapter, we will look at how sociology fits into the curriculum in England and Wales, what is commonly taught and what you should consider when choosing a GCSE or AS/A Level syllabus for your students.

Sociology as a GCSE and AS/A Level

As sociology is not part of the National Curriculum, you will undoubtedly be teaching GCSE or AS/A Level sociology in your school or college. This means you will have to familiarise yourself with the specifications for the syllabuses on offer from the various exam awarding bodies (exam boards) and consider which topic areas you feel you are best equipped to teach.[1] In addition to this it is vital that you consider what will most appeal to the students in your school or college. If you are starting up a sociology department or considering switching exam boards, it is worth canvassing the views of colleagues and students to see what they would most like to teach or study. In my school, I was initially keen to introduce units on *religion and belief* and *power and politics*, but the students had a preference for the *mass media* and *crime and deviance*.

In terms of syllabus content most exam boards have very similar, almost identical, assessment objectives and topics for study. A new programme of study for GCSE courses was brought in by exam boards in 2014 and fresh guidance was issued in 2016 for teaching from 2017 onwards (see Department for Education, 2016) and A Level courses have all been revised as recently as 2015 (see Department for Education, 2014); this is why I am referring to AS and A Level as opposed to AS and A2. Nonetheless, these changes have not really impacted the key assessment objectives and topic areas and any future changes are unlikely to be radically different. Therefore, we can identify and discuss the common skills (by way of assessment objectives), themes and perspectives found in most exam syllabuses quite easily.

Task 2.1 Review exam board specifications

It is essential that you thoroughly know and understand the syllabus specifications at both GCSE and AS/A Level. It is well worth printing out all of the specifications from the different exam boards and distributing them to your colleagues to see which specification is best for you and your students. Although they are very similar, there are slight differences. Once you have decided on a specification and feel you can deliver that syllabus, ensure that you are all fully aware of the expectations stated in the specification and audit your knowledge in relation to content of the specification. This will then inform your planning (see Chapter 10).

Assessment objectives

At GCSE level the main assessment objectives (AOs) are referred to numerically as AO1, AO2 and AO3 (see Table 2.1 below). These objectives are often focused on specific sociological skills, which makes Durkheim's notion of specialist skills central to GCSE syllabuses. In all the syllabuses *knowledge and understanding* is the main focus of AO1 whereas AO2 focuses on the *application* of knowledge and understanding in exam questions (or, away from exams, to issues in sociology). For example, an AO2 question may ask how you would apply labelling theory to teacher-student interactions in schools. Lastly, AO3 objectives examine the all-important skills of *selecting information, interpretation, analysis* and *evaluation*. Following on from the example above, this could involve debating the strengths and weaknesses of labelling theory and whether other ideas, such as poor socialisation at home, are more significant.

Table 2.1 Adapted from various exam boards' GCSE assessment objectives

GCSE assessment objectives	Key skills
AO1	Students should demonstrate their knowledge and understanding of social issues, processes and structures by recalling, selecting and communicating relevant information.
AO2	Students should demonstrate that they can apply basic sociological terms and concepts to a range of social issues both familiar and unfamiliar.
AO3	Students should show that they can select, interpret, analyse and evaluate sociological information from a variety of sources.

Table 2.2   Adapted from various exam boards' AS/A Level assessment objectives

AS/A Level assessment objectives	Key skills
AO1	Students should demonstrate their knowledge and understanding of sociological theories/perspectives, concepts and evidence as well as research methodologies.
AO2	Students should demonstrate that they can apply sociological theories/perspectives, concepts, evidence and research methodologies to a range of social issues.
AO3	Students should demonstrate analysis and evaluation of sociological theories/perspectives, concepts, evidence (including famous studies) and research methodologies so that they are able to present sound sociological arguments, make judgements and draw conclusions.

At AS/A Level the assessment objectives are very much the same (see Table 2.2 above) and include: AO1, which again includes knowledge and understanding as well as the communication and explanation of that knowledge and understanding; AO2, which includes the interpretation and application of sociological theories, concepts, research methods and studies to a range of issues; and, lastly, AO3, which includes the analysis and evaluation of sociological theories, concepts, research methods and studies. Most boards now specify that students should use the AO3 skills to present arguments, make judgements and draw conclusions.

It is worth noting that different exam boards may weight their assessment objectives differently in that some may award more marks for AO1 than AO3 or vice versa on different papers. Also, it is important to read the exam boards guidance on how they will mark the quality of written communication (QWC) at AS/A level or spelling, punctuation and grammar (SPaG) at GCSE.

Knowledge and understanding

To gain successful grades in sociology students must be able to demonstrate that they understand sociological theories, perspectives, research methods and key themes/issues. Most exams in sociology have simple closed response questions at the start of the paper. These questions can simply ask students what things mean, such as 'What does IMR stand for?' or they can ask for more explanation, for example, 'Explain what is meant by the nuclear family?' In slightly larger questions students may be asked to identify a given number of sociological ideas or reasons, such as three reasons why the infant mortality rate has decreased over the last 150 years, as well as briefly explain them (for examples, see Chapter 10).

Although short answer AO1 questions seem easy, students often lose marks on them in exams. This is partly due to the fact that exam boards use short answer questions to test the specific sociological meanings of key words like *socialisation* and key concepts such as *secular society*. Unlike other subjects where you may be able to write an essay on a subject despite forgetting a particular aspect of a historical event, a certain quote from a holy book or even a minor character, sociology students need to know all of the key words, concepts, major studies and theories associated with the syllabus specification as they could face narrow and specific questions on any part of any topic area studied.

However, students' knowledge and understanding will only properly be explored by longer questions or essay questions. At GCSE level 'long' questions can range from 6 to 12 marks and at A Level essay questions can range from 12 to 33 marks. Of course, these longer questions will also assess other skills, but the students' knowledge, especially at A Level, will need to be extensive if they are to sustain up to 50 minutes of writing on a given topic.

Helpfully, many questions have prompts that can really help with jogging students' memory, but they are literally just prompts and students will have to use *knowledge from elsewhere* to build up a relevant and successful answer.

Selection, interpretation and application skills

Although the exam boards will place these assessment objects in different AO categories, many books on studying sociology, including textbooks, put these skills in the same category as they all involve the processing and communication of sociological information (see, for example, Marsh et al., 1999). For instance, the skill of *selection* is essential in sociology as students will need to consider all of the information they have been taught, which will be substantial, and select what is relevant to a particular exam question or sociological issue discussed in class. This skill is obviously key to other social sciences and humanities, but the amount of potentially relevant material available for any given question is one of the key things that worry students in exams. For instance, an exam question on how audiences react to violence in a *sociology of the media* question could include the hypodermic syringe model, the uses and gratification model, the cultural effects model, reception theory, the 'Bobo Doll' experiment, various studies by sociologists and psychologists as well as relevant examples from the media, such as the murder of toddler James Bulger, which in turn could lead to a discussion on moral panics, folk devils and deviancy amplification. Therefore, one of the key skills taught to students at both GCSE and particularly AS/A Level is the ability to select and understand the relevance of information.

Selection, however, is dependent on the skill of *interpretation*, which centres on how a student has interpreted the question as well as any stimulus material and data given in the exam. A key part of sociology in schools is teaching students how to interpret questions, stimulus material (often in the form of text) and data. Of course, in exams this will build upon what you have taught students in class; specifically, how they interpret sociological ideas or research in relation to social issues, such as what Marxism has to say about middle class people committing 'white collar crimes' like fraud or tax evasion. If we are to look at data, students may have to interpret what statistical trends or correlations tell us about the effect of, say, lifestyle on health.

It will then be incumbent on you to teach students how to apply their interpretations of sociological theories, perspectives and studies to relevant social issues and exam questions. Although similar to interpretation, *application* basically involves applying the selected sociological ideas and studies to sociological issues and exam questions in a precise, coherent and relevant way that justifies their interpretations. This skill obviously transcends sociology as students will need to select and organise information, interpret information and then articulate what they are saying in all kinds of situations from problem solving at work to debating with friends. In others words, application is how one explains, articulates and justifies the sociological ideas they have selected and interpreted in relation to a particular issue or question.

Analysis and evaluation

In sociology an *analysis* is a detailed examination of the key elements or structure of a theory, perspective or social study. For example, it could involve going through an idea, such as situational crime prevention theory (Clarke, 1995), unpacking it bit by bit and seeing if the evidence used to justify it (or similar studies) stacks up. By doing this the student proves they fully understand the theory, perspective or study and it also gives them scope to explore and examine the benefits and limitations of it further.

Subsequently, an analysis paves the way for an *evaluation*. Here, the student can make judgements about the strengths and weaknesses of a theory or the relevance and significance of a piece of research. However, one of the difficulties of getting students used to the social sciences is that personal opinions need to be kept in check so that an objective evaluation can be made on the evidence presented for the conflicting ideas being studied. In many ways this is the beauty of sociology, in that it teaches students to respect other views, consider them and evaluate them fairly *vis-à-vis* their own views. Although this will be discussed in the next chapter in relation to the *sociological imagination*, I think it is one of the defining features of sociology and the reason why it is such an important subject.

Syllabus content and topic areas

If you are starting out in terms of teaching sociology or if you are switching from another subject, knowing what to teach can be daunting. Nonetheless, I am sure that you will find most of the topic areas on GCSE and A Level syllabuses intrinsically interesting and will actually enjoy discovering what sociology has to offer. However, if we are to look at what topics are taught, it is worth at this point looking at GCSE and AS/A Level syllabuses separately.

GCSE units of study

Three major exam boards currently offer sociology at GCSE and they tend to offer very similar choices for students in terms of topics to be studied. All of them introduce the key words, terms and concepts used in sociology. For example, their GCSE syllabuses will often involve learning about social processes, including basic ideas on socialisation, social control and social change; social structures, which may include looking at units on the family, education or power and politics; and, lastly, social issues stemming from these processes and structures, such as whether power is concentrated amongst the few or examining the causes and consequences of changing family types.

In addition to the above, GCSE students are expected to develop a basic understanding of sociological research, especially how sociologists go about collecting evidence for their studies. However, the GCSE syllabuses stop short of going into the main theoretical perspectives in any real depth and there will be none of the deep analysis of the theories' underlying philosophies and contributions to the development of the subject like there is at A Level.

For those new to sociology and those switching from other subjects, what follows is a breakdown of the common topic areas found in the three exam board syllabuses (see Table 2.3 below). This is included so that you can get your head around what will be taught in terms of content.

Table 2.3   Common themes and content in GCSE syllabuses

Topic/unit	Common themes/content	Exam boards
Key ideas and concepts	These type of units are useful at the start of GCSE courses as they introduce students to the core themes that run through the syllabuses.	AQA, OCR, WJEC
	Key ideas and concepts can include learning about social norms, values, socialisation and identity.	
	These units can also include learning about social processes, structures, agency and key debates in sociology.	
	Not all syllabuses offer this as a discrete unit. However, it is implicit in all of them.	
Research methods	These units include types of data collection, such as the difference between quantitative and qualitative data. This could involve learning about surveys and observations.	AQA, OCR, WJEC
	Units on research methods may also cover how research is designed and used, especially in terms of ethics as well as practicality.	
	Moreover, students will need to have an elementary grasp of how to interpret research; how to assess the strengths and weaknesses and, in some cases, explain how they would plan their own survey.	
	This unit can build on a lot of PELTS and BLP learning skills (see Chapter 4) as students can collaborate on designing and collecting their own research data. It also makes for good cross-curricular links with maths and citizenship due to the possible use of quantitative data and 'active citizenship' respectively.	
Families and households	Units on families and households invariably look at types of family, such as nuclear, lone-parent and reconstituted families; they will also look at the functions of families and how the family socialises the young.	AQA, OCR, WJEC
	Also included in most units on families is the changing nature or structure of families as well as relationships within the family, such as ideas on the symmetrical family etc.	
	Although popular and engaging, some issues can be quite sensitive and it is worth checking with your head of year as to whether any students may be upset by the content (see Chapter 13).	
Education	Education is a popular unit with schools for obvious reasons. It can include the functions or role of education; how education socialises the young as well as how government policies influence education, such as the tripartite system of the 1944 Butler Act.	AQA, OCR, WJEC
	Most education units also emphasise research on student attainment, which may include looking at ethnic minorities, gender and socio-economics as reasons for academic success or failure.	

Table 2.3 continued

Topic/unit	Common themes/content	Exam boards
Mass media	Often a favourite of students, units on mass media can cover the ownership and control of media organisations; the effects and influence of new media; and the effect of the media on audiences, especially from violence in the media. Other issues covered may include stereotypes, moral panics and the social construction of the news. The mass media unit allows for an awful lot of references to pop culture and social media/networking (see Chapter 12). It is also a good choice if media studies is popular in your school.	AQA, OCR, WJEC
Crime and deviance	Another unit very popular with students is crime and deviance, which can also be topical, controversial and emotive. It can include defining crime and deviance; analysing the causes, consequences and patterns of crime; as well as the methods and concepts used in the control of crime. Units can also look at issues such as socialisation and whether crime is down to nurture or nature. This unit has cross curricular links to most religious education syllabuses at GCSE, which often overlap as they focus on the ethics of crime and punishment.	AQA, OCR, WJEC
Power and politics	Although the title of this unit may vary, it is a good optional topic to have if you have a popular history department that also focuses on British politics. It can also be a useful subject to go alongside citizenship at GCSE. Most units include participation in democracy, such as voting patterns, elections and the influence of the media. These issues may also include the exclusion or apathy of particular social groups. Another key area is the analysis of political structures that affect the UK, such as local government, parliament and the European Union.	AQA, WJEC
Work and the workplace	An important unit considering the world students are heading for. These units introduce students to key definitions that we may take for granted, such as the differences between employment, unemployment and leisure. A key component of these units will be learning about life chances, inequality in the workplace and the law surrounding equality. Another aspect of work related units is discussion on key concepts and issues, such as alienation and workers' views of their roles and status in the workforce as well as looking at key pieces of legislation, such as the minimum wage, and laws on unionisation.	OCR, WJEC

This is not an exhaustive list and other topics, such as *social inequality, youth* and *global citizenship* are available in some syllabuses. Personally, I would argue social inequality/stratification is underrepresented considering its importance, but perhaps that is my own bias. It is essential that you read through all the GCSE syllabus specifications if you are starting a department and if you are considering changing exam boards.

AS/A Level units of study

The GCSE syllabuses offered by exam boards offer a firm foundation for students going onto AS or A Levels as most A Level specifications/syllabuses build upon the same skills and themes. However, the knowledge and understanding required will be deeper, especially the use of *technical terms*, which will include using more key terms, words and concepts when explaining theoretical perspectives and research findings. Moreover, AS and A Levels tend to be more theoretical and there will be greater emphasis on the application of key perspectives (including functionalism, Marxism, feminism, social action theory, the new right and postmodernism) to the themes studied. There are also more theoretical debates in most syllabuses, such as whether sociology is a science and whether it can be objective and value free. In essence, whereas the GCSE involves *basic* knowledge and understanding of the key ideas in sociology, AS and A Levels develop an *advanced* knowledge and understanding of the subject.

Although students who have benefited from sociology at GCSE will be at an advantage studying AS and A Levels, there is no reason why students cannot start it at A Level despite not having a GCSE; so long as they have the ability to deal with abstract concepts and are willing to engage with the content. However, I would suggest having some entry criteria for those opting without a good sociology GCSE. In my current school we require students to have a B in English as well as another humanities subject (or equivalent) as they will need sound essay writing skills in order to succeed.

In a similar fashion to the above table on GCSE themes and content, I have drawn up a table of common AS and A Level themes (see Table 2.4 below). Of course, this is designed to help you consider, perhaps think about auditing, your subject knowledge if you are starting out, but it may be worth considering these topic areas if you already teach sociology in case you feel there is a subject you are better suited to teach. Please note that exam boards may not title the units as I have and they often combine units, particularly with research methods. Moreover, I have not differentiated between AS Level and A Level (the old A2) units – so you will need to look at the actual exam board specifications to get a better idea of what is on offer.

As with the GCSE table earlier, this is not an exhaustive list and some boards include units on *global development, power and politics* and *youth subcultures* amongst others.

Another important aspect in choosing a syllabus is being fully aware of the type and length of questions being asked. For a general overview of some of the differences between the Assessment and Qualifications Alliance (AQA), Oxford Cambridge and RSA (OCR) and Eduqas boards see Table 2.5. It does not include the Welsh Joint Education Committee's (WJEC) Welsh only specification.

Table 2.4 Common themes and content in AS/A Level specifications/syllabuses[2]

Topic/unit	Common content/themes	Exam boards
Culture and identity	Culture and Identity is a good topic choice for developing the 'sociological imagination' (see Chapter 3) as it gets students thinking about their own lives in relation to the wider society.	AQA, OCR, WJEC, Eduqas
	The identity component would consider how one defines their identity, especially considering their gender, ethnicity, sexuality etc. It would also consider how these identities are formed through the processes of socialisation in the family, school and other institutions.	
	The culture aspect would look at the influence of subcultures, pop culture, high culture etc. on identity and society as a whole. An evaluative aspect here would be how culture influences norms and values; for example, an evaluation may include viewing the effects of culture on society from a Marxist, feminist and postmodern perspective.	
Families and households	This seems to be a popular option with many schools and is very topical, especially as at the time of writing there is lots of discussion in the news about 'broken homes', gay marriage and cutting welfare spending; this reinforces the importance of the topic to students.	AQA, OCR, WJEC, Eduqas
	Most units on families include defining types of families, looking at relationships within the family and debating the functions of the family. However, an AS or A Level analysis of these issues will include evaluating the strengths and weaknesses of the different sociological perspectives in relation to these issues, such as how the new right contrasts to feminism.	
	At AS and A Level there is also more detailed analysis on demographics and how these not only impact the family, but have impacted the family over time. Of course, all analysis and evaluation will consider sociological perspectives on these and a deeper understanding of the economic consequences and policy options for governments.	
	Childhood may be another area of study at AS or A Level, especially theoretical arguments on whether it is socially constructed or is disappearing.	
Education	Again, this topic area can build on the GCSE syllabuses, but goes into far more theoretical and empirical depth.	AQA, WJEC, Eduqas
	A key area of study is evaluating the role of education from different perspectives, which include functionalism, Marxism, feminism, social action theories and the new right. In many ways understanding these theoretical perspectives informs a lot of the rest of the content from looking at gender gaps in attainment (feminism) to considering the marketisation of education (new right).	
	These units also focus a lot of attention on patterns of educational attainment in relation to socio-economics, ethnicity and gender as well as addressing issues such as cultural and linguistic deprivation. By applying the above theoretical perspectives here, the syllabuses highlight teacher/student interactions as an area of study and, in particular, labelling theory.	
	Government policy will also be looked at theoretically, empirically and historically.	

Topic/unit	Common content/themes	Exam boards
Health	Units on health can also be topical as long as the public remains passionate about the NHS.	AQA, WJEC, Eduqas
	Health units cover definitions of health and illness and considers whether they are socially constructed; for example, what does it mean to be unhealthy; what is a lifestyle illness and why are some illnesses blamed on the patient whereas others are not.	
	Inequality will be a big factor when looking at health, especially whether different social groups are prone to certain types of illness. Inequality would also cover access to health care and whether there is fair access for all groups within society, including geographical discrepancies. Of course, this would include looking at health policies in some detail alongside theoretical perspectives on health care.	
	Lastly, there will probably be some opportunity to look at issues associated with mental health.	
Mass media	The media is a great unit to cover if you like using music, YouTube clips and other media resources in your classroom (see Chapter 12). It is also an area of sociology that the students arguably have more awareness of than other issues.	AQA, OCR, WJEC, Eduqas
	At AS and A Level, media units build on the GCSE content, but obviously go into more depth. Issues such as the ownership and control of the media will involve more analysis of concepts like vertical and horizontal integration as well as theoretical perspectives such as neo-Marxism and neo-pluralism.	
	Additionally, topic areas like globalisation, new media and the social construction of the news pay more attention to theoretical ideas than at GCSE level, such as neo-Marxist views on the *digital divide* and *public sphere*.	
	Other areas to look at are stereotyping, which is far more theoretical than at GCSE, and audience theories, which include analysing the theoretical ideas behind the conceptual models on audience behaviour as well as greater evaluation on the empirical studies justifying them.	
Crime and deviance	Again, due to its topical and often controversial nature, this unit is well liked by students, especially when looking at deviant subcultures and criminal gangs.	AQA, OCR, WJEC, Eduqas
	Starting with definitions and examples on what crime and deviance actually are, units will often go over the theoretical perspectives on crime as well as what they say about social order and crime prevention.	
	Most units also look at patterns of crime in some depth, which includes its social distribution by ethnicity, gender and social class. This includes how we measure crime using statistics and surveys, how these crimes are socially constructed and the importance of victim studies.	
	Another key area of study is globalisation, especially in relation to state crime, green crime and human rights abuses.	
	In addition to the above, crime and deviance units also look at criminal justice systems, punishment and surveillance of crime.	

Table 2.4 continued

Topic/unit	Common content/themes	Exam boards
Religion and belief	The idea of studying this unit is often dismissed if students in very secular schools are given the choice to study it, but the topic is purely sociological and not faith based in any way. It is also one students appreciate and enjoy if given a chance.	AQA, OCR, WJEC, Eduqas
	The unit would include an analysis of what religions are in comparison to ideology and science before looking at religious organisations from churches and denominations to sects and cults. This can make for good independent research projects as students can find out about different groups etc.	
	Another key element is trends in religious belief and the secularisation of society. There may well be a national and global element in this part of the unit.	
	Units on religion and belief will also look at the impact both religion and secularisation have on social change, stability and social policies.	
Social inequality/ stratification	All main exam boards include units on social inequality, but they may label them differently.	AQA, OCR, WJEC, Eduqas
	Social inequality/stratification can include looking at the relative position of different socio-economic groups (or classes) in society as well as where other groups, such as ethnic minorities, fit in. This would include analysing both the material and cultural factors involved, such as wealth, poverty, social status and power.	
	An important element here would be comparing the key sociological perspectives of Marxism, functionalism, feminism and the new right to each other and analysing how they justify their positions in relation to empirical evidence/studies.	
	Key concepts such as life chances and social mobility would be evaluated in relation to statistical data on current trends as well as the impact of government policies on inequality.	
	All units will critically examine how inequality is defined and measured by sociologists.	
Research methods	Units on research methods vary. Some are combined with the topics above whereas other exam boards combine them with units on theory. However, if a student wants to take sociology further, research methods are essential and will be compulsory at some stage in all AS and A Level syllabuses.	AQA, OCR, WJEC, Eduqas
	Research methods will cover research design, formulation and implementation. More specifically, students will look at qualitative research, such as unstructured interviews and observations, and quantitative research, such as large scale postal surveys and use of official statistics, in far more evaluative depth than at GCSE.	
	Students will also look at the ethical and practical strengths and weaknesses of conducting research as well as the theoretical underpinnings and bias found in research.	
	A key element at AS and A Level will be examining the differences between interpretivist and positivist approaches to research and whether this can ever be scientific or value free. It also looks at the benefits and limitations of macro and micro studies (see Chapter 8 for more on teaching about research).	

Topic/unit	Common content/themes	Exam boards
Theory	Theory is a major part of any AS and A Level syllabus and the theoretical perspectives covered carry far more weight than they do at GCSE. Firstly, students will need to be familiar with the main sociological perspectives of functionalism, Marxism, feminism, social action theory, the new right and postmodernism. In some exam boards these perspectives are studied in and of themselves and students may have to analyse and evaluate their strengths, weaknesses and contributions to sociology. Nevertheless, all boards specify that students should consider them in relation to most topics. Importantly, theory overlaps with research methods here (although the two topic areas inform each other and are often combined), especially the importance of macro and micro approaches to research, debates about structure and agency and whether sociology can be a science (see Chapter 7 for more on teaching about theories).	Implicit in all syllabuses

Table 2.5 Comparing selective aspects of AS/A Level sociology specifications from 2015 onwards[3]

	OCR	AQA	Eduqas
AS *Paper 1*	**Socialisation, Culture and Identity** is assessed by 4, 6, 8 and 12 mark questions. All these questions must be answered. **Youth Subcultures, Families and Relationships** and **The Media** are all assessed by 5, 8, 12 and 20 mark questions. Students choose only one of these topic areas. There is no choice of questions in this paper. In total students can gain 75 marks over 90 minutes by answering 8 questions.	**Education and Methods in Context** is assessed by 2, 2, 6, 10 and 20 mark questions on education and a 20 mark question on research methods. The paper lasts for 90 minutes and is worth 60 marks in total. AQA use a question paper with lines on and limited space for writing (as with GCSE papers). There is also no choice of questions and students answer 6 questions in total.	**Socialisation, Culture and Identity** is assessed by 5 and 10 mark questions. **Youth Subcultures and Families and Households** are both assessed by 10 and 15 mark questions then a choice of two 25 mark questions. Students choose either topic area. **Education, Media and Religion** are all assessed by two 10 mark questions and then a choice of two 10 and 25 mark questions. The exam lasts 2 hours 30 minutes and is worth 120 marks in total. It has 8 questions with choices.
AS *Paper 2*	**Researching and Understanding Social Inequalities** is assessed by 4, 9, 12, 20, 10 and 20 mark questions. There is no choice of questions. In total there are 75 marks to be answered in 90 minutes. This is a total of 6 questions.	**Research Methods** is assessed by a 4 mark and 16 mark question. **Culture and Identity, Health, Families and Households** and **Work, Poverty and Welfare** are each assessed by 2, 2, 6, 10 and 20 mark questions. Students choose one of these topic areas. Once the topic area has been chosen there is no choice of questions. The paper is worth 60 marks over 90 minutes with 7 questions in total.	**Methods of Sociological Enquiry** is assessed by 5, 10, 10 and 25 mark questions. All must be answered. The exam last for 1 hour and 15 minutes, is worth 50 marks in total and comprises 4 questions.

	OCR	AQA	Eduqas
A Level Paper 1	**Socialisation, Culture and Identity** is assessed by 6, 12 and 20 mark questions. These questions must be answered. **Youth Subcultures, Families and Relationships** and **The Media** are all assessed by 12, 16 and 24 mark questions. Students choose one of these topic areas to answer from. There is no choice of questions aside from choosing the topic areas and the exam lasts 90 minutes and is worth 90 marks. There are 6 questions in total.	**Education, Methods in Context** and **Theory and Methods** is assessed by 4, 6, 10, and 30 mark questions on education and a 20 mark question on methods in context and a 10 mark question for theory. As at AS, there are lines to write on in the booklet. The exam is worth 80 marks and lasts 2 hours and has 6 questions in total. There is no choice of questions.	**Socialisation, Culture and Identity** is assessed by 5 and 15 mark questions. **Youth Subcultures** and **Families and Households** are both assessed by a 15 mark question and a **choice** of two 35 mark questions. Students choose either topic area. **Education, Media** and **Religion** are all assessed by a 15 mark question and then a choice of two 35 mark questions. Students must choose one topic area. The exam is 2 hours 30 minutes in total, is worth 120 marks and students answer 6 questions in total.
A Level Paper 2	**Researching and Understanding Social Inequalities** is assessed by 4, 6, 10, 25, 20 and 40 mark questions. There is no choice of question and the exam lasts 2 hours 15 minutes with 105 marks in total. There are 6 questions.	**Culture and Identity, Health, Families and Households** and **Work, Poverty and Welfare** are each assessed by 10, 10 and 20 mark questions. One topic area is chosen. **Beliefs in Society, Global Development, The Media** and **Stratification and Differentiation** are all assessed by 10, 10 and 20 mark questions. There is no choice in the exam other than the chosen areas of study; students choose one of the topic areas. The exam has 6 questions in total and lasts for 2 hours. It is worth 80 marks in total.	**Methods of Sociological Enquiry** is assessed by 5, 5, 25 and 30 mark questions totalling 60 marks overall. The exam last for 1 hour 45 minutes. In total there are 4 questions. There is no choice in this paper.

Table 2.5 continued

	OCR	AQA	Eduqas
A Level Paper 3	**Crime and Deviance, Education** or **Religion, Belief and Faith** are assessed by 10, 20 and 40 mark questions. Students choose one of these topic areas. **Globalisation and Digital Media**, which is compulsory, is assessed by 9, 10 and 16 mark questions. This means there are 105 marks in total and the exam lasts 2 hours 15 minutes. It has 6 questions in total.	**Crime and Deviance** is assessed by 4, 6, 10 and 30 mark questions. **Theory and Methods** is assessed by 10 and 20 mark questions. The student booklet has lines to write on. They must answer all questions. The exam lasts 2 hours, is worth 80 marks and has a total of 6 questions.	**Social Differentiation and Stratification** is assessed by a 20 mark question then a choice of two 40 mark questions. **Crime and Deviance, Health and Disability, Politics** and **World Sociology** are all assessed by a 20 mark question then a **choice of two** 40 mark questions. Students choose one of the topic areas. The paper is worth 120 marks in total, lasts 2 hours 30 minutes and has a total of 4 questions.
Total number of questions	32	31	28
Total time	9 hours	9 hours	10 hours 50 minutes

Choosing the right syllabus for your students

Although all the topics discussed above can be engaging and beneficial to students, it is worth thinking about the types of issues that most interest your students. One way to do this, especially if you have been asked to introduce sociology to your school or college is to survey your students (using ideas from the research methods unit, see Chapter 9). I have used a mixture of closed question surveys and small focus groups to do this when asked to take over a department that had seen all its teachers move on. I initially wanted to teach units on *religion and belief* and *power and politics* partly because they interest me and also because that is what I remember studying at A Level. However, teachers can be quite egocentric and the students, when asked, had other ideas. Their preference was clearly for *mass media*, especially as many were also studying media studies, and *crime and punishment* (this was at a time when the US TV show *The Wire* was popular with students in my class). Objections to the *religion and belief* unit centred on, perhaps unfairly, the fact that they had not opted for religious education and *power and politics* seemed less exciting than *crime and deviance*. Of course, the units I preferred were outlined and defended in some detail, but the students made their choice.

Lastly, it is important that you play to your strengths and choose, in consultation with colleagues, topic areas you know fairly well or think you will find interesting. Teaching any subject for the first time is hard and choosing something you are completely unfamiliar with or apathetic towards may mean spending more time reading up on the subject than planning, creating and preparing engaging and successful lessons.

Further reading

GCSE and AS/A Level exam specifications

To fully comprehend what is taught and required in terms of syllabus content at both GCSE and AS/A Level, read the exam board's specification. Specifications will list all of the key areas you need to cover in your courses. Moreover, even if you are using a particular specification, it is worth keeping a copy to hand and occasionally checking you are covering everything it specifies. These documents are available from all exam board websites.

GCSE and AS/A Level textbooks

These are great for ensuring your subject knowledge is at the level it should be and that you are up-to-date on sociological developments. Buy a number of these textbooks as some are better and more comprehensive than others. However, read these well in advance of your lessons so you can plan effectively. Also, avoid death-by-hand-out; do not simply teach from the textbook. Textbooks are often linked to particular exam boards, but a good general example is Haralambos, M. and Holborn, M. (2008), *Sociology themes and perspectives* (7th ed.), Glasgow: Collins.

Notes

1   All the exam awarding bodies put their sociology specifications online alongside past papers and support materials. For AQA see: www.aqa.org.uk; for Edexcel see: www.edexcel.com; for OCR visit: www.ocr.org.uk; for Eduqas, which is part of WJEC, see: www.eduqas.co.uk; and, lastly, if in Wales check: www.wjec.co.uk. All of these boards have subject specific advisors you can contact if you request information or advice.

2   The WJEC AS/A level is only available in Wales. In England and Northern Ireland, the board operates as Eduqas.
3   This table is adapted with kind permission from Dr. Denise Jackson.

Bibliography

Clarke, R. V. (1995). Situational crime prevention. *Crime and Justice*, 19, 91–150.
Department for Education. (2014). *GCE AS and A Level subject content for sociology.* London: Department for Education.
Department for Education. (2016). *Sociology: GCSE guidance.* London: Department for Education.
Haralambos, M. & Holborn, M. (2008). *Sociology themes and perspectives* (7th ed.). Glasgow: Collins.
Marsh, I., Trobe, K., Griffiths, J., Hope, T., Best, S. & Harris, G. (1999). *Sociology: Dealing with data.* Harlow: Longman.

3 Sociological pedagogies

This chapter includes:

- What is meant by pedagogy?
- The importance of Mills' concept of the sociological imagination in developing a sociological pedagogy.
- How pedagogy based on the sociological imagination could be informed by the main sociological perspectives. Including:
  - functionalism
  - Marxism (and critical pedagogy)
  - social action theories
  - feminism
  - and postmodernism.
- Concluding thoughts linking the above perspectives to the sociological imagination.

As teachers we talk about 'teaching and learning' all the time; at staff meetings, when giving or receiving lesson observation feedback and when we plan lessons and schemes of work collaboratively with colleagues. Therefore, in most books on teaching and learning there will be a chapter on *pedagogy*, which is often defined as 'the methods and practice of teaching' (Capel, Leask & Turner, 2013, p. 7). Bearing this in mind, it is obvious that thinking about pedagogy is crucial to teaching successfully. However, the scope of pedagogy is huge and includes theories and research from the fields of psychology, neuroscience, educational development and, of course, the sociology of education. Some, therefore, prefer to call pedagogy the art or craft of teaching in the classroom (Gershon, 2015, p. 21); whether this is delivering activities in actual lessons or planning activities beforehand, pedagogy is often seen as the skills, strategies and methods employed by the teacher to support students' learning.

However, thinking deeply about pedagogy transcends any focus on teaching strategies and should encompass more than the 'best methods' of teaching. As Smith (2012) argues, pedagogy 'is concerned not just with knowing about things, but also with changing ourselves and the world we live in' (par. 10). In this sense, pedagogy is not just about the practicalities of teaching, but also the philosophy of education; thinking about pedagogy should challenge us to question why we are teaching and what we hope to achieve by teaching it. Smith suggests that as well as being concerned with a process of 'inviting truth' about what is being studied and the possibility of advancing our students knowledge and development of a given subject, pedagogy should also centre around certain values and commitments inherent in that subject, such as fostering respect for others and for one's self. In fact, 'Education is born, it could be argued, of the hope and desire that all may share in life and *be more*' (Smith, 2012, par. 8; my italics).

The sociological imagination

In a similar vein, the American sociologist Charles Wright Mills argued that sociology should invite students to 'share in life'. Mills' argument was formulated in his book *The Sociological Imagination* (1959), which encouraged students to imagine, explore, develop and articulate the connections between their personal histories and the social world they live in. For Mills this would combine 'biography' and 'history' as students start to see the 'self' as part of the wider 'whole' (p. 4).

Mills (p. 8) recognised that our 'private troubles', such as worrying about career progression or concern for a friend in an abusive relationship, are often reflected in less personal 'public issues', such as a lack of job opportunities in society or a statistical increase in recorded incidents of domestic abuse. If we have experienced these 'troubles' or have family and friends that have, then it is arguably incumbent upon us to think about the wider social causes of these issues or trends as they could shed light on a potential way to prevent them. Here, our 'personal troubles' may be bound up in these larger 'public issues' or vice versa.

This has two main pedagogical impacts: firstly, developing the sociological imagination furthers students' understanding of everyday events, such as getting a doctor's appointment or choosing subjects for A Level, as it presents various sociological arguments, or perspectives, as to why these things happen. Could their inability to get an immediate doctor's appointment be due to the marketisation of the NHS? Are they socialised in a way that made them opt for sociology, psychology and English literature as opposed to chemistry, physics and further maths? It is here that the sociological imagination comes into play as students are invited to imagine why their life is set up and organised the way it is.

Secondly, the sociological imagination is a beneficial pedagogical concept as it allows the student to compare and contrast the life they live and the experiences they have had with the results and findings of sociological studies. For example, does Willmott and Young's (1972) research on gender and housework contrast to who does the household chores in the students' homes. Moreover, do statistical trends on secularisation mirror the religiosity of the communities the students live in? By combining their personal biographies with these wider social histories or studies, it can be said that Mills' concept of the sociological imagination is a good starting point when considering what constitutes a sociological pedagogy, especially one that engages and develops students' view of themselves in the world as well as what it might be like for others. Once this approach to teaching the subject has been established, we can start to think about the most appropriate strategies and methods that will help us develop our students' sociological imagination.

Nevertheless, just focusing on Mills' concept would be a great injustice to all the other potential pedagogies in sociology. All of the classical theories can be said to offer valuable pedagogical insights. Moreover, it is worth considering these pedagogies after discussing Mills' core ideas as in some ways they are all compatible with attaining the outcomes of the sociological imagination and can all be seen as developing students' ability to contemplate the world beyond themselves.

As Halasz and Kaufman (2008) have argued, 'By viewing our classroom as a social space, our discipline can explore a range of sociological themes such as interactional dynamics, identity formation, institutional effects, structural inequalities, and knowledge production. If sociologists already study these levels of social analysis, why not capitalise on this for the betterment of teaching and learning?' (p. 301).

Functionalist pedagogy

In the introduction I suggested that Durkheim's ideas on education could be appropriated as a *modus operandi* for teaching sociology. This is because his work on education clearly categorises the purpose of education: to teach specialist skills, embed social solidarity and prepare students for life in society through their participation in school life, which is a microcosm of the wider society. However, according to Halasz and Kaufman (2008), the pedagogical possibilities of Durkheim's writing are mainly to be found in his concepts of *solidarity* and *anomie*. As I have already argued, Durkheim's conception of solidarity centres on looking at how we as well as other people live, behave and are affected by political decisions – this can create a sense of common purpose or shared values and students may be compelled to participate in public life through a realisation of social solidarity with others. In some ways this is comparable with Mills' sociological imagination as we have to conceptualise the self as part of the wider whole, but in essence Durkheim is arguing that education – and, therefore, any sociological pedagogy – should seek to enhance and maintain social cohesion amongst the citizenry. Otherwise society would experience instability due to heightened anomie, which is often referred to as normlessness as there is a breakdown of social norms and shared values between individuals.

For Durkheim (1997), modernity has increased society's tendency towards individualism, which could lead to isolation, normlessness and a lack of social cohesion as individuals become less socially integrated because the old bonds found in familial networks of kinship, small local communities and religion are eroded or at least seem less important (p. 354). However, in his 1893 work *The Division of Labour in Society,* Durkheim describes an *organic society* in which interdependence between individuals arises from the specialisation of work and the consensual relationships between people (see Durkheim, 1997, p. 79). This avoids the potential pitfalls of anomic individualisation as, although the individual is rational and aware of the self and the opportunities open to them, they are still dependent on others and understand, perhaps subconsciously, the importance of society's norms and values in maintaining order, stability and harmony; this then develops into a *collective conscience* as society is 'increasingly to be made up of generalised modes of thought and sentiment, which leave room for an increasing multitude of individual differences' (Durkheim, 1997, p. 172). It is here, then, that Halasz and Kaufman (2008) argue that a pedagogy aiming to create a miniature organic society in the classroom has real benefits to education as: 'interdependence would be strong, cooperation would be expected, and positive individualism in the form of inventiveness, innovation, and imagination would be welcome. A classroom modelled on Durkheim's organic solidarity would demonstrate cohesiveness, reciprocity, and respect amongst teachers and learners' (p. 305). Moreover, if we take functionalism at face value, this would also fulfil a school's purpose of establishing a microcosm of society.

A sociology teacher applying these pedagogical ideas in the classroom may emphasise collaborative learning or group work so that students understand the importance of relying on each other. By setting up and facilitating activities that create interdependence between learners, the teacher would ultimately aim to increase levels of cooperation and reciprocity as students work together to attain an end goal. Whether this is a substantial research project or short activity where students seek information from each other to find answers to questions set by the teacher, a scaffolded learner-centred activity could also set rules or guidelines, such as stipulating certain levels of politeness and interaction between students, to establish the norms and shared values of constructive collaborative learning. Even if this learning environment is engineered by the teacher and not necessarily spontaneous between the students, it is still an attempt to establish a cohesive and interconnected classroom. Importantly, this collaboration, or *collective conscience*, still allows for some individualism as students pursue their own targets, build on previous individual feedback on assessed work and are encouraged to offer their own ideas and talents to this collaboration, especially if they are to maximise their personal outcomes. Also, if we really want to establish a Durkheimian organic society, we could allocate roles within each group to create a 'division of labour', but perhaps this is labouring the point!

Halasz and Kaufman (2008) further develop the idea of functionalist pedagogy by looking at the contribution made to sociology by Robert K. Merton (1957), especially his development of *strain theory* (p. 306–307). Strain theory is often taught as part of *crime and deviance* units in school as Merton (1938) analyses the strain between the consensual goals within society, such as legitimately obtaining the material affluence of the American Dream, and the means at people's disposal to achieve these goals (p. 676). Merton (1938) goes on to identify five ways – or *typological modes* – in which people adapt to their social positions or circumstances, which are paramount as they can either provide people with the means to attain society's consensually constituted goals or prevent them from doing so. These are:

- conformity
- innovation
- ritualisation
- retreatism
- rebellion.

Put simply, those that lack the means – intellectual or otherwise – to attain given goals will forego conformity and *rebel*, which could include poor behaviour, or *retreat*, which could include truanting or even substance abuse in an educational context. Students who fit the typological mode of *ritualism* reject the goals and just carry on with the means and those who fit *innovation* reject the means and accept the goals as they try to obtain them by any means possible. In terms of learners, the ritualistic are just going through the motions – perhaps taking A Levels as they are at a loss as to what to do next in life – and innovators are arguably going to cheat.

As education is becoming more and more goal orientated at secondary level with Fischer Family Trust (FFT), ALPS and ALIS targets (see Chapter 10) cemented in teachers everyday practice; let alone senior school and college leaders worrying about their institution's position in league tables and whether they meet the Ofsted criteria for 'good' or 'outstanding', it is obvious that Merton's strain theory has something to say about pedagogy today.

Firstly, teachers need to personalise learning to ensure students can find their own pathways to attaining the stated goal or target of their learning, which is undoubtedly – and perhaps cynically

– their end grade. Otherwise students may succumb to one of Merton's other typological modes; for example, messing around in class (rebelling). Secondly, teachers will have to be aware of whether students' goals are the same as those of their schools or colleges. For instance, some students may decide to study a subject because their peers have chosen it; they may not have a real intrinsic interest and merely enjoy coming to school for the social relationships it provides; and, as a result of this, they may not be too fussed about their final grade (ritualism). The second situation would undoubtedly cause strain not just between the student and the school, but will also exasperate their teacher who is probably performance managed on their students' attainment.

So what? What can we do? Importantly, this is where Merton's ideas are useful as part of our pedagogical approach: by understanding whether students are adapting to the goals set by schools through conformity, innovation, ritualisation, retreatism or rebellion we are better placed to help them. If they are, for example, plagiarising (innovation), handing in lacklustre essays (ritualism), skipping classes (retreatism) or making wholly inappropriate or deliberately stupid comments in class (rebellion), we need to figure out ways of engaging, encouraging and nurturing an interest in sociology through listening, personalising and facilitating different types of activities for different learners. For examples of how these strategies or activities may look in practice it is worth reading about learning styles, personalised learning, planning and differentiation in later chapters.

Lastly, Robert Agnew's (1992) development of strain theory could be useful in how we understand and manage the behaviour of students (pp. 51–57). Importantly, Agnew focused less on the wider social structure and societal goals and more on an individual's emotional responses to their immediate social environment. He suggested that actual or anticipated failure to achieve socially constituted goals can result in immense strain, which leads to anger, frustration and negative relationships. In a student this could manifest from frustration at getting consistently poor grades, feeling that they are unsupported or are being put under too much pressure to attain their targets or goals. Subsequently, Agnew has identified the application and development of temperament, intelligence, interpersonal skills, self-efficacy and a supportive environment as conducive to combatting strain amongst criminals or deviants. In many ways, these capacities and skills need to be nurtured amongst our students as well as in our own relationships with them. Therefore, any pedagogical approach that incorporates functionalist thinking should bear in mind Agnew's (1992) call for an awareness of our students' emotions (p. 65). Incidentally, this arguably corresponds to our teaching standards as we are required to build positive and constructive relationships with students in order to facilitate cohesion in the classroom.

Nevertheless, some teachers may have concerns at this formation of functionalist pedagogy for various reasons. Firstly, it is arguably theoretically weak as I have attempted to draw on theoretical ideas that do not concern themselves with pedagogy directly; it would be wrong, therefore, to claim any of this as representative of functionalist thinkers themselves. Secondly, functionalist theory and arguably any potential pedagogy owes a huge debt to the ideas formulated in Durkheim's *The Division of Labour in Society* (1893), which subsequently runs into some difficulty in explaining how class conflict, economic disadvantage and elitism emerges in a modern society. For example, Giddens (1971) argues that whilst Durkheim recognises that 'class conflict between capital and wage labour has accompanied the expansion of the division of labour… It is, however, fallacious to suppose that this conflict results directly from the division of labour' (p. 80). What Giddens is suggesting is that the economic differences between classes in society are disproportionate due to the 'division of economic functions' (disparities in pay and widening social inequality) outstripping the moral regulation of these divisions. This could be seen as the economic mismanagement of equality and social justice. In turn, the interdependence of the collective conscience could breakdown as there is not a fair distribution of talents and capacities, especially when higher positions in society are overwhelmingly occupied by privileged groups.

Although this may seem irrelevant to teaching and learning, schools cannot guarantee that students will not perceive a lack of moral regulation in how they are set or streamed, allocated targets and affected by out of school factors, such as the need for some A Level students to work extra shifts if asked to pay rent by parents; in other words, it is harder for some students to pay rent than others. Although strain theory goes some way towards explaining this, it may be beyond the teacher to simply recognise 'issues' and deal with them sufficiently. Any sociology teacher will know that functionalism, especially through the work of Talcott Parsons, generally sees school as meritocratic, but this is arguably a simplistic way of looking at the myriad of social, personal and economic problems faced by supposedly 'equal individuals' in the classroom.[1] Therefore, many teachers may prefer the more radical pedagogical alternatives offered by Marxism and feminism or be interested in what social action theories have to say about pedagogy.

Task 3.1 Strain theory in practice

At your next department meeting, review your students' data and identify any underachievers and/or behavioural concerns. Then think about the students' attitudes to learning, their engagement or apathy with the subject and whether there are any issues affecting them away from school. Finally, map these students and their issues against the 5 typological modes formulated by Merton. Discuss whether any are applicable and whether these modes can help you come up with any solutions to the problems the students have.

Marxist pedagogy

Marxism has a lot to say about education and, therefore, has influenced a whole raft of pedagogical ideas, including the highly influential philosophy cum social movement known as *critical pedagogy*. In the same way that most of us will teach the functionalist ideas of Durkheim and Parsons to our students in relation to the sociology of education, we will also probably teach the counter-hegemonic ideas of Marx and Engels as well as those of Althusser, Bourdieu, Bowles and Gintis; all of whom offer criticism of how things are taught in school.[2] Essentially most Marxists see education as reinforcing the class system and reproducing inequality. Althusser (2001) saw this as part of the ideological state apparatus that brainwashes us into a false class consciousness of accepting our position in life regardless of our true potential (pp. 85–126). Bowles and Gintis (1976) developed this further to discuss how we are taught to be deferential to bosses and obey authority in later life as our school rules and hierarchies correspond to the world of work and future exploitation. They go as far to say that Parsons' view that school is a meritocracy is a myth and that schools also operate a hidden curriculum that aims to teach us the selfish and unequal norms and values of the capitalist system. These ideas clearly pose problems for the advancement of a liberating sociological imagination, especially if we are ideologically hindering students' ability to see the world as it is as well as stifling their views and opinions. However, Marxism does offer radical alternative pedagogies to help students break free of a life of false conscience and exploitation.

Importantly, Marx and Engels argued that without education the working class were condemned to 'lives of drudgery and death, but that with education they had a chance to create a better life' (Kellner, n.d., p. 2). Both Marx and Engels believed that with education and experience the *proletariat* (working class) could eventually use it to fight the *bourgeoisie* (ruling class). However, they acknowledged that in order to facilitate this any revolution would need a 'radical intelligentsia' that would leave the bourgeoisie and live alongside and help further the education of the proletariat. The radicals are those who will raise 'themselves to the level of comprehending theoretically the historical movement as a whole' (Marx & Engels, 1975, p. 494 as cited in Kellner, n.d., p. 2). It is here, of course, that a radical pedagogy will be needed to reveal to the working classes not only the systems and structures that exploit them, but also the eventuality of their own emancipation.

For Marx and Engels, the importance of education cannot be underestimated as it is needed to create a harmonious socialist society. Nonetheless, neither Marx nor Engels were pedagogues and, as stated by Kellner (n.d.), they lacked a fully articulated theory of education and subjectivity, which suggests they did not consider what sort of pedagogy is needed for the working classes to discover their own class consciousness as well as the potential of their own agency, or individual capacity, to organise themselves collectively to change their economic position or exploitation (p. 2).

Marx argued that a revolutionary consciousness would develop amongst the masses as they became aware of their exploitation; perhaps all the revolutionary teacher should be doing is 'painting this picture' through formal teacher centred 'chalk and talk'. The radical pedagogue Paulo Freire (1970), however, cautions that the 'oppressed must be their own example in the struggle for their redemption' (p. 54). What a teacher should do is to make it possible for the students to become themselves. Moreover, although I am not directly linking Mills' thinking to critical pedagogy in the same way that I did not wish to link him with functionalism, Freire's ideas do lend themselves to enhancing a sociological imagination of sorts as they encourage students to be conscious of their personal histories and biographies in relation to their current social position or context.

Of course, Freire was known for his criticisms of the *banking model* of education, in which the student's mind is viewed as an empty account to be filled by the teacher's knowledge. He argued that the banking model simply 'transforms students into receiving objects. It attempts to control thinking and action, leads men and women to adjust to the world, and inhibits their creative power' (Freire, 1970, p. 77). Freire believed, therefore, that teaching methods that centre on rote learning, even if well meaning, create a 'culture of silence' that could well lead to students simply accepting everything they are taught without really thinking about it, questioning it and challenging the teacher's or subject's assumptions (see Giroux, 2001, pp. 77–86). Freire also believed that this culture of silence suppresses students' *self-image* as they will not find their voice nor realise the impact their intellect, views and actions can have. Therefore, for Freire, the learner must develop a *critical consciousness* in order to recognise their self-worth and potential.

Another sociological thinker whose work is relevant to this discussion is Pierre Bourdieu, especially his ideas on *habitus*, cultural capital and cultural deprivation. Although Bourdieu himself was neither a pedagogue nor a Marxist,[3] his views on how individual behaviour is constrained by the hierarchical and socially unjust structures that are prevalent in modern society are useful in furthering a Marxist pedagogy. These structures, in Marxist tradition, exist independently of our individual consciousness and include the material and economic structures that shape the class system. However, Bourdieu (1990) is also concerned with the social, symbolic and cultural structures that shape our lives and our perception of ourselves within society (pp. 66–67). Bourdieu called this *habitus*, which suggests these structures can socialise us with an inhibiting perception of our place in society. This can be as much a burden as any material or economic structure. For instance, after reviewing various studies on cultural habitus and *cultural capital*, Halasz and Kaufman (2008) state that, 'those students socialised with the cultural habitus, cultural capital and practices of the dominant class are more likely to succeed in the educational field than those who find the cultural codes foreign and more difficult to acquire' (p. 311). Furthermore, Bourdieu and Passeron (1990) argue that formalised testing is inherently biased as students who come from working class backgrounds will lack cultural capital, which makes their comprehension of questions, texts and wider cultural references found in exams harder than their middle class peers (p. 142); this theory was tested in the UK by Basil Bernstein (2003) and his research suggested Bourdieu and Passeron's ideas are evident in the English educational system. Moreover, this also affects the eloquence in which students write, their articulation in discussion and debate and their teachers' perceptions of them. Here, middle class students are seen as having more *elaborate speech codes* whereas working class students have *restricted speech codes*. It is here, then, that cultural capital is mistaken for merit and students' mistakes are often due more to cultural deprivation than innate intelligence.

This is certainly true of my experience of teaching sociology in mixed comprehensive schools. Often the whole language of sociology – even the content of school textbooks – is so dense that intelligent children from families with no academic background or support at home will struggle more than their classmates from more 'professional' or 'university educated' backgrounds. Although a potentially patronising assertion, I have had students from 'working class families' struggle with words like 'class', 'revolution' and 'merit' – let alone 'meritocracy' – at A Level. Of course, although these words are new to many of them, some students from 'middle class' or 'professional' families have discussed or heard these words at home already. Interestingly, at GCSE level I have come across children with high Cognitive Attainment Test (CAT) scores struggling to explain words like 'community', 'individual' and 'society' whereas others in the class have not suffered these linguistic hindrances despite performing worse in linear subjects like maths. It is arguably incumbent on an outstanding sociology teacher to be aware of cultural deprivation and the barriers it can erect for some of our most intelligent students. As Halasz and Kaufman (2008) suggest, even if you have reservations about Bourdieu's thinking, his 'sociology encourages us to suspend such impulsive reactions and instead implores us to be reflexive about our social practices' (p. 312).

In terms of teaching sociology, we can arguably apply Bourdieu's ideas by simplifying our own sociological language as students start our GCSE and A Level courses. Sociological terms and concepts may be obvious to us, but we cannot assume that all of our students have come across or used the words we are using. Also, we could offer students a variety of activities to build up their confidence prior to the usual written assessments; this could include creating posters championing theoretical perspectives or PowerPoint presentations. Perhaps expressing ideas in ways that are less academically formal could allow students to better comprehend the deeply abstract ideas found in sociology. Away from class, offering students flexible homework options where they can negotiate what they do if resources are a problem, may be of help. Here, it would also be useful to check that students have the time and space to complete them. By the same token, offering activities that stretch and challenge is important, too. Although it might sound as if I am contradicting myself, ensuring we are using difficult words, terms and concepts with students who have demonstrated that they are picking up sociological language is essential, too, even if their own general vocabulary is not particularly academic or articulate.

In some ways this ties in with Freire's critical pedagogy as a teacher should always endeavour to make it possible for the students to 'become themselves' by reaching their potential. There are many ways to do this, but one is clearly to be self-aware of one's own biases. We should also look at how we are planning, differentiating and giving feedback to students as it may not just be a case of ability that is hindering their progress. A Marxist pedagogy would require a teacher to plan for socio-economic differences: have we considered the limits of some students speech codes; have we thought about whether we are taking it for granted that students know our own vocabulary; do they fully understand our cultural references; have they been to libraries, museums and historical sites; have their family members experienced many of the 'common' life events we have, such as going to university or foreign holidays; and, importantly, have they met, got to know and accepted people from or with different cultures, ethnicities and sexualities? Another key issue is taking their access to books and resources for granted. I would argue that many schools are a little hasty in assuming all students have proper access to the internet, for example.

Social action theory as pedagogy

Any general overview of *social action theory* begins with the ideas of Max Weber. Weber (1978) sees social action as how an individual 'attaches a subjective meaning to his behaviour – be it overt or covert, omission or acquiescence. Action is social insofar as its subjective meaning takes account of the behaviour of others and is thereby oriented in its course' (p. 4). In terms of pedagogy, it could be argued that Weber's writings on understanding social action are a useful tool for conceptualising how we understand other people's actions in social situations, especially as it treats students as *subjective agents* with individual perceptions, emotions and motives. Subsequently, Weber identified two main types of understanding. The first was *aktuelles Verstehen*, which is direct *observational understanding*, and the second was *erklärendes Verstehen,* which is often referred to as *empathetic understanding*. Building on the second type, Weber argues that sociologists should interpret the meaning of an act in terms of the thoughts, feelings and motives that have given rise to it. Many sociology textbooks simplify this as understanding social actions by 'putting yourself in the shoes of the person you are studying' in order to comprehend their feelings and motives (Giddens, 2009, p. 6). In some ways, this is very similar to Mills' sociological imagination as the idea of empathising is central to one's ability to imagine the feelings and motivations of others.

However, what would a 'Weberian pedagogy' actually look like? A Weberian teacher may endeavour to set up learning activities that get students thinking about others; exploring their emotions and own motivations towards similar situations to those they are studying in order to reach some degree of empathetic understanding. Of course, this theory is not designed to engineer revolutionary sentiments amongst students, but should allow them to interpret what they see and make value judgements on this (say what they think). Of course, one student's feelings towards a particular issue may not be the same as another's, but this will then allow for debate and evaluation of the subject matter. This is not purely emotive as the first type of understanding, *aktuelles*

Verstehen, suggests the student needs to consider all the factors that could lead to the person or people being studied behaving in such as way. In this sense, there is still room for objective analysis of the facts.

Importantly, the teacher must let students decide to what extent they empathise with others and should remain impartial in order to retain some level of overall objectivity, especially in lessons where emotions may run high. For example, Weber (1978) stated that the role of the teacher in sociology is 'to subordinate himself to his task and to repress the impulse to make an unnecessary spectacle of personal tastes or other sentiments' (p. 493). Therefore, Weber felt that the teacher should have an ethical neutrality, which would certainly put him at odds with advocates of critical pedagogy. Nonetheless, there is scope here for teachers to employ *erklärendes Verstehen* towards understanding their students' circumstances. For example, we try to empathise with how they learn, their so-called learning styles, or even – in a similar way to the ideas of Bourdieu – with their personal circumstances.

How would a Weberian learning activity work in practice? A lot of the content of Chapter 6 on teaching sociological skills will give implicit insights into this, especially how the teacher can act as an objective facilitator of activities that engage students' opinions. If we are to explore others emotions whilst remaining objective as teachers, perhaps there is room for us to act as *'devil's advocates'* in discussion so long as this is to give an alternative perspective. Furthermore, in discussion the teacher could also take the role of a *neutral judge* or a *committed participant in role*, but not as a 'committed participant in a personal capacity'; the former type of participant adds points to discussion to further evaluation whereas the latter gives their opinion (again, see Chapter 6 for more on this). I am sure a lot of politicians and parents would prefer the former types of teacher debate as the teacher's views can unduly influence the students' opinions on things and, perhaps, this runs counter to their freedom to make up their own mind on issues (see Chapter 13 for a discussion on politics and teaching).

In addition to *erklärendes Verstehen,* teachers can further benefit from Weber's thinking by being aware of his concern with the rationalisation of modern society and, in particular, the overarching power of bureaucracy. In a society where critics of modern education often refer to schools as 'exam factories' or, in some cases, 'sausage factories', Weber's work is particularly relevant to our understanding of how schools operate and the impact these operations have on our students. For example, as schools test, set or stream and target students using statistical data and as our own approaches to pedagogy have to increasingly conform to others' view of what Ofsted wants or what senior leadership deems the right way to plan, teach and assess, it often feels like we are placed in a bureaucratic straightjacket that saps all originality, creativity and flexibility from our own classroom practice. Similarly, although Weber acknowledged the benefits of bureaucratic rationalisation, especially our ability to calculate results, he also looked into the dysfunctions of bureaucracy, including its inability to deal with individual cases that do not conform to the norm (see Croser, 2003, p. 230). This is especially important if we take into account our students' lives outside of school, their interactions with peers and other contextual and subjective elements of their day-to-day lives that cannot be calculated or factored into statistical predictions of their ability, potential and/or suitability for certain academic or vocational pathways. Bearing this in mind, it is essential that we remain aware of our students' feelings, individual situations and their own aspirations, in the sense that they are human beings and not learning machines, as well as our own understanding of their ability, potential and interests, regardless of what the bureaucracy (data and management) tell us. For an interesting and deeper discussion on this and how rationalisation can lead to depersonalisation and disenchantment in an educational context, see Halasz and Kaufman's (2008) article 'Sociology as Pedagogy' (pp. 303–304).

Considering the points made above, it is now worth looking at the concept of *symbolic interaction*, which is another area of sociological thinking that can be seen as coming under the wider umbrella of social action theory. Symbolic interaction builds on the Weberian notion of *erklärendes Verstehen* as it seeks to understand how our relationships with other people impact on our own individual behaviour. Although symbolic interactionism originated with George Herbert Mead's work on the meaning and symbolism of 'significant gestures' between individuals, it was further developed by his student Herbert Blumer who believed that people act toward things or phenomena and behave in certain ways based on their understanding of the meanings these things or phenomena have for them (see Ferris & Stein, 2012, p. 30). A simple example is the colour red, which is often associated with danger or caution if on a sign or light. Consequently, people will tend to stop or think twice when faced with a red sign or light. In an educational setting, such things or phenomenon could include the stern unwavering stare of a teacher who is unimpressed with a particular student's behaviour; the stare symbolises a warning to stop. Importantly, Blumer believed these meanings were derived from social interactions with others. Therefore, the stern stare will only have any symbolic meaning if others act in the same way. Moreover, it may take on more significance if others look concerned or become silent as the teacher stares at the student in question.

Building on the ideas of Mead and Blumer, Giddens (2009) suggests that understanding our everyday *social interaction* is an essential aspect of sociological thought and has three key uses:

- firstly, we can learn a great deal about social life and ourselves as social beings from studying our day-to-day routines;
- secondly, we see how individual actions can help us creatively shape and even change social reality within certain social structures;
- and, thirdly, how our everyday social interactions can add to our more holistic understanding of larger social systems and institutions affecting social life (p. 251).

These sociological concepts can arguably be applied to pedagogy as we need to be aware of how our day-to-day interactions with students impacts on their learning. In practice, symbolic interaction can be played out in the application of learning styles in the sociological classroom. As Powers (1999) suggests, we need to comprehend how our students learn (how they act towards learning) in order to apply the best strategies for maximising their learning and academic progress (as cited in Halasz & Kaufman, 2008, p. 308). In Chapter 4, I will go through various conceptions of learning styles that, whilst disputed by some, may enable us to identify students' preferences for activities that they feel improve their knowledge and understanding of the subject. For example, using diagrams for visual learners or setting up active learning activities for those who like learning kinaesthetically. Also, ideas associated with *personalised learning* can be appropriated here as, according to the National College of Teaching and Leadership (NCTL), it aims to provide a tailored education for every learner; including an in-depth understanding of each learner's needs in order to identify and provide learning opportunities that challenge and support students in their learning (NCTL, n.d.). The NCTL states that personalised learning should include 'active commitment from pupils', individual 'responses from teachers' and, if possible, 'engagement from parents'. This is significant to symbolic interactionist approaches to pedagogy as it recognises the importance that these individual interactions can have on shaping student behaviour in the classroom.

Although he did not consider himself a social action theorist nor a symbolic interactionist, it is worth briefly looking at how Erving Goffman's (1990) *dramaturgical analysis* of social action can be applied to our understanding of pedagogy in addition to symbolic interaction (see also Halasz & Kaufman, 2008). Goffman argued that individuals put on acts in front of different people in order to fit in or impress others. This is relevant to teachers as we are constantly being reminded that we are role models and that we have certain professional standards that might make us hide or subdue some aspects of our personalities, thoughts or emotions in front of our classes (or, rather, audience). This is no doubt true of students, too. I have often felt guilty about putting shy students on the spot in class discussions or forgetting that young people are not always going to gel with every other student in the class as they are concerned about their 'performances' in front of others.

It may be less obvious, however, how we apply these ideas to the classroom. Nonetheless, we can give students particular roles in social situations that are either suited to them or will allow them to participate in a way that does not cause anxiety or stress. For example, pair work that involves two people working together before the more extroverted student adds their ideas to a debate or discussion is one way round this. Another could be the use of information and communications technology (ICT), which may allow students to engage with discussion on social media or even in anonymous chat rooms set up for the purpose of studying sociology (obviously, any teacher doing this must be aware of the dangers of this as well as being able to monitor discussion).

Lastly, perhaps we can also use Hargreaves (1998) research on *labelling theory* to see how Goffman's dramaturgical analysis, and social action theory more generally, can be applied to students' behaviour and subsequent achievement in school. Labelling theory examines how the self-identity and behaviour of individuals is often influenced by the words used to describe them. For instance, labelling by teachers or peers can lead students to perform or act in line with these labels. This can lead to a *self-fulfilling prophecy* based on the student's self-identification with others' stereotyping of them. In his study, Hargreaves linked the existence of non-conformist and conformist subcultures in secondary modern schools to the effects of labelling and streaming by teachers. Importantly, Hargreaves found that students placed in lower sets (or streams) were almost immediately labelled as 'trouble-makers' or even 'worthless louts' whereas students in more academic sets or streams were seen as well behaved and academic. This distinction inevitably had a knock-on effect for the trouble-maker's self-esteem and they would often seek out fellow trouble-makers and give up on behaving well and progressing academically; in other words, failure and poor behaviour brought prestige in their subculture. Unsurprisingly the opposite was true for those labelled as well behaved. It is essential, then, that as teachers we are aware of how our own prejudices can affect the students' perception of self and try to be mindful of how our day-to-day interactions can impact on their learning.

Of course, one major criticism of these approaches is that they can burden the teacher with more work, especially if we are to unpack individual students' behaviour, emotions and perceptions of themselves and others. Moreover, it will also lead to teachers spending more time on figuring out students' individual needs or the dynamics of the groups within the class at the expense of other aspects of curriculum and lesson planning. And, lastly, by centring pedagogy on individual

---

Task 3.2 Assess whether students in your school feel labelled

Although you could get students to research this issue (see Chapter 8), it may be interesting for you to see whether labelling theory works in practice by doing some one-to-one meetings with students who may be causing 'trouble' in your school or those that are considered little angels. Perhaps come up with some structured, but open ended questions that implicitly ask the students whether they are labelled and whether this affects their behaviour. You could, for example, do this as part of your pastoral role as a form teacher. The point of this research, quite simply, is to better understand the students you are teaching and perhaps be more cautious in how you interact with them.

---

actions and interactions within the classroom we may be ignoring the wider implications of social structure discussed already with Marxism and to be highlighted by feminism below.

Feminist pedagogy

Although all of sociology's 'founding fathers' are male, sociology is one of the few subjects in school to make the male domination of academic, public and, more often than not, family life, an overt and explicit area of study. Not only is it one of the main theories, but feminism has something to say on almost every area of sociology from *family and households* to *power and politics*. However, it could be argued that both teacher training courses and continuing professional development (CPD) courses pay little attention to *feminist pedagogy* despite concern at gender differences in attainment.

So, what would a feminist pedagogy look like? A good starting point is Allen, Walker and Webb's *Feminist Pedagogy: Identifying Basic Principles* (2002), which is a review of the literature on feminist pedagogy and identifies six general principles of a feminist approach to teaching and learning. These include:

- reformation
- empowerment
- building community
- privileging voice
- respecting personal experience
- challenging traditional pedagogical assumptions.

The first principle, *reforming* the teacher's relationship with the student, is key to overcoming gender inequalities both in and beyond the classroom. The domination of teacher over student transcends gender here as young girls socialised to accept patriarchal authority at home would undoubtedly be conditioned to accept other types of authority elsewhere. In too many situations the teacher dominates the student as power is knowledge and, therefore, the students' experiences and opinions count for less. Here, we see that feminist pedagogy, as a *conflict theory*, builds on some of the ideas of Freire and critical pedagogy. Indeed, many feminist thinkers on education, such as bell hooks, have acknowledged the importance of Freire's work on feminist pedagogical thinking.

The second part of the formulation is *empowerment*, which again follows critical pedagogy's emphasis on liberation and the rise of critical consciousness. Female students must be allowed to participate in the class, to shape discussion and not be judged by prejudicial views of their experiences. They must be seen as members of a democratic process that is compatible with the 'decentering, antihierarchical perspective of feminism' (Woodbridge, 1994, p. 133 as cited in Allen, et al., 2002). A teacher, female or male, must encourage female participation and be aware of inhibitions that might arise from their socialisation at home and elsewhere.

The third principle identified by Allen et al. (2002) is *building community*. In this they talk of establishing learner-centred collaborative activities that allow students to participate in learning as the domination of traditional teacher-led learning is bypassed (this type of teaching is discussed in Chapters 4, 5 and 6). Importantly, this principle puts the previous two principles into some sort of practice as we can see what sort of activities can give rise to independence and voice in their learning. Collaborative activities, such as projects where students all share in producing presentations, documents or research can give female and male students an equal share in input and control; so long as these activities are facilitated properly (discussion on collaborative learning can also be found in Chapters 5–8). Moreover, collaboration can take place between the teacher and student whereby the students help the teacher and other students to suggest solutions to points that the teacher may struggle with. Through a 'problem solving dialogue' students can tackle controversial and topical issues, such as areas of social policy dealing with welfare, in a way that builds on the students' own experiences and 'harmonises well with feminist theories of [liberating] theory and praxis' (Allen et al., 2002).

The next two principles in many ways reflect the importance of bringing in the sociological imagination to feminist thinking on pedagogy as they highlight the importance of individual experience. This is similar to Mills' emphasis on biography and social context. The next two principles, then, are *privileging the individual voice* as a way of knowing and a *respect for the diversity of individual experience*. The latter is not only important for females if they are to participate and feel empowered, but is also important for males to understand female experiences from hearing about their opinions and views; for many boys, a girl's perspective may be new to them. Moreover, the former point raises the importance of mixing personal 'biography' or experience with the social context of what is being studied in that the feminist project has always encouraged an analysis of personal experience through validation. In the 'feminist classroom' girls will be able to shed light on the meaning of the subject being studied through their own personal experiences and this is no less relevant to sociology than any other subject, especially as girls will be able to add voice to their experiences of, say, gender inequalities in schools if studying the sociology of education. The point here is that liberation can only be achieved if students learn to respect each other's opinions and experiences. Importantly, for Allen et al. (2002), 'respect can replace fear when students articulate unique personal experiences based on diverse backgrounds'.

The last principle is *challenging traditional assumptions*. Sociology is arguably uniquely placed to do this due to the substantial contribution of feminism to the subject. Not only does this principle tie up all the previous principles, but it also highlights an important element of feminist thinking on the sociology of education itself; this includes the domination of male writers, historical figures and role models across the curriculum. A sociology teacher, therefore, should not only challenge the dominance of male thinkers such as Talcott Parsons and Charles Murray, but should also emphasise the work of female sociologists like Ann Oakley or Fran Ansley, especially when challenging

Parsons' and Murray's views on the nuclear family, for instance.[4] Moreover, female sociologists must be given voice throughout all areas of the syllabus so that girls can see the importance of their contributions and the potential of their own sociological abilities. A cynic may argue that some areas may be lacking feminist perspectives and that male writers are more important due to their work and not their gender, but in sociology there are relatively few areas where both feminist and female voices cannot be heard.

Task 3.3 Do you include enough female sociologists?

Go through your lesson plans, teaching resources and hand-outs and tally up how many references you make to male and female sociologists. Of course, it may be wise to narrow this down to a scheme of work or even a sub-section of a particular topic, but the results could suggest that your teaching is dominated by the ideas and research of men. If so, can you find any female sociologists to balance the discrepancies?

However, some feminists may argue that pedagogy needs to be aware of more than just a female experience, especially if we consider *black feminism* and *queer theory*. Whilst any formulation of a feminist pedagogy will be built on inclusion, equality and collaboration between students of different genders, a conception of these differences as purely male and female can lead to the marginalisation of other groups, especially where a white liberal feminist narrative becomes the dominant way of defining these differences. For example, a sociology teacher should be aware that the experiences of minority students, both male and female, will sometimes be very different to those of their white peers. There will be complex sensitivities and issues here that may involve different solutions than the more dominant narrative would assume. For instance, advances and changes in the law may have less impact for women in some communities or religious groups than others. Further still, the experiences of gay and lesbian students may not be resonant with changes in gender equality let alone be included in all areas of sociology. Here, areas of sociological interest such as education rarely involve discussion on issues surrounding sexuality, for example. It is in this vein that feminist and critical pedagogue bell hooks (1994) argues that the classroom can help students to *transgress* racial, sexual, and class boundaries that inhibit their freedom – so long as teachers see this as the purpose of education.

Postmodern pedagogy

The last sociological theory we will view in relation to pedagogy is postmodernism. Postmodernism can arguably inform pedagogy in a world that is rapidly changing and where knowledge and access to knowledge is becoming less dependent on trained professionals, such as us teachers, as students today have access to so much information through digital media and the internet. However, writing on adult education, Campbell (1993) has argued that the pedagogical nature of postmodernism is difficult to conceptualise as its central characteristics resist a fixed and stable definition (p. 3). Nonetheless, between writers interested in postmodernism and education there is some agreement on postmodernism's central features, which include the importance of heterogeneity (difference) of subject content, the plurality and choice of views and the fragmentary nature of what is being studied. In some ways due to the ever changing nature of sociology and the emergence of new studies and critiques of previous studies, a postmodernist approach may be beneficial, especially as the traditional theoretical aspects embedded in modernism are often seen, especially by students, as outdated.

Perhaps a postmodernist pedagogy for teaching sociology would centre on criticising subject content and challenging students to question whether sociology itself is part of an outdated modernist enterprise. Of course, this may seem impractical when so much of the subject content is focused on traditional sociological theories, but the inclusion of a postmodernist critique will allow for students to easily evaluate the main theories in relevant exam questions. In most syllabuses, especially at A Level, not only is postmodernism included as a perspective, but there is no reason why students cannot bring postmodernist views into their learning or assessments to counter the dominant views of functionalism, Marxism and feminism in particular. For example, the work by Hareven (2000) on *life course analysis* can be used to challenge the traditional views of Talcott Parsons that the nuclear family is the 'best fit' for society. Here, a teacher can set up activities that allow students to compare people's 'life courses' in the so-called modern and postmodern eras (this includes accounting for changes in the chronological order of our lives, such as getting married for life in your 20s in the modern era to getting married in your mid-30s and even re-married thereafter in the postmodern era; for an example, see Chapter 7). Again, and in line with the sociological imagination, this type of analysis can allow the students own situations to be used as a tool for comparing and contrasting the worth and significance of traditional sociological theories.

Moreover, a postmodernist pedagogy would emphasise the *politics of difference* which notices, names, and respects difference as opposed to accepting a *politics of unity* that works towards consensus or sameness (Campbell, 1993, p. 4). Here, students would be encouraged to see that there is no one dominant view and that all views in sociology need to be taken seriously with some degree of respect. Some sociologists have characterised the postmodern world as being one of individuality, incessant choice and constant change; and it can be argued that sociology offers choice for the individual amongst very fragmented subject areas that can jump from culture and identity to health.

In a practical sense, then, if a teacher is to take a postmodern approach, they will employ teaching techniques that allow the students to decide for themselves what theories and perspectives they side with whilst allowing space for the criticism of all of them as well as the subject itself. In some ways, these would not be dissimilar to techniques used to teach from a critical, social action or feminist perspective, as they would all inspire students to think critically about sociology as a subject. It is in this sense that postmodernism is arguably conducive to the sociological imagination.

Another aspect to consider is that the students may see the world completely differently to us teachers. Giroux argues that a postmodern pedagogy needs to be aware of our students changing views, attitudes and desires in the context of the historical, economic, and cultural times they are living in (see Castells et al., 1994). Their reasons for studying sociology, their views of education and their ways of viewing society will be highly nuanced to the context of their lives and it is important that we do not make assumptions about shared understandings and meanings. However, perhaps a criticism of postmodernism is that, firstly, we need to teach a syllabus that is geared towards common views of sociology and, secondly, that the pedagogy here – that we should be aware of inter-generational understandings of society – is not unique.

Conclusion

Although all the theories discussed here are different, they all offer some ideas for teaching sociology. Moreover, as we started with Mills' sociological imagination, it seems clear that all five theories aim to recognise that our private troubles are often reflected in less personal public issues. Whether it is a functionalist approach that allows an element of individualism to be seen alongside a wider collective conscience of accepted norms and values or the more radical views of Freire in his argument for critical consciousness, it is clear that sociology works best when students realise that the subject impacts on them and that they impact on the subject.

Of course, the methodologies employed by sociologists often favour objectivity over subjectivity (positivism over interpretivism), especially when looking at the macro structures of society. However, it is still possible to get students to understand these theories by 'imagining' how their own lives fit within the patterns and trends evident in the wider social world. The same imaginative process can be reversed for micro studies focusing on small groups or individuals. Here, students can imagine how the motives, feelings and actions of each agent plays out in the wider world, especially when considering how certain social issues are presented via less subjective statistics or research. The sociological imagination, then, is a conceptual tool that transcends agency and structure in the context of pedagogy as it aims to give students a greater connection to the subject they have chosen to study. Moreover, it can be applied to each perspective in its own way, although this is dependent on the teacher using their own sociological imagination.

Further reading

Mills, C. Wright (1959). *The sociological imagination.* New York: Oxford University Press.
> This book is a good call to arms for sociology. In the book, Mills tries to conceptually bridge the two very big ideas of 'the individual' and 'society' and argues that by studying sociology students can see how the two concepts relate, interact and influence each other. Therefore, through their studies of the subject, students will be better placed to both understand and change society.

Halasz, J. R. & Kaufman, P. (2008). Sociology as pedagogy: How ideas from the discipline can inform teaching and learning. *Teaching sociology, 36,* 301–314.
> This is one of the few expositions of sociological theories and pedagogy. Although written for those that are well versed in sociological perspectives, it does give a clear and concise overview of some key sociologists' ideas and how they can be applied to pedagogy.

Freire, P. (1970). *Pedagogy of the oppressed.* New York: Herder and Herder.
> This book has had a massive impact on the philosophy of education. Despite Freire's background in adult literacy, his ideas on empowering the oppressed may inspire you to see the transformative nature of education, especially if you teach disadvantaged students. It is Marxist in tone, but I have a number of somewhat non-political colleagues who have found Freire's student-centred methodology useful in their everyday practice.

Notes

1   Despite the vast amounts of books by Talcott Parsons as well as those about him, one of the best places to start is in the education section of most general textbooks, especially Webb, Westergaard, Trobe and Townsend, (2015), *AQA A Level sociology book one including AS Level*, Bath: Napier Press. Even if you are not using AQA, this has an excellent sociology of education section.
2   Again, most A Level textbooks cover these thinkers.
3   It is worth noting that Bourdieu never identified as a Marxist, but his arguments are conducive to neo-Marxist views.
4   All good AS/A Level textbooks will cover these thinkers in relation to the nuclear family.

Bibliography

Agnew, R. (1992). Foundation for a general strain theory. *Criminology, 30*(1), 47–87.

Allen, M. W., Walker, K. L. & Webb L. M. (2002). *Feminist pedagogy: Identifying basic principles.* Retrieved from www.thefreelibrary.com/Feminist+pedagogy%3a+identifying+basic+principles.+(The+scholarship+of...-a085916959

Althusser, L. (2001). Ideology and ideological state apparatuses: Notes towards an investigation. In *Lenin and philosophy and other essays* (pp. 85–126). New York: NYU Press.

Bernstein, B. (2003). *Class, codes and control: Applied studies towards a sociology of language.* London: Psychology Press.

Bourdieu, P. (1990). *The logic of practice.* Cambridge: Polity Press.

Bourdieu, P. & Passeron, J. C. (1990). *Reproduction in education, society and culture.* London: Sage.

Bowles, S. & Gintis, H. (1976). *Schooling in capitalist America: Educational reform and the contradictions of economic life.* New York: Basic Books.

Campbell, P. (1993). *Pedagogical implications of postmodernism in adult literacy.* Retrieved from http://files.eric.ed.gov/fulltext/ED400416.pdf

Capel, S., Leask, M. & Turner, T. (Eds.). (2013). *Learning to teach in the secondary school: A companion to school experience.* London: Routledge.

Castells, M., Flecha, R., Freire, P., Giroux, H. A., Macedo, D. & Willis, P. (1999). *Critical education in the new information age.* Lanham: Rowman and Littlefield Press.

Croser, L. A. (2003). *Masters of sociological thought: Ideas in historical and social context.* Long Grove: Waveland Press.

Durkheim, E. (1997). *The division of labor in society* (W.D. Halls, Trans.). New York: Free Press.

Ferris, K. & Stein, J. (2012). *The real world: An introduction to sociology* (3rd ed.). New York: W. W. Norton.

Freire, P. (1970). *Pedagogy of the oppressed.* New York: Herder and Herder.

Gershon, M. (2015). *Teach now! History: Becoming a great history teacher.* London: Routledge.

Giddens, A. (1971). *Capitalism and modern social theory: An analysis of the writings of Marx, Durkheim and Max Weber.* Cambridge: Cambridge University Press.

Giddens, A. (2009). *Sociology* (6th ed.). Cambridge: Polity Press.

Giroux, H. A. (2001). Culture, power and transformation in the work of Paulo Freire. In F. Schultz (Ed.), *Sources: Notable selections in education* (3rd ed.) (pp. 77–86). New York: McGraw Hill Dushkin.

Goffman, E. (1990). *The presentation of self in everyday life.* London: Penguin.

Halasz, J. R. & Kaufman, P. (2008). Sociology as pedagogy: How ideas from the discipline can inform teaching and learning. *Teaching Sociology, 36*, 301–314.

Hareven T. (2000). *Families, history, and social change: Life course and cross-cultural perspectives.* Boulder: Westview Press.

Hargreaves, D. (1998). *Social relations in a secondary school.* London: Routledge.

hooks, b. (1994). *Teaching to transgress: Education as the practice of freedom.* London: Routledge.

Kellner, D. (n.d.) *Marxian perspectives on educational philosophy: From classical Marxism to critical pedagogy.* Retrieved from www.gseis.ucla.edu/faculty/kellner/

Marx, K. & Engels, F. (1975). *Collected works.* London: International Publishers and Lawrence & Wishart.

Merton, R. K. (1938). Social structure and anomie. *American Sociological Review, 3*(5), 672–682.

Merton, R. K. (1957). *Social theory and social structure.* New York: Free Press.

Mills, C. Wright (1959). *The sociological imagination.* New York: Oxford University Press.

National College of Teaching and Leadership. (n.d.). *ADSBM phase 3 module 1: Enabling learning.* Retrieved from www.nationalcollege.org.uk/transfer/open/adsbm-phase-3-module-1-enabling-learning/adsbm-p3m1s 2/adsbm-p3m1s2t4.html

Powers, G. T. (1999). Teaching and learning: A matter of style. In Pescosolido, B. A. & Aminzafe, R. (Eds.), *The social world of higher education: Handbook for teaching in a new century* (pp. 435–446). Thousand Oaks: Pine Forge Press.

Smith, M. K. (2012). What is pedagogy? In *The encyclopedia of informal education.* Retrieved from http://infed. org/mobi/what-is-pedagogy/

Webb, R., Westergaard, H., Trobe, K. & Townsend, A. (2015). *AQA A Level sociology* (book one). Bath: Napier Press.

Weber, M. (1978). *Economy and society: An outline of interpretive sociology.* Oakland: University of California Press.

Willmott, P. & Young, M. (1972). *Family and class in a London suburb.* London: Routledge and Kegan Paul.

Woodbridge, L. (1994). The centrifugal classroom. In S. M. Deats & L. T. Lenker (Eds.), *Gender and academe: Feminist pedagogy and politics* (pp. 133–151). Lanham: Rowman & Littlefield.

4 Thinking about learning styles, skills and capacities in relation to sociology

This chapter includes:

- The importance of active learning.
- What learning styles are.
- The simple ideas of VARK as a tool for thinking about learning in sociology.
- Howard Gardner's multiple intelligences and their possible application to sociology.
- David Kolb's experiential learning cycle as a strategy for developing students' ability to learn complex ideas.
- Learning skills: the importance of Bloom's taxonomy and higher order thinking skills in relation to sociology.
- The personal, learning and thinking skills (PLTS) framework in the context of sociology.
- How Building Learning Power (BLP) capacities can aid students' progress in sociology.
- Developing students' Growth Mindset in sociology.
- A word on personalising learning.

In order to teach sociology successfully you must be able to teach. This statement might seem self-evident, but it is not as straightforward as it sounds. An effective sociology teacher has to do three things when they teach the subject. First, they have to know how students learn. Second, they have to apply this knowledge on learning to sociology. And, thirdly, they have to be able to deliver it in the classroom. Therefore, this chapter largely covers the first aspect of the above assertion whereas the following four chapters address the latter aspects.

Active learning

Put simply, *learning* is the acquisition of knowledge and skills by being taught, through study or from experience. However, many educationalists emphasise that learning should be *active*. According to Michelle Lowe (2013) this 'occurs when a learner takes some responsibility for the development of the activity, emphasising a sense of ownership and personal involvement is the key to successful learning' (p. 328). Essentially, our job as teachers is not only to tell the students what they need to know in order to pass exams, which would be *passive learning*, but is also about getting students to see the importance and value of what they are learning. Therefore, the process of learning needs to give them a sense of purpose, fulfilment and pride as they interact with the material they are studying. In this sense, active learning is highly conducive to the development of a sociological imagination as students will actively engage with the sociological content of lessons by contributing to discussion and debate and critically analysing and evaluating sociological ideas. Nonetheless, if we are to promote active learning in sociology we need to consider how students learn in some depth. A good starting point here is with the students themselves and how they prefer to learn.

Learning styles

Academics have spent a great deal of time studying how students learn. Although their studies can often be abstract and full of psychological jargon, sociology teachers should pay some attention to them as they can be useful in understanding how students learn best. The concept of *learning styles* refers to students' preferences for the sort of tasks and activities they find engaging and most effective in developing their own knowledge and skills. Chris Kyriacou (2014) states that the students' preferences 'in regards to the physical and social characteristics of the learning situation' can be taken into consideration as well (pp. 70–71). This would include considering whether they enjoy interacting with others and how far they are willing to participate in group activities. By way of example, Kyriacou lists a number of activities that could be seen as learning styles, such as whether students like to read as opposed to listen, work alone rather than in pairs or groups, find things out for themselves or have the teacher spell things out for them and, lastly, have learning proscribed and scaffolded as opposed to being left to figure things out for themselves.

It is arguably important in sociology, if we are to work on the pedagogies suggested in the last chapter, to explore these learning styles further in order to put students in the driving seat of their own learning. Nonetheless, Kyriacou does caution us here to be wary of trying to please all the people all the time. Firstly, it is important that students build up a variety of skills and this will inevitably mean taking them away from the comfort zone of their preferred learning style. He states that, 'Pupils who are taught overwhelmingly in their preferred learning style may not be able to develop a full range of learning skills' (Kyriacou, 2014). Secondly, Kyriacou believes that learning styles are hard to determine and teachers may misjudge the students if they try to make a permanent match. Moreover, most students will be able to apply various learning styles and will adapt different learning styles to different activities, tasks and lessons. Interestingly, this caution has also been highlighted by the sociologist David Hargreaves who has chaired a report into learning styles for the Demos think tank. The report stated that the evidence for learning styles was 'highly variable' and that teachers and educators championing learning styles were 'not by any means frank about the evidence for their work' (Hargreaves et al., 2005, p. 11).

The useful simplicity of VARK

Although there are plenty of theories and research on learning styles, such as Robert M. Gagné's (1985) five categorisations for learning and Peter Honey and Alan Mumford's (1982) *Learning Styles Questionnaire*, perhaps a good place to start is Neil Fleming's (1995) VARK model, which is probably the most common and widely taught categorisation of learning styles. Despite being criticised as simplistic and too restrictive, as well as drawing flack for being built on questionable evidence, it is still taught on many teacher training courses, CPD courses and is part of the language of teaching and learning. Fleming's VARK model includes:

- Visual learners;
- Auditory learners;
- Reading and writing preference learners;
- Kinaesthetic learners.

The premise here is straightforward: *visual learners* have a preference for seeing things and may benefit from pictures or other types of visual aids that represent ideas. In terms of sociology, this is a very useful conceptualisation when considering that abstract and theoretical aspects of the subject are highly conducive to visualisation. Abstract ideas, such as Marx's theory of society's economic base and superstructure, can easily be depicted as a diagram. Students may also benefit from mind mapping concepts associated with sociological themes and perspectives, such as family types, and be able to create flowcharts and diagrams for demographic changes etc. (see Chapter 7 for more on this in relation to teaching sociological theories). Moreover, statistics can be depicted in bar graphs and pie charts etc. which means that something a visual learner may have found extremely difficult to comprehend suddenly becomes more comprehensible.

Fleming's second categorisation is *auditory learning*. Auditory learners can benefit from listening to others, listening to lectures and, if applicable, music. One of the main staples of any sociology lesson at any level is a good old discussion or debate on a topical issue. For students who like to listen to, if not always take part in, discussion and debate the benefits are intrinsic. Be that as it may, it is imperative in discussion and debate to ensure learners are listening and not passively sitting there doing nothing (this is discussed in-depth in Chapter 6). Of course, part of my argument so far is that teachers need to be wary of too much chalk and talk, but many students still prefer to learn that way. Although my evidence is anecdotal, I have been the recipient of numerous protests, especially in the run-up to exams, when students 'just want to know' what they 'need to know'. For these learners there are a vast amount of resources available outside of class. Good examples include the numerous YouTube channels set up by teachers and students that talk students through aspects of sociology as well as various documentaries and television shows that are available on the internet. For students who can listen well and have a real interest in learning more about the subject, radio programmes such as BBC Radio 4's *Thinking Allowed*, which is presented by the sociologist Laurie Taylor, is an excellent introduction to the variety, richness and importance of sociological studies (see Chapter 12 for more on using YouTube and *Thinking Allowed*).

Furthermore, music can be used as a way to engage *auditory learners*. There is plenty of music, especially in pop culture, which can be used to introduce students to sociological topics. There is more on this idea later in the book, but examples could be using Bob Marley's *Them Belly Full (But We Hungry)* to teach about stratification and Pulp's *Common People* to teach about the stereotyping of the working class (see Chapter 12). Using pop music not only adds a bit of street cred to your lessons, if you can fathom the current trends and tastes of your students, but often lyrics are highly, if not implicitly, sociological.

The third part of VARK highlights learners with a preference for *reading and writing*. Students who have this preference will obviously prefer reading text in print or even online and may be note takers and bullet pointers as opposed to mind mappers or flow charters. Some students with this preference may also have a tendency to write extensive notes, create lists, categorise things under headings and consult dictionaries and glossaries as well as being very appreciative of hand-outs.[1] If you are giving out hand-outs or copying articles or sections of textbooks, it may be worth having sets of highlighters to help these students make sense of all the paper they will end up stuffing into lever arch folders.

However, on a practical level, these preferences can be a danger if you put too much on a whiteboard or PowerPoint; students will attempt to copy everything down and complain that you are moving on too fast. Moreover, students who prefer learning this way may not necessarily produce the best essays despite a preference for 'writing'. You will need to be wary of homework that has been copied or taken verbatim from something you said in class. Remember, it is a learning style which does not automatically turn into academic prowess due to its scholarly sounding title. Students who prefer this type of learning will always need scaffolding, guidance and formative feedback in order to reach their potential. As discussed in the following chapters, writing sociologically is different to the writing styles found in other subjects; some of the biggest challenges my students have faced is learning to write sociology essays without using 'I' all the time to denote their own personal opinion as opposed to a sociological argument.

The last part of VARK is *kinaesthetic learning*, which means students prefer to learn through activities that involve moving, touching, and doing. There are plenty of ways in which to incorporate kinaesthetic learning into lessons. Getting students to move around, perhaps through games or role play, is one obvious method. There is no reason why students studying sociology at GCSE, AS/A Level or even in higher education should not be playing active games, such as 'walkabout bingo' or producing role plays to demonstrate social situations. Moreover, for those that like to create through touch, investing in Lego can be a wise use of departmental budgets. In the past, I have used Lego to get students to recreate their best childhood memories (the social construction of childhood) or to attempt to create structural theories such as functionalism and Marxism in AS/A Level lessons (see Chapter 8).

The application of VARK learning styles to sociology allows us to prepare classes that address some of our students' learning preferences. Subsequently, despite the simplicity of this model and

---

Task 4.1 Case studies of different learners

To understand how different students learn, it may be worth selecting a number of them that have identified a preferred learning style. By selecting 4 students based on the VARK styles, you could then set them differentiated work both in class and away from class. For example, visual learners could be set mind mapping activities for home work; you could identify podcasts (see Chapter 12) for auditory learners to listen to and feedback on; and you could select readings with scaffolded note taking exercises for students with a reading and writing preference. Kinaesthetic is harder, but they could be given key texts and ask to 'do' their own small surveys and compare their results to the arguments or findings in the text. Over time, monitor how the students acquisition of knowledge and skills increases and ask them if they enjoy learning this way; this may then inform how you differentiate and personalise learning (see Chapter 9 for more on differentiation).

concern that it is too broad ranging and that the research behind it is questionable, we can arguably use it to help our students maximise their understanding of sociology by thinking about how they prefer or even like to learn.

Multiple intelligences

If you feel that VARK is too simplistic and we need to think about learning styles in more depth, Howard Gardner's theory of *multiple intelligences* is a useful conceptual model. Although Gardner (1993) has his critics – these critics, like those of VARK, often see his categories of intelligence as too simplistic, broad ranging or, reversely, too narrow – his theory gives us useful categorisations in which to think of learning styles. Importantly, for Gardner, intelligence is the ability to resolve 'genuine problems or difficulties' and, therefore, by harnessing these intelligences we, as sociology teachers, can better inform our methods of teaching to suit our students needs or, rather, intelligences so that they can solve sociological problems or, at least, better understand them (p. 60).

Gardner (1999) originally listed seven intelligences, but this has increased to eight as he has developed his ideas; he has debated the inclusion of 'existential' and 'moral intelligences' as well, but has decided that the concept and evidence is not strong enough at present. Despite questions on the relevance, practicalities and actual evidence for these categorisations, I feel they have helped me understand how children learn; so long as you see them as a tool to think about the processes of learning and, subsequently, teaching. The eight intelligences are listed below and I have endeavoured to suggest how they can relate to sociology.

- **Linguistic intelligence:** Gardner believes that linguistic intelligence includes sensitivity to spoken and written language, the ability to be articulate and persuasive as well as the capacity to learn languages. Subsequently, learners with this preference would benefit from discussions, debates and written tasks in class. As Gardner sees this as benefitting professions such as writing, law and anything involving public speaking or debate, teachers can rest assured that developing linguistic intelligence is giving students an important specialist skill (see the points made about Durkheim in Chapter 1).
- **Logical-mathematical intelligence:** this intelligence is most often associated with scientific and mathematical thinking, which includes the ability to think logically, solve mathematical problems and investigate issues using a scientific methodology. Importantly, Gardner claims that this intelligence gives learners the ability to recognise patterns and logically deduce reasons for causes, effects and correlations. This intelligence, therefore, is of use to sociology as a lot of positivist studies rely on statistical data that needs to be analysed mathematically. For students with this learning preference, you could consider activities based around analysing raw empirical data, especially official statistics, on anything from free school meals to stop and search statistics (for ideas on how to set up activities based on numbers, see Chapter 8).
- **Musical intelligence:** this intelligence centres on the performance, composition and appreciation of musical patterns. Gardner argued that it is similar to mathematical and linguistic intelligences due to the skills of recognising patterns and it is, therefore, also similar to the idea of auditory learning in VARK. This narrower categorisation may seem irrelevant to sociology, but you can consider bringing music into lessons on a range of things, such as

using music to get students thinking about postmodernism. Jazz or various forms of *avant garde* classical music can be compared to more traditional forms of classical music to explore the lack of structure and predictability in the former in contrast to the latter.

- **Bodily-kinaesthetic intelligence:** this intelligence involves using the body or parts of the body to solve problems and stems from the brain's ability to coordinate bodily movements. Again, it may seem an intelligence that is largely redundant in an academic subject like sociology, but there is no reason why students should not use their fine motor skills in lessons. 3D puzzles and challenges, such as constructing things out of straws, Play-Doh or even Lego, appeal to these learners as they have to use their hands to create sociological structures to represent key concepts or theories (see Chapter 7).

- **Spatial intelligence:** this intelligence includes the skill of understanding and utilising space and confined areas in productive ways. In sociology, there is no end of conceptual ideas that can be explored through the use of spatial awareness. One area is arranging artefacts in a classroom to represent the concepts studied in *urban criminology*. For example, the work of sociologists aligned to the Chicago School on concentric rings, which are zones of desirability/ liveability within cities, can be redefined as comfort zones within the classroom. Quite simply, if one part of the classroom is undesirable due to the teacher's leftover lunch being left there or another has an overflowing bin, where would students position themselves in relation to them? Students could be tasked with zoning the space within the classroom to mirror the concentric rings described by Park and Burgess in their book *The City* (1967).

- **Interpersonal intelligence:** this intelligence is very relevant to sociology, especially when dealing with interpretivist approaches to the subject. It involves understanding the intentions, motivations and desires of other people, which is similar to the principle of *Verstehen* (empathetic understanding) as advocated by Weber and discussed in the previous chapter. Nurturing it through appropriate learning activities can make students more empathetic towards those affected by the issues they are studying. Moreover, it has a more practical use in the classroom as these learners will be able to work effectively with others whether in pairs, groups or with the class as a whole. Interestingly, creating activities based on this intelligence would also relate to the ideas of social solidarity discussed in relation to Durkheim in Chapter 1. Importantly, Gardner argued that, in later life, educators, salespeople, religious and political leaders and counsellors all need a well-developed interpersonal intelligence (Smith, 2008).

- **Intrapersonal intelligence:** this intelligence allows the individual to understand her or himself better, to appreciate their feelings, fears and motivations. Activities that get students to think about their positions on various sociological themes and perspectives would be relevant here. Do they feel angry when confronted by certain sociological perspectives? (This often happens when I teach the ideas of Charles Murray (1999) on welfare dependency, single parents and the 'underclass'). Simple activities that get the students to identify their positions will appeal to these types of learners and are some of the simplest to set up; often via straightforward questioning (see the next chapter for ideas on this). Importantly, the ideas of intrapersonal and interpersonal intelligences are central to building up a sociological imagination as advocated by Mills.

- **Naturalistic intelligence:** although this was not included in Gardner's initial list, this intelligence has to do with an awareness and appreciation of one's natural surroundings. In some ways it is an extension of interpersonal intelligence, which is applied to the natural world as learners' need to have a 'sensitive, ethical, and holistic understanding' of it (Morris, 2004, p. 159). This may seem less tangible in terms of activities, but sociology does include reference to environmentalism; for example, most *crime and deviance* syllabuses include green crime.

Of course, as briefly touched upon, critics of multiple intelligences argue that they are not particularly well defined and can be hard to implement in the classroom. However, it is again worth stressing that these intelligences are not necessarily separate nor are they always fixed; children's minds develop at various rates (despite what target data tells us) and their ability to adapt and learn new skills should not be underestimated. In fact, Gardner himself has suggested that you can substitute 'intelligences' for 'thought processes', 'cognitive capacities' or 'forms of knowledge' (Gardner, 1993, p. 284), which means it is not entirely clear whether these 'intelligences' are innate or learned (Ireson & Levinson, 2013, p. 238). However, I would suggest that the main purpose of using 'multiple intelligences' as teachers is to get us to think about the variety of intelligences students might have and not to categorise or label them with any particular one; they are a useful conceptual tool for thinking about ways in which to engage students with active learning.

Task 4.2 Observe other subjects

If you are somebody with a humanities or social science degree, you may be unsure how to set up activities around mathematical, auditory and visual intelligences. However, you will have a wealth of ideas within your school on how to adapt your teaching to suit multiple intelligences. Firstly, arrange to observe colleagues in maths, music and art, for example, to see how they teach and what activities they use. Secondly, you could then think about adapting some of those activities for use in sociology lessons. For instance, I learnt to incorporate simple activities on percentages in sociology lessons from observing similar activities in Year 8 maths lessons; here, my students turned raw data from the British Crime Survey into percentages, see Chapter 8 for more on this type of activity.

Kolb's experiential learning cycle

As mentioned above, one key objection to allowing students to learn via their preferred learning style is that it will not allow them to develop new abilities and skills. Moreover, these students will not cope when different learning styles are used in other lessons and in higher education. However, in order to address this issue, we can apply David Kolb's *experiential learning cycle* as a way of developing learning styles that may be outside of students' comfort zones (Kolb, 2014). Kolb uses this cycle to conceptualise the 'stages' of learning and, subsequently, apply it as a strategy for getting students to complete various learning tasks successfully. Therefore, it can be used as a strategy that gets students to attempt and eventually comprehend new and often daunting learning situations. It also endeavours to get them actively involved with the process of learning.

The strategy is broken down into four stages: concrete experience, reflective observation, abstract conceptualisation and active experimentation (see Figure 4.1). Despite the long words, the strategy is relatively simple in that the *concrete experience* involves the initial learning

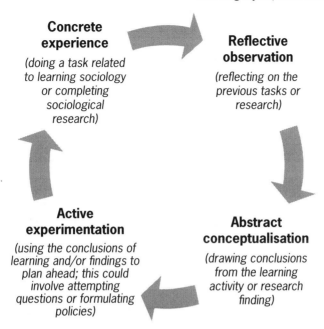

Concrete experience

(doing a task related to learning sociology or completing sociological research)

Reflective observation

(reflecting on the previous tasks or research)

Active experimentation

(using the conclusions of learning and/or findings to plan ahead; this could involve attempting questions or formulating policies)

Abstract conceptualisation

(drawing conclusions from the learning activity or research finding)

Figure 4.1 Kolb's learning cycle adapted for teaching sociology

experience. Once the student has been immersed in that type of learning (whether we call it an activity, style or process), they then need to reflect on what they learnt or understood from it. Of course, they may have found it useful or difficult, but they will need to reflect on and observe why this is in order to better understand what the objective of the learning task was. Here, a teacher can scaffold activities to point out what should have been learnt as well as the common misconceptions or mistakes made by students when attempting that task or type of learning activity. The third stage follows on from the second as through *reflection* students start to integrate their observations of what they are learning into an *abstract conceptualisation*. This stage then allows students to use these conceptualisations to solve problems in the final *active* implementation stage (Fielding, 1996 as cited in Burton, 2013).

Kolb's strategy is particularly useful when setting up learning activities focused on sociological theories and perspectives. The initial immersion into theory can often startle students, especially if it is explored via a learning style that they find difficult. For example, a student who does not make regular use of visual aids, such as diagrams, may be puzzled by the use of a triangle to explain stratification from a Marxist perspective (the *proletariat* as the mass at the bottom and the *bourgeoisie* as the minority at the top). However, when learning this students must be given time – perhaps through another activity such as discussion – to reflect on why the triangle has been used to represent the relative position of socio-economic groups in the class system. This reflection/activity should then allow students to think about why some people represent it that way. The process should, therefore, help the students gain a better abstract conceptualisation of the class system as a whole. Perhaps the active experimentation stage can then involve students adding more complicated strata or social groups to explain more complex ideas of Marxist views of stratification.

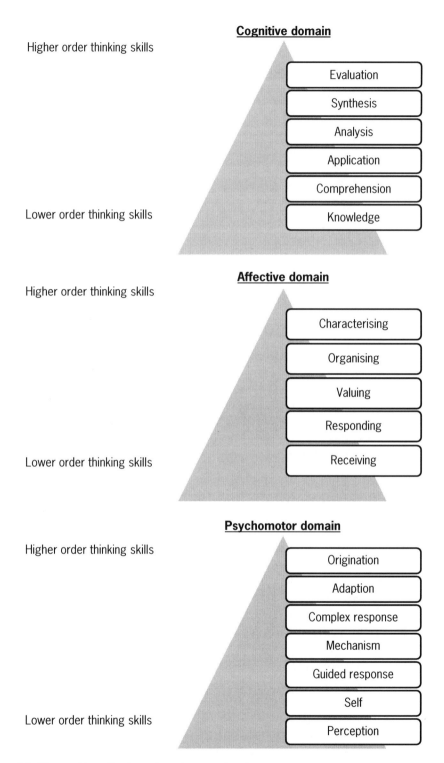

Figure 4.2 The cognitive, affective and psychomotor domains
Source: Adapted from Bloom, 1956; Krathwohl, Bloom and Masia, 1964; and Simpson, 1972.

Learning skills: The importance of Bloom's taxonomy

Aside from learning styles and strategies, it is also worth thinking about the generic learning skills that students need to succeed in school and how they relate to sociology. Any discussion on academic skills should include a brief overview of *Bloom's Taxonomy* (Bloom, 1956). This staple of teacher training, CPD and general best practice has been used from the 1950s and is still popular today.

The taxonomy was the result of a number of conferences on learning chaired by Benjamin Bloom. However, Bloom only edited the first of three key handbooks that have since been revised and updated.[2] Nevertheless, the taxonomy identifies three key *domains of learning*, which are: cognitive, affective, and psychomotor (see Figure 4.2 on previous page). Each domain in turn classifies six levels of learning and essentially ranks them in order of difficulty. For instance, the most commonly used is the *cognitive domain*, which starts by classifying the *lower order thinking skills* of knowledge, comprehension and application and then moves onto the *higher order thinking skills* of analysis, synthesis and evaluation.

This taxonomy is useful to sociology as, firstly, it mirrors the key skills of knowledge and understanding, interpretation, application, analysis and evaluation. If we are to use Bloom's levels as a ladder for building up our students' sociological abilities, then we will be building not only the skills just listed, but also contributing to the skills looked for by examiners at both GCSE and AS/A Level. Secondly, as Bloom was interested in seeking ways to structure, develop and progress learning through using skills for objective setting, the taxonomy is helpful when planning schemes of work and lesson objectives. Quite simply, we start with baseline ideas (knowledge) and build up centring on, say, key words and – through various activities – gradually introduce the higher order skills of analysis, synthesis and evaluation as activities get harder and more complicated.

Another point to make here is that the other domains can aid aspects of learning and teaching in sociology. For example, the *affective domain*, which centres on values, can support Durkheim's belief that education should promote social solidarity or even Weberian notions of *erklärendes Verstehen*. It would also help in the development of our students' sociological imagination. Moreover, the *psychomotor domain* can be useful when considering strategies for active learning. *Bloom's Taxonomy* is widely discussed, so it is wise to leave it for now and refer back to it in later chapters. Nonetheless, it is worth reading up on and, if you have the time, it is also worth looking at alternative ideas stemming from *SOLO Taxonomy*, which is briefly discussed in relation to teaching sociology theories in Chapter 7.

Personal, learning and thinking skills (PLTS)

Bearing in mind that Bloom only gives a taxonomy of skills to develop, it is now important to consider strategies for developing those skills in practice. The now defunct Qualifications and Curriculum Authority (QCA) developed a popular framework for outlining essential learning skills, which was referred to as *personal, learning and thinking skills* (PLTS). The idea was to champion these skills in schools and colleges and embed them in the national curriculum at secondary level (QCA, 2007). Although the QCA has been abolished for some time, the term PLTS is still used and often crops up on courses and in popular books on teaching; for example, Jackie Beere lists them in her book *The Perfect Ofsted Lesson* (2012). To be fair, it was a good framework for thinking about learning and, I would argue, thinking about sociology in particular. The PLTS framework comprises six groups:

- independent enquirers
- creative thinkers
- reflective learners
- team workers
- self-managers
- effective participants.

All of these skills are discussed at various points throughout this book and Table 4.1 on page 54 summarises the focus of each PLTS group next to an example of their use in sociology.

Building learning power

If the intelligences defined by Gardner seem too narrow or impractical, it is worth looking at the ideas behind *Building Learning Power*, or BLP, which has been developed by Guy Claxton (2007) amongst others as a framework for identifying and nurturing *learning capacities*. BLP can be seen as an alternative to thinking of individual learning styles and more about the skills intrinsic to all styles of learning as well as types of intelligence. Importantly, learning capacities are not specific to a particular intelligence, such as logical/mathematical intelligence, but can be applied to learning more generally; BLP capacities are not, therefore, an intelligence *per se*, but they do involve strengthening a student's character or personality in order overcome difficulty or frustration, which is essential in a subject like sociology that will present them with a whole new vocabulary, way of thinking and way of arguing. Claxton often refers to the capacities as *learning muscles* as they give the student the resilience, resourcefulness, reflectiveness and ability to learn through reciprocity with others. It is then possible to uncover a student's intelligence, ability or passion for a given subject as they are better placed to learn in the first place.

Claxton and his associates at *The Learning Organisation* (TLO) initially divided various learning capacities and put them into 'four learning clusters'. These are:

- **Resilience:** this is the emotional and attentional aspects of learning, such as perseverance, absorption, managing distraction (concentration) and attentive noticing (perceptiveness).
- **Resourcefulness:** this is the cognitive aspect of learning, such as questioning and answering, imagining, reasoning, making links (connecting), and making smart use of resources.
- **Reciprocity:** this is the social dimension of learning, which includes interdependence, collaboration, listening and empathy, and imitation (learning from others strengths).
- **Reflection:** this is centred on building up learners' strategic management and self-awareness skills. For example, the ability to plan effectively, self-evaluate or revise and look for further applications of what is learnt (referred to as distilling).

The idea here is that students build these capacities and subsequently become better learners; thus, achieving their (and our) goals or targets and becoming better educated in general. I have worked in two schools that have adapted Claxton's ideas and feel that identifying learning skills can

Table 4.1 PLTS in sociology

PLTS group	Example in sociology
Independent inquiry: these skills enable students to process and evaluate information independently as well as conceptualise and plan strategies on how learn by themselves.	Any activities that encourage students to find, compare and contrast different pieces of information can be seen as encouraging this. Regularly giving them a selection of key ideas and/or shortened texts and asking them to go away and evaluate the text is a good way of turning these skills into a habit. Over time you can give less help as they start to identify the sources of information and apply the scaffolded skills automatically (see Chapter 11 for more ideas).
Creative thinking: these skills aim to get students thinking creatively by generating and exploring ideas in ways that encourage originality. This can be done by getting them to think of different ways to tackle a problem, such as welfare dependency, and getting them to work with others to find realistic yet imaginative solutions and outcomes.	Most areas of sociology involve some discussion on social policy and getting students to come up with their own 'policies' can encourage creative thinking. For example, activities that involve role plays where students are 'the secretary of state for education' and get to redesign the curriculum are relevant here (see Chapter 6).
Reflective learning: these skills get students to evaluate their strengths and weaknesses and encourage them to set realistic goals. They also learn to monitor their own progress, give and receive feedback from peers and adapt their learning accordingly.	Although this would not be unique to sociology, getting students to understand key sociological skills, such as explanation, analysis and evaluation, in order to self and peer assess is essential. Moreover, creating trackers that audit their learning and progress is essential here – so long as they take ownership of them (see an example in Chapter 9).
Team working: these skills get students working cohesively with others, especially when assigned groups, as well as taking responsibility for their own part in collaborative learning. They listen to and respect other people and use each other's various abilities to reach solutions etc.	There is no end of ideas for collaborative/team work in sociology. Obvious examples include setting up research projects on, say, students' use of social media (on units examining new media versus old media). Students can use different research techniques and allocate roles, collate information and write up their findings amongst themselves (see Chapter 8).
Self-management: here students are able to organise themselves, take responsibility and show initiative in their learning. They would be motivated to improve through self-reflection and be proactive in doing so. They can deal with new challenges, change and disruption optimistically and look for opportunities in all situations.	Again, this is clearly a generic skill that sociology would benefit from, especially when it comes to revision. As most sociology courses are focused on exams, self-management is essential for organising revision as well as dealing with stress. Sociology poses difficulties for revision due to the vast amount of topic areas (see Chapter 11).
Effective participation: these skills get students to engage with both the academic issues discussed in class as well as the wider issues that affect them and their peers.	Sociology allows for discussion and debate. This means students can participate in class debates on health policy, for example, and ask 'should smokers receive treatment paid for by the taxpayer'. If they are introvert, they can still work in smaller groups to participate or simply vote on hot topics. If their teacher is tech savvy, they can also take part in anonymous debates online (in a safe environment).

Source: Adapted from the QCA's PLTS framework.

improve students' application of them. In both schools, students had lessons at key stage 3 on *Learning to Learn*, which basically got them to practise the capacities above. However, we broke these somewhat abstract concepts down into simple 'BLP skills', such as 'noticing skills', 'listening skills', 'collaboration skills' and 'independent learning skills', in order to apply the theoretical framework implicitly and in a way that students would understand.

The application of BLP to sociology is straightforward – perhaps a 'no-brainer' – but once students are well versed in using these simple learning skills it makes setting up activities and identifying the strengths and weaknesses in how they learn very easy. For example, collaboration (*reciprocity*) is key to students working on tasks together, especially in activities that involve debating or peer teaching, and 'noticing skills' are useful when getting students to watch documentaries and make connections (*resourcefulness*); this allows students to think about and audit their learning skills and to improve those areas they feel they struggle with. The example of making connections, for example, is very useful in sociology where students need to make connections between themes and perspectives in different topic areas, such as the application of feminist thinking on the family as well as on the media. A connecting idea, of course, is that both institutions arguably reinforce patriarchy. Moreover, these capacities aid the sociological skills discussed in Chapters 2 and 3 as well as build one's sociological imagination; they also link nicely with some of the 'sociological pedagogies' discussed in the last chapter and PLTS discussed earlier.

However, I would argue one of the most essential elements of BLP in relation learning about sociology is *resilience*, especially at key stage 5 where the amount of content that students have to learn can be overwhelming. Resilience, as mentioned above, includes the emotional and attentional aspects of learning. At times students will feel like they are drowning in work, especially when sociology is one of three or four subjects they will be studying. Here, developing their perseverance is paramount. Students need to know they are not alone if struggling, so any teaching methods that reinforce the idea that sociology is difficult, but that the difficulties can be overcome, are useful. A simple idea is to build testimonies from former pupils into your lessons so students can recognise that others have experienced what they are going through and have succeeded in the end. Another idea is 'buddying up' Year 10 students with Year 11 students or Year 12s with Year 13s in order to act as mentors to guide students through the highs, lows and frustrations of studying sociology.

Growth mindset

If you are new to teaching, changing schools or in a school undergoing a transformation in how senior leaders view teaching and learning, you may come across the ideas referred to as *Growth Mindset* in addition to things like BLP. Growth Mindset is very much in vogue, but to many of us it simply seems like common sense. The term is mostly associated with the work of Carol Dweck and her colleagues who have spent years researching students' responses to failure, especially how some students show resilience in the face of challenge whereas others are thrown of course and even give up when things do not go their way. Therefore, Dweck (2006) has identified two types of mindset, namely fixed and growth, from her research of children in education. Those children with a fixed mindset will see setbacks as evidence of their limited abilities or capacity to learn. Moreover, they will adapt and accept labels based on these experiences. However, children with a growth mindset will endeavour to improve and progress regardless of their mistakes.

It is well worth reading up on growth mindset as it is becoming more and more prevalent on CPD courses and as part of many schools overall teaching and learning ethos. Nevertheless, Dweck has made the case that it is not merely an idea, but – like BLP – needs to be taught to students and seen as an intervention strategy. Of course, students' ability does vary and some personality traits are partially predisposed, but the argument is that every child can change, improve and progress given the right frame of mind or mindset. Here, even simple things such as praising how a child has attempted a learning activity can improve students' view of their potential to succeed (see, for example, Cimpian, Arce, Markman & Dweck, 2007). Importantly, this praise must not centre on their intelligence or abilities *per se*, but the processes of learning and improving. It is obvious, then, that growth mindset can be applied to sociology students. As I have emphasised already, sociology is a juggernaut of information, new words and new ideas that will overwhelm many students when they start their courses. Furthermore, the skills needed to attain high grades are not easy to master either, particularly when jumping from KS3 to GCSE and then GCSE to A Level. Thus, if we accept that mindsets, like intelligence, are not fixed, we will be better able to see and nurture the potential in our students and help them overcome their early mistakes and setbacks. We could also apply this to learning styles as well as these should not be seen as fixed in any way; students need to be challenged and encouraged to learn in new ways. However, with the latter, I would not rule out their relevance as a tool for engaging, encouraging and enabling students to explore the subject in their own way when appropriate.

Personalising learning

All of the above can be applied to *personalising learning*. Essentially, personalising learning advocates matching activities to the ways in which students learn best; this is in many ways similar to learning styles, but advocates of personalising learning often emphasise interactive whole-class activities with particular interventions for students who need additional support (Winstanley, 2013). Importantly, personalised learning looks at how teachers can design activities, lessons and schemes of work that will reach as many students as possible. In this sense, a teacher will have to think about how a particular cohort learns, especially in terms of the level of diversity of learning preferences, ability and needs. The term personalised learning often crops up in texts on learning to teach as well as CPD courses, but is also evident in the fifth teacher standard, which states we should, 'Adapt teaching to respond to the strengths and needs of all pupils' (Department for Education, 2013, pp. 11–12).

Thinking about learning, including how we get students to learn actively, their preferred styles, the strategies we use to understand the learning process and the skills we are trying to teach are not only relevant to sociology, but are part and parcel of good practice generally. Therefore, as a successful sociology teacher, you would need to consider all of the ideas in this chapter as well as many more.

Further reading

Capek, S., Leask, M. & Turner, T. (Eds.). (2013). *Learning to teach in the secondary school*. Abingdon: Routledge.
This book has been complied for trainee teachers, but is still valuable to those who have been teaching for years. Various chapters will tackle issues related to how students learn. Good

examples are those by Lowe, Burton and Winstanley who look at active learning, ways students learn and personalised learning respectively.

Gardner, H. (1993). *Frames of mind: The theory of multiple intelligences*. New York: Basic Books.
A good starting point if interested in Gardner's ideas. After a discussion on the traditional and biological explanations of intelligence, Gardner goes into each part of his original theory in more depth. Well worth reading if you are interested in further understanding his theory of multiple intelligences.

Claxton, G. (2007). *Building learning power*. Bristol: The Learning Organisation Limited.
BLP is used in lots of schools and is often simplified into straightforward PLTS skills. Unfortunately, very few teachers ever read further into Claxton's ideas. If you want to better understand the importance of resilience, resourcefulness, reflectiveness and reciprocity in students learning, then I would recommend having a look at this book.

Dweck, C. (2006). *Mindset: The new psychology of success*. New York: Ballantine Books.
This book outlines Dweck's key ideas on mindsets and explains that peoples' abilities do not necessarily lead to success. Her view is that success results from moving beyond a fixed mindset to a 'can do' growth mindset. Although this may seem like common sense and many teachers have this view anyway, her ideas are becoming more influential in British schools and you may come across them on teacher training courses, CPD courses and at teaching conferences.

Notes

1   For an extensive list, see the '*VARK: A guide to learning styles*' website at: http://vark-learn.com/strategies/readwrite-strategies/
2   See, for example, Anderson, L. W. and Krathwohl, D. R. (Eds.), (2001), *A taxonomy for learning, teaching, and assessing: A revision of Bloom's taxonomy of educational objectives*, New York: Longman.

Bibliography

Anderson, L. W. and Krathwohl, D. R. (Eds.). (2001). *A taxonomy for learning, teaching, and assessing: A revision of Bloom's taxonomy of educational objectives*. New York: Longman.
Beere, J. (2012). *The perfect Ofsted lesson* (2nd ed.). Bancyfelin: Independent Thinking Press.
Bloom B. S. (Ed.). (1956). *Taxonomy of educational objectives: The classification of educational goals* (Handbook I: Cognitive Domain). New York: McKay.
Burton, D. (2013). Ways pupils learn. In Capek, S., Leask, M. & Turner, T. (Eds.), *Learning to teach in the secondary school* (pp. 307–324). Abingdon: Routledge.
Capek, S., Leask, M. & Turner, T. (Eds.). (2013). *Learning to teach in the secondary school*. Abingdon: Routledge.
Cimpian, A., Arce, H. C., Markman, E. M. & Dweck, C. S. (2007). Subtle linguistic cues affect children's motivation. *Psychological Science, 18*(4), 314–316.
Claxton, G. (2007). *Building learning power*. Bristol: The Learning Organisation Limited.
Department for Education. (2013). *The teachers standards*. Retrieved from www.gov.uk/government/uploads/system/uploads/attachment_data/file/301107/Teachers__Standards.pdf
Dweck, C. (2006). *Mindset: The new psychology of success*. New York: Ballantine Books.
Fielding, M. (1996). Why and how learning styles matter. In Hart, S. (Ed.), *Differentiation and the secondary curriculum: Debates and dilemmas*. London: Routledge.

Fleming, N. D. (1995). I'm different; not dumb: Modes of presentation (VARK) in the tertiary classroom. In Zelmer, A. (Ed.), *Research and development in higher education: Proceedings of the 1995 Annual Conference of the Higher Education and Research Development Society of Australasia (HERDSA)* (pp. 308–313). Retrieved from www.vark-learn.com/wp-content/uploads/2014/08/different_not_dumb.pdf

Gagné, R. (1985). *The conditions of learning* (4th ed.). New York: Holt, Rinehart & Winston.

Gardner, H. (1993). *Frames of mind: The theory of multiple intelligences.* New York: Basic Books.

Gardner, H. (1999). *Intelligence reframed: Multiple intelligences for the 21st century.* New York: Basic Books.

Gardner, H. (2006). *Multiple intelligences: New horizons* (2nd ed.). New York: Basic Books.

Hargreaves, D., Beere, J., Swindells, M., Wise, D., Desforges, C., Goswami, U., Wood, D., Horne, M. & Lownsbrough, H. (2005). *About learning: Report of the learning working group.* Retrieved from www.demos.co.uk/files/About_learning.pdf

Honey, P. & Mumford, A. (1982). *Manual of learning styles.* London: P Honey.

Ireson, J. & Levinson, R. (2013). Cognitive development. In Capek, S., Leask, M. & Turner, T. (Eds.), *Learning to teach in the secondary school* (pp. 234–253). Abingdon: Routledge.

Kolb, D. A. (2014). *Experiential learning: Experience as the source of learning and development.* Upper Saddle River: Pearson FT Press.

Krathwohl, D. R., Bloom, B. S., & Masia, B. B. (1964). *Taxonomy of educational objectives: The classification of educational goals* (Handbook II: Affective domain). New York: McKay.

Kyriacou, C. (2014). *Essential teaching skills.* Oxford: Oxford University Press.

Lowe, M. (2013) Active learning. In Capek, S., Leask, M. & Turner, T. (Eds.), *Learning to teach in the secondary school.* Abingdon: Routledge.

Morris, M. (2004). The eighth one: Naturalistic intelligence. In Kincheloe, J. L., *Multiple intelligences reconsidered.* New York: Peter Lang.

Murray, C. (1999). *The underclass revisited.* Washington, DC: AEI Press.

Park, R. E. & Burgess, E. W. (1967). *The city.* Chicago: University of Chicago Press.

Qualifications and Curriculum Authority. (2007). *The six areas of the PLETS framework.* Retrieved from www6.plymouth.ac.uk/files/extranet/docs/SOPEPS/Personal,%20Learning%20and%20Thinking%20skills.pdf

Simpson, E. (1972). *The classification of educational objectives in the psychomotor domain: The psychomotor domain* (Vol. 3). Washington, DC: Gryphon House.

Smith, M. K. (2008). Howard Gardner and multiple intelligences. In *The encyclopedia of informal education.* Retrieved from www.infed.org/mobi/howard-gardner-multiple-intelligences-and-education

Winstanley C. (2013). Personalising and individualising learning. In Capek, S., Leask, M. & Turner, T. (Eds.), *Learning to teach in the secondary school* (pp. 372–381). Abingdon: Routledge.

5 Thinking about teaching skills and styles in relation to sociology

This chapter includes:

- What teaching skills are.
- Using a teaching skills framework to improve practice.
- Adapting teaching frameworks for use in sociology.
- The strengths and limitations of teacher-centred approaches to teaching.
- The general strengths of student-centred approaches to teaching and methods used to deploy these.
- The idea of the Teacher's Palette and its usefulness for teaching sociology.

Having established how students learn, it is now incumbent upon us to teach in a way that appeals to their different learning styles and in so doing meets the needs of all our students. Here, it is worth considering how we can develop our skills as sociology teachers before looking at more concrete examples of *teaching styles*. I use the term teaching skills as a precursor to teaching styles as it is essential that we think about what we are going to do in the classroom as well as reflect on the impact of our teaching rather than just delivering content in lessons. By this, I mean that we cannot just replicate other people's teaching styles, methods or ideas without establishing a framework in which to evaluate them in relation to our overall strengths and weaknesses as well as those of our students.

There is a whole host of academic research on teaching skills, just like there is on learning styles, but delving into this research is time consuming and often distracts from the practicalities of day-to-day life in schools. However, in summing up much of this research, Chris Kyriacou says that academic studies view teaching as a complex cognitive skill that is centred on knowledge about how to construct and conduct lessons as well as adequately conveying the content to be taught. If this sentence seems obvious, Kyriacou (2014) identifies three tangible 'key elements' of teaching to help us reflect on some of our skills. These are: knowledge, decision making and action (pp. 12–13).

Kyriacou has identified these three as, firstly, *knowledge* comprises what you know about the subject taught and an awareness of what the curriculum entails, which is essential in sociology as it is such a wide ranging subject (see the discussion in Chapter 2). Knowledge also includes an awareness of the learning skills discussed in the last chapter as well as knowledge of your own strengths and weakness as a teacher (see below for further discussion on this). Second, Kyriacou identifies *decision making* as a key factor in teaching as it occurs before the lesson, during the lesson and, of course, after the lesson; when you reflect on how well everything panned out. Of course, decision making is also essential in planning schemes of work to fit around syllabuses. In this sense, sociology is a decision-making intense subject as you will have to decide what to include in lessons and what choices of topics your students will be most engaged in. More importantly, you will have to assess the content of lessons, especially key words, vocabulary and terms, to decide whether students can access them with or without further elaboration. For example, do not take it for granted that students understand terms like *social class* or *secular*. This has already been briefly touched on in Chapters 2 and 3, but will be further developed in the chapter on planning. And, lastly, Kyriacou identifies *action* as a key element in teaching. This would be how you perform in the classroom; whether you act on your decisions and, therefore, effectively impart your knowledge to the students.

Using a teaching skills framework

Although the identified key elements above are intrinsic to teaching, they do not fully guide us as teachers in that they are somewhat abstract and broad ranging. Therefore, Charlotte Danielson suggests that a teaching framework for professional practice can be used to get us thinking about our own teaching skills. A framework can be used for a variety of purposes and by new and experienced teachers alike. Danielson (2007) argues that because teaching is complex, it is helpful to develop a 'road map through the territory, structured around a shared understanding of teaching'. Accordingly, teachers new to sociology will need a road map as they will inevitably be concerned with their day-to-day survival in the classroom whereas experienced teachers may want to improve and/or review their overall skills and benefit from reviewing a 'road map' or framework of essential teaching skills. For experienced teachers switching to sociology from other subject areas, a skills framework may be a good tool to ensure they are embedding best practice, whilst having the extra burden of learning enough to confidently teach the students.

Subsequently, in his review of the literature on teaching skills, Kyriacou (2014) has made a distinction between 'three dimensions' that affect the quality of teaching (see also Fauth, Decristan, Rieser, Klieme & Buttner, 2014). The idea here is to set up a framework in which to assess the overall quality and effectiveness of our teaching skills; do we or don't we fulfil these three dimensions when teaching and, if not, will there be barriers to learning? The three dimensions/categories identified are cognitive activation, a supportive climate and classroom management. The framework identified is conducive to teaching sociology as it enables both new teachers and experienced teachers to think and adapt their classroom practice to the needs of their students. In relation to sociology, their application can be broadly summed up as:

- **Cognitive activation:** this could also be called thinking skills as it refers to the development of challenging learning activities that actively engage students and, subsequently, develop their knowledge and understanding of sociology. In some ways this aspect of the framework for assessing teaching skills combines thinking skills with engagement – in that, if you can kill two birds with the same stone, you've nailed it.

- **Supportive climate:** this involves building effective relationships with students by being positive about their studies, giving informative and constructive feedback and generally showing that you care. In sociology, feedback will be essential (and is discussed in Chapter 10) as your students will be writing plenty of essays and will want to know that they are read thoroughly and marked. Additionally, displaying a caring side will be extremely fruitful when students really need your support and reassurance near exams.
- **Classroom management:** as sociology can be a topical and controversial subject, you will need clear rules and procedures in the classroom to effectively organise debates, discuss sensitive issues and maintain the peace amongst students with differing views (see Chapters 6 and 13 for ideas). Also, as students will need to show that sociology has many perspectives, a mutually respectful classroom environment where other people's views and opinions are listened to respectfully rather than being shouted down or dismissed out-of-hand, is essential.

The point of having a framework of teaching skills is, of course, a point of reference for us to refer back to regularly and to see if our professional practice properly fulfils the framework. On a day-to-day basis Kyriacou's three dimensions can be extremely useful. However, from time to time it may be worth thinking about our practice in more depth. Probably one of the most extensive frameworks is Danielson's *Framework for Teaching* (2007). The use of this framework is as a classroom observation instrument, but it can be used to reflect on our own professional practice, especially if you are considering teaching sociology for the first time; whether new to teaching or experienced, it can give you a fresh outlook on what you need to do to teach sociology successfully. Importantly, Danielson's *Framework for Teaching* was arrived at through extensive research on essential teaching skills and is made up of various components, but these can be simplified as:

1. Planning and preparation

a   Demonstrating knowledge of content and pedagogy
b   Demonstrating knowledge of students
c   Setting instructional outcomes
d   Demonstrating knowledge of resources
e   Designing coherent instruction
f   Designing student assessments

2. Classroom environment

a   Creating an environment of respect and rapport
b   Establishing a culture for learning
c   Managing classroom procedures
d   Managing student behaviour
e   Organising physical space

3. Instruction

a   Communicating with students

b   Using questioning and discussion techniques
c   Engaging students in learning
d   Using assessment in instruction
e   Demonstrating flexibility and responsiveness

4. Professional responsibilities

a   Reflecting on teaching
b   Maintaining accurate records
c   Communicating with families
d   Participating in the professional community
e   Growing and developing professionally
f   Showing professionalism

Adapted from Coe, Aloisi, Higgins and Major (2014).

In terms of sociology, this framework can be really useful. For instance, component 1, part d is useful for considering the appropriateness of resources in line with the other components listed in that section, such as knowledge of learners (1 b), especially as you will need to choose resources that appeal to the learners learning styles or particular needs. Additionally, ensuring the instructional outcomes (1 c) are accounted for relates not just to differentiated outcomes, but whether the resources of 1 d are clear enough for your learners to comprehend.

For our purposes, the framework is first and foremost a tool for auditing your teaching skills to see if you are encompassing the essentials of outstanding teaching. However, as already stated, Danielson (2007) sees her framework as useful to all those in the profession; 'The responsibilities of a first-year teacher are just as complex (in some situations, more so) as those of a 20-year veteran... they are plunged immediately into the full responsibilities of a teacher. A newly licensed architect, for example, would never be asked to design a major building the first week on the job, all alone. But this is exactly what teachers are asked to do.' It would be an unfair 'veteran' who does not acknowledge the immense task of a trainee or newly qualified teacher. Moreover, the depth of knowledge needed to teach sociology, especially if the syllabus is not the same as their degree syllabuses or even degree subject, makes it even more daunting. It is important, then, that an extensive framework is available as a scaffold to support and remind the new teacher of their professional duties in and outside of the classroom.

This framework can also be of use to experienced teachers as Danielson argues it can help answer the questions, 'What does an effective teacher know?' and 'What does an accomplished teacher do in the performance of her duties?' By reflecting on this framework and auditing their skills, experienced teachers can aim to be outstanding in all areas (of course, additional ideas can be added, especially if conducive to teaching sociology). Danielson feels that as teachers we rarely devote our precious time to professional dialogue and sharing best practice. Therefore, this framework provides the structure for discussions on how to improve our overall effectiveness. It can be very useful to collaborating colleagues getting ready to teach sociology for the first time or looking to improve their department's practice.

Developing a skills framework specifically for sociology

Although Danielson's generic framework is helpful, it may be worth developing a specific sociology framework to improve our success of teaching sociology. A useful starting point is the six 'common' components of great teaching as identified by Coe et al. (2014) in their report *What Makes Great Teaching?* This is a list of the six common components that they think teachers should consider when assessing teaching quality. In their 2014 report for the Sutton Trust education charity, they researched these six aspects of teaching in depth to show how strongly they improved the outcomes of students. Again, for new teachers, Coe et al. (2014) stated that this framework can be seen as offering a 'starter kit' for thinking about effective pedagogy. In a similar but slightly different vein to Danielson, they identify 'pedagogical subject knowledge', 'quality of instruction', 'classroom environment', 'classroom management', 'teacher beliefs' and 'professional behaviours' as the six components. The list is also essential for experienced teachers as, they argue, 'Good quality teaching will likely involve a combination of these attributes manifested at different times; the very best teachers are those that demonstrate all of these features' (Coe et al., 2014, pp. 2–3). Below, I have developed their ideas in relation to the teaching of sociology to demonstrate how this framework can be applied successfully. Of course, what I have added to their initial ideas is not conclusive, but does illustrate how teaching frameworks can be adapted for specific subjects.

1   **(Pedagogical) content knowledge:** firstly, sociology teachers must have a detailed knowledge of the subject, including an understanding of theories, concepts and key vocabulary as well as names, studies and relevant examples. What makes sociology even more knowledge based is that the examples used will constantly be evolving and changing as society changes. A teacher who does not try to incorporate all of this knowledge into their teaching will have less to offer their students and may even hinder them. Sociology teachers must also have a strong understanding of how students think about these theories and ideas. This will include the ability to evaluate the thinking behind students' own understanding of the subject and to identify students' common misconceptions. This component was also highlighted by Kyriacou in his shorter three dimensions and, interestingly, the inclusion is backed up by empirical research as Coe et al. found that pedagogical subject knowledge shows strong evidence of impacting on student outcomes.

2   **Quality of instruction:** sociology, like many subjects, combines abstract ideas with empirical research and students will be new to many of the perspectives taught. Therefore, teachers must endeavour to 'get across' these ideas in clear and concise ways. Here, effective questioning and answering and the constructive use of assessment will be needed to communicate what students are doing well, not so well and badly. It is important that this is done with accuracy to be effective. As with pedagogical knowledge content, the quality of instruction has been shown to have a strong impact on student outcomes. Coe et al. (2014) suggest specific practices, like reviewing previous learning, providing model responses and giving adequate time for practice, especially timed essays, are essential (pp. 2–3). They also discuss scaffolding, which is needed for mixed ability sociology groups in and outside of the classroom and the importance of providing students with handbooks, reference glossaries, plans of the year and past papers to guide them through their studies (see Chapters 9 and 11 for more on planning this).

3 **Classroom climate:** this component covers the quality of interactions between teachers and students, which can have an impact on students' confidence. Although teachers should always be positive and have high expectations, sociology is a subject of competing ideas and teachers, as well as students, need to be mindful of their own biases that may surface when dealing with students' views and understanding of the subject. There is also 'a need to create a classroom that is constantly demanding more, but still recognising students' self-worth. It also involves attributing student success to effort rather than ability and valuing resilience to failure (grit)' (Coe et al., 2014, p. 3). Although an important component, Coe et al. (2014) found that classroom climate showed moderate evidence of impact on student outcomes.

4 **Classroom management:** pace, resources and space are essential to outstanding teaching. Here, a sociology teacher's abilities to make efficient use of lesson time, especially managing the amount of teacher talk versus student centred learning, can impact learning. There is plenty of evidence and research that demonstrates that children can get bored by endless didactic monologues by teachers. Therefore, effective time management, such as pace and breaking up lessons into various activities, can really help keep students focused on learning. It is also important that we manage our resources well, too; always ensuring that students find them accessible (again, do not take for granted that the students will find newspaper articles etc. as interesting or as relevant as you think they are). It is also important to manage space, especially setting up the room in a way conducive to learning and creating the right atmosphere in the class. Of course, it is also vital to manage students' behaviour with clear and agreed upon rules that are consistently enforced in all lessons. Coe et al. (2014) suggest this component has a moderate impact on student outcomes (p. 3).

5 **Teacher beliefs:** we need to have a belief in the importance of our subject, ourselves and in the students we teach. Our beliefs, though, are wide ranging and can be applied to our adoption of particular teaching practices, styles and methods and what we hope to achieve by teaching sociology. In some ways we could see ourselves as 'committed sociologists' – those sociologists who admit that they want their sociology to change society for the better – as opposed to teaching just an intrinsically interesting subject. We need to believe, therefore, that sociology is beneficial and believe that we are teaching it in an engaging and relevant way. Otherwise, what's the point? The researchers found that teacher beliefs show some evidence of impact on student outcomes (Coe et al., 2014).

6 **Professional behaviours:** lastly, the behaviour exhibited by sociology teachers has an impact on learning too. Coe et al. (2014) identified reflecting on and developing professional practice (CPD), participation in professional development, supporting colleagues, and communicating with parents as key areas. Some of these, for instance CPD and reflection, are evident in the application of these frameworks when auditing our teaching skills. Moreover, we can join interest groups, such as the *British Sociological Society's* Teaching Group, to further our professional interest in the developments in sociology.[1] And, of course, we can keep parents informed of what we are delivering. A lot of our topic areas are quite sensitive and it exhibits professionalism if we keep parents informed and interested in the important things we teach their children.

Task 5.1 Audit your teaching skills

Use either Danielson's teaching skills framework or the six components selected by Coe et al. (2014) and create a checklist to audit your own skills. This could include using red, amber and green (RAG) colours to say which components are strengths and which are weaknesses. If using the six components from the Sutton Trust's report, you may have to identify and decide on tangible examples of practice within each component in order to measure or get a sense of how well you are performing. This could be a useful CPD exercise itself, especially if completed with other colleagues.

Teaching styles

The term teaching styles is interchangeable with teaching methods. Essentially, a teaching style comprises the methods and strategies used for instruction in the classroom. Common examples would include demonstration, recitation, memorisation and ways of facilitating class participation or group work. Most books or websites on teaching styles start by distinguishing between 'teacher-centred' approaches and 'student-centred' approaches. However, the reality is that most teachers mix these two approaches up and, although many criticise teacher-centred approaches, they both have their uses. Of course, outstanding teachers tend to use combinations of these either within a lesson or across a scheme of work. To help us fully understand these different styles it is worth looking at the ideas of Anthony Grasha in his book *Teaching with Style* (1996). Although developed for teaching in higher education institutions, they are still useful for thinking about secondary teaching. Grasha identifies five main 'styles', which include 'expert', 'formal authority', 'personal model', 'facilitator' and 'delegator'. These five models can be fitted into the teacher and student centred approaches respectively.

Teacher-centred approaches

Quite literally, in this approach, teachers are the centre of attention. The teacher's function is to instruct or lecture students on the subject to be taught and the students' role is to receive the information; they may listen, take notes or even answer questions that the teacher asks. Importantly, the teacher is the font of knowledge and the students are like glasses that need filling up. If we reflect back on students' learning styles, a teacher-centred approach may suit auditory learners – so long as the teacher is engaging!

Student-centred approaches

These approaches shift the focus from the teacher to the students. Of course, the teacher still retains authority in the classroom, but they will set up and facilitate activities the students will carry out themselves. The teacher's main function is to coordinate student learning and ensure that they learn through the tasks set. Obvious examples of student-centred approaches include pair work, group work, student projects and student organised debates.

Table 5.1 Teacher-centred approaches and their application to sociology

Teacher-centred approach	Use in the sociology classroom
Formal authority: these teachers are a source of authority and leadership. They have more knowledge than the students and they want to directly impart it. Classroom management is through traditional rules and expectations as is the classroom layout. The model centres on the power and authority of the teacher.	Although most educational theorists would shun this style, it does have its uses. It can be useful when explaining ideas prior to setting up other activities, especially in rowdy GCSE classes. It may be useful with selected groups of students in revision or intervention sessions on the run up to exams. However, the students selected should be those with a preference for this style.
Expert: these teachers see themselves as there to guide and direct their students in their learning. The teacher is seen as knowing everything and the students have complete faith and trust in their ability to deliver knowledge. The students are the beneficiaries of the teacher's expertise. Unlike the above, this model centres on deference to the teacher's own knowledge and experience.	This style is similar to the above. Nonetheless, there is no harm in occasionally explaining theories and concepts, such as Marxism or postmodernism, to the class as a whole. At A Level, many students request these whole class 'lecture-style' explanations from time to time. However, this should not be too long to prevent passive learning and needs to be buffeted by other student-centred activities.
Personal model: this model sees the teacher as a role model. They demonstrate how to find information, how to analyse it and how to understand it. The students will learn by watching, listening to and copying what the teacher does.	Although a teacher-centred approach, there is nothing wrong with modelling things for students. For example, demonstrating how a student would use an online referencing system is fine so long as it is limited timewise. Nevertheless, as with all of these teacher-centred approaches, the personal model should not be used as a dominant way of teaching.

Source: Adapted from Grasha (1996) and www.teach.com (see the further reading section below).

Table 5.2 Student-centred approaches and their application to sociology

Student-centred approach	Use in the sociology classroom
Facilitator: teachers who use a facilitator teaching style tend to focus on student centred activities. Teachers set up activities and let the students get on with them. Ideally, there will be minimal input from the teacher once the students have started the activity. Therefore, students take responsibility for finding information, analysing it and deciding what it means. They must use their initiative to achieve the goal of the activity. This type of approach often involves active learning, such as group discussion and/or varied collaborative activities incorporating various learning styles.	There are so many activities that can be covered by this approach. A good example would be setting students research tasks. For example, at A Level my colleague often sends students off to make PowerPoints on school subcultures. They can choose from subcultures such as 'goths' or 'lads' and have to link their general information to sociological ideas. The PowerPoints are peer assessed by the students in other groups. Although criteria are given out with key requirements, once the students are sent off the teacher has no input unless the students come back to ask questions.
Delegator: this approach places responsibility for learning with the students. It is slightly different to the facilitator as the teacher delegates specific responsibilities to individuals or groups. Whereas the facilitator will design, set up and ensure there is a uniform progression during the activities, the delegator will allow students to choose, design and implement their own activities, which will often centre on in-depth projects. The teacher's main role is to act as an advisor or consultant when requested by the students.	Although compact syllabuses often limit this type of learning in sociology, it is possible to set up projects of this kind from time to time; these can be short activity centred projects or longer research projects. For example, when looking at sociological research methods in education, students can be left to design their own Ofsted inspection of the school (see Chapter 8). You can give specific roles to the students, such as 'lead inspector' or 'observers' or even just give them some end goals – i.e., they are to organise themselves to complete a report on the school that includes a variety of research methods.

Source: Adapted from Grasha (1996) and www.teach.com (see the further reading section below).

Although all of the learning styles can be useful when conceptualising how we approach our practice in the classroom, the styles we use in our day-to-day teaching are obviously going to be far more mixed up and varied than the five narrowly identified by Grasha (for an alternative take on teaching styles, see Leask, 2013). Therefore, we need an approach that allows us to mix-and-match various styles within lessons in a way that fits with students learning styles and/or BLP capacities.

Task 5.2 Video observations

To get a sense of your own teaching style, it may be worthwhile filming yourself teaching. There are plenty of video observation cameras on the market and plenty of schools are now investing in them.

   Filming yourself may seem extreme or even bizarre to the un-initiated, but colleagues of mine have used filmed observations to review their own performance. They have often been surprised that they taught slightly differently to how they imagined. When I did this myself, I realised I was far too didactic than I wanted to be; too much 'formal authority' in Grasha's words. Importantly, video observations should not be considered as too Big Brother, especially as nobody other than the teacher being filmed needs to see the recording.

The teacher's palette

In a similar vein to their BLP framework, Guy Claxton and the TLO have now devised a framework for teachers that 'maps the ingredients of a school and classroom culture that help to cultivate those habits of mind' (TLO, n.d.; see also, Claxton, 2007). In some ways this bridges the gap between learning styles and teaching styles as it asks how getting the students to build on their learning capacities, or learning muscles, impacts on the planning and structure of our lessons. For example, the framework asks, 'If we want [students] to become more willing to take risks in their learning, and more tolerant of making mistakes, how should we alter the way we mark their work, or the choices we make about what to display on the walls of the classrooms and corridors?' (Claxton, 2007).

   Claxton's framework for teachers, therefore, is called the *Teacher's Palette* as it provides us with an overview of useful tools that we can use to build the learning capacities discussed in his BLP framework. The idea is that teachers and schools build up a learning culture that nurtures the development of inquisitiveness, responsibility and independence amongst students. Of course, this is exactly what a sociology teacher needs to do, especially considering the development of the 'critical' and 'social' consciousness we were discussing in previous chapters. According to Claxton, this framework provides a basis for long-term planning that is centred on cultivating 'learning power'. He states that teachers can promote outstanding learning by (a) discussing their explicit values with the whole class; (b) how they talk to students about their learning (including learning styles); (c) the activities they choose on the back of these conversations; and (d) how we model learning (Claxton, 2007, p. 69). More specifically the *Teacher's Palette* includes:

- **Explaining:** this is telling students directly and explicitly about their learning. This includes informing them of the purpose of their learning; reminding them of how they are learning, which means they are self-aware of their learning; discussing their learning, especially their own ideas on how they learn; and training them through direct tips and techniques on learning.

- **Commenting:** this is conveying messages about learning through informal discussion and evaluation with students. It includes nudging their attention towards their own learning; replying to their questions and queries about their learning; evaluating learning with them; and tracking their progress, which must be shared with them.
- **Orchestrating:** this is selecting activities and making sure the environment is arranged correctly for learning. For example, it entails ensuring activities are developed for the four clusters of the BLP framework; clarifying to students the learning intentions or purpose of the activities completed in class; helping them set their own targets and facilitating their own monitoring of their progress; and making use of the physical space of the classroom and things like displays in order to maximise learning.
- **Modelling:** this centres on demonstrating to students what it means to be an effective learner. Here, we must respond to unseen events in appropriate ways in order to model behaviour; we must think aloud, or rather 'learn aloud', to model decision making etc.; we must demonstrate learning and make sure learning projects or work is visible in the classroom; and, importantly, we must share in both our and our students learning by discussing our learning in the past in comparison to learning in the present.

I would argue that the *Teacher's Palette* offers us the chance to consider how our students learn whilst engaging them in that consideration as well. In some ways it complements the other theoretical frameworks discussed in the previous chapter, including VARK and multiple intelligences, as it not only allows students to implicitly think about so-called learning styles, but also to be resilient and resourceful in the face of those learning styles that they find difficult or frustrating. This is why BLP is important, as to succeed academically, our students need to learn in various ways and if we can build the learning capacities, or muscles – or whatever we want to term the ability to learn well – we must get all our students to overcome the aspects of learning they are uncomfortable with.

Further reading

Kyriacou, C. (2014). *Essential teaching skills*. Oxford: Oxford University Press.

This book covers key areas of practice and references plenty of evidence for championing a vast array of teaching skills and methods. It is ideal for trainees, but also of use to experienced teachers.

Coe, R., Aloisi, C., Higgins, S. & Major, L. E. (2014). *What makes great teaching*. London: Sutton Trust.

This is a really good review of research on teaching skills and how it impacts learners. It references Danielson's framework and other studies as well as incorporating the authors' own research. Although academic, it does give a very comprehensive overview of what makes great teaching. It is available online at: www.suttontrust.com.

www.teach.com

This website, run by 2U Inc. and USC Rossier, has a section on 'Teaching Methods' that explains Grasha's ideas on teaching styles concisely and clearly. Grasha's book is, of course, very interesting, but at the same time very technical and full of data. The 'Teaching Methods' web page is available online at: http://teach.com/what/teachers-teach/teaching-methods [retrieved 23/06/16].

Note

1   The BSA Teaching Group offers resources, ideas and support to secondary teachers of sociology. They also have an online journal, *The Sociology Teacher*, which is available to members. Visit their website at: http://www.britsoc.co.uk/study-groups/bsa-teaching-group.aspx.

Bibliography

Claxton, G. (2007). *Building learning power*. Bristol: The Learning Organisation Limited.

Coe, R., Aloisi, C., Higgins, S. & Major, L. E. (2014). *What makes great teaching*. London: Sutton Trust. Retrieved from http://www.suttontrust.com/wp-content/uploads/2014/10/What-makes-great-teaching-FINAL-4.11.14.pdf

Danielson, C. (2007). *Enhancing professional practice: A framework for teaching* (2nd ed.). Alexandria: ASCD. Retrieved from http://www.ascd.org/publications/books/106034/chapters/The-Framework-for-Teaching@-An-Overview.aspx

Fauth B., Decristan, J., Rieser, S., Klieme, E. & Buttner, G. (2014). Student ratings of teaching quality in primary school: Dimensions and prediction of student outcomes. *Learning and Instruction, 29*, 1–9. Retrieved from http://www.sciencedirect.com/science/article/pii/S095947521300056X

Grasha, A. F. (1996). *Teaching with style*. Pittsburgh: Alliance Publishers

Kyriacou, C. (2014). *Essential teaching skills*. Oxford: Oxford University Press.

Leask, M. (2013). Teaching Styles. In Capel, S., Leask, M. & Turner, T. (Eds.), *Learning to teach in the secondary school: A companion to school experience* (pp. 345–359). Abingdon: Routledge.

The Learning Organisation Limited. (n.d.). *How it's done*. Retrieved from http://www.buildinglearningpower.co.uk/how_its_done.html

6 Practical teaching strategies for developing sociological skills

This chapter includes:

- A description of some simple starters and their use for checking knowledge and understanding.
- Using games in sociology for checking knowledge, understanding and even getting students to analyse and evaluate.
- How questioning can check more than knowledge and be applied to higher order thinking skills.
- Techniques to get the most out of discussion.
- The different uses of card sorts and how they can develop different skills.
- An explanation of how group work can develop both sociological skills and learning skills.
- Using role plays and drama to further students' sociological thinking skills.
- How to scaffold and support students' essay writing skills.

In Chapter 1, I suggested that part of the *modus operandi* of this book is exploring Durkheim's suggestion that a key aspect of education is to teach specialist skills. Moreover, in Chapter 2 we discussed some of the key assessment objectives in sociology at GCSE and AS/A Level as well as the skills needed to succeed in sociology generally. This included knowledge and understanding, interpretation, application, analysis and evaluation. The sociological skills listed here also fit into *Bloom's Taxonomy* and the PLTS framework highlighted in Chapter 4. Whereas the latter offers a strategy for building these skills, the former almost mirrors the AO1, AO2 and AO3 skills identified in Chapter 2. Considering the importance of these skills to sociology, this chapter discusses some common teaching strategies that can develop them.

Starters

Starters, which are small activities used at the beginning of lessons to engage, recap on previous learning or introduce the main objectives, are an excellent way of checking, revisiting and introducing knowledge and understanding. Simple starters that can check basic knowledge of key words and terms include:

- anagrams
- word searches
- crosswords
- true or false quizzes
- other games (see below).

These are easy to create using websites on the internet. The drawback is that these starters merely test knowledge – although crosswords can be cryptic and, therefore, demonstrate a deeper understanding of the knowledge being sought. Cryptic crosswords can get students to both interpret and analyse the meaning of the questions by making connections between the cryptic clue and their sociological knowledge. For example, see Figure 6.1 that explores previous knowledge taught on functionalist theory.

If you prefer getting students to think more deeply, using photographs and pictures to engage them in discussion is a good way to introduce interpretation and application skills at the start of

REACP: Basic Functionalist Ideas

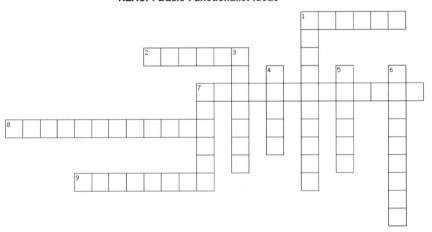

Across
1. We all follow these norms.
2. The theory formulated by Merton.
7. This is needed to produce order, stability and productivity in society.
8. Society is made up of these and they are designed to fill different needs.
9. Functionalism's 'founding father'.

Down
1. Skills taught by schools.
3. Type of family preferred by functionalists.
4. Functionalism sees society as a large structure.
5. We share these.
6. When everyone agrees.
7. All of society's institutions fit together to form a social...

(Answers (across and then down): 1, social; 2, strain; 7, socialisation; 8, institutions; 9, Durkheim; 1, specialist; 3, nuclear; 4, macro; 5, values; 6, consensus; 7, system)

Figure 6.1   AS Level crossword on functionalist theory

lessons. For instance, pictures of social deprivation, such as run down city centres, vandalism and graffiti can get students interpreting what social issues are depicted and debating why the situations are of importance to sociology. Students can then apply their sociological knowledge by suggesting how particular sociologists or sociological perspectives would view the issues.

Games

There are all sorts of games you can use for checking the basic skills of knowledge and understanding. They can be used as starters, breathers from more serious activities or even plenaries. These activities can include:

- **Guess the sociologist:** get your students to describe a famous sociologist's work, perhaps in teams, as others try to guess who it is. At the end of term, they could even create a sociological version of the famous board game *Guess Who?*
- **Guess the key word:** this can be done in pairs, teams or as a class. The idea is similar to the game *Pictionary* as students draw words, concepts or theories as others try to guess what they are drawing. This can also be done by using simple word-fill sentences, for example, 'I believe the bourgeoisie look after the proletariat's health so they can _____ them.' Guessing games can involve mime and actions, too.
- **Definition bingo:** students draw a 3 x 3 grid. Then, as a class, they suggest 14 useful words on a topic area. These are written on the board. Each student then randomly fills in their grid with 9 of these words. Next, in pairs, they come up with a definition for the words on the board. Then you go around the class asking students to read out one of their definitions and students mark of the words accordingly.
- **Keyword relay races:** here the teacher (or students) write key words or terms on the board. Then you need to split the class into two teams before giving a red and blue pen to each team respectively. Then you call out the definition at which point a student from each team races to circle the right word; then they pass on the pens to the next team member.
- **Walkabout Bingo:** give the students a grid with 9 to 12 squares on it. In the grid write questions on a sociological subject. Then get the students to walk around the room asking each student in turn a question. The rules are that they can only use a student's name once and cannot use their own. The first to fill the grid with names is the winner.

I like to use 'walkabout bingo' when teaching Hockey and James' (2002) theories on how students 'act up' and 'act down'. Although you would need to ask appropriate questions, this game allows the students to answer questions about their behaviour and have some fun before evaluating whether they 'act up' or 'act down' when breaking rules or going against social norms (see Figure 6.2).

Lastly, at the end of term you can always get students to make their own board games. An easy game to create is a sociological *Snakes and Ladders*, where students can design the board on the concepts of, for example, *life course analysis* if they are revising the topic of *family and households* or even try to have squares that explain meritocracy (where you go up) or the myth of meritocracy (where you go down) if they are revising a unit on education. If students create games, such as a *Monopoly* board based on urban criminology, they will need to use their higher order learning skills to conceptualise how the game will work.

Someone who has lied about completing homework: Mark	Someone who has made silly noises in class: James	Someone who has sent a text during a lesson: Sarra	Someone who regularly chews gum in school: Jenny
Someone who has refused to sit in the right place: Chelsea	Someone who has gone out (of their home) without their parents' permission: Tara	Someone who has walked out of a class: Edward	Someone who has had a stand up row with their parents: Emir
Someone who has thrown an object across the classroom: Charlie	Someone who has told a teacher they 'don't care': Teresa	Someone who has cried when they did not get what they want: Ted	Someone who has been in a fight at school: Clare
Someone who has scribbled on a desk: Jordan	Someone who has worn too much make up to school: Tamara	Someone who has gossiped about friends at school: Demi	Someone who has shouted at a teacher: Charmaine

Figure 6.2 Walkabout Bingo based on 'acting up' and 'acting down' (used at AS Level)

Task 6.1 Linking games to learning styles

At a department meeting, staff meeting or CPD study group, list all of the learning games you and your colleagues can think of. Write each game on a sticky note or small piece of card or paper. Once you have done this, think about the different learning styles discussed in Chapter 4. This could be the basic VARK styles or even Gardner's multiple intelligences. Then match the games to the different learning styles in order to see how you can select games to suit the general learning styles preferred by the students in your classes. This activity could also give you an indication of how regularly you should alternate between certain games so that you are offering students a variety learning activities.

Questioning and answering

It is estimated that on average teachers like us ask 300 to 400 questions a day, which could equate to 70,000 a year and around 3 million by the time we retire (Leven and Long, 1981 as cited in Brualdi, 1998, p. 1). We ask questions all the time in lessons; from recapping on last lesson, to ensuring students understand instructions and checking that the students have learnt what has been taught. However, questioning is not as simple as it sounds and there are multiple techniques that can be deployed to get students engaged, thinking and collaborating through effective questioning.

Too often poor teachers just ask basic questions; these are normally *closed* questions that have specific short answers. An example of a closed question is, 'Who wrote *Simulacra and Simulation?*' This is closed as there is only one correct answer, which is 'Jean Baudrillard'. Although this may be useful for occasionally checking knowledge, it does not get the students thinking or using their analysis and evaluation skills. Moreover, really bad questioning will allow students to answer closed questions by putting their *hands up*. This is now considered a general 'no-no' by many educationalists as it means those students not wanting to participate will sit there passively whilst the others answer. It also means that you cannot target questions at students by ability or see if a wide range of students have understood what is being taught.

One way around this it to use the *pose, pause, pounce and bounce* (PPPB) technique advocated by Ross McGill (2011) and attributed to Pam Fearnley. The idea is to engage all students by posing a question that any one of them may have to answer; this would be a *hands down* activity and would involve giving students thinking time. McGill breaks the technique down like this:

- **Pose:** explain the PPPB technique to your class so they know what you are doing; make sure students know it is a hands down approach and they will be selected randomly; and ask questions that the students will have to think about in some depth. For example, 'Are nuclear families better at bringing up children than lone parent families?' You can ask them to consider a variety of responses to this, such as, 'Explain why a feminist may agree or disagree with your view?'
- **Pause:** give the class thinking time. This could be anything from 30 seconds for short explanations or longer for more reflective ones. McGill advocates holding the silence for a while if the students are captivated and engaged.
- **Pounce:** think about who you will ask. This can be useful for targeting questions at certain students to see if they have understood. You could, therefore, ask in a way that a student of a particular ability would comprehend or be able to answer.
- **Bounce:** once one student has answered, ask another to respond. This is how the question is 'bounced' between students. If you are dealing with competing sociological perspectives, you could bounce the question to see if students can come up with an alternative. For instance, 'Why might some sociologists disagree with the student X's opinion on this?' This could be made more specific, 'Why might the new right disagree with student X's opinion?' Of course, you can develop higher order thinking skills by asking students to develop points. An example could be, 'So if a feminist believes lone parents can provide a supportive environment for a child, especially if an abusive partner is out of the relationship, would a Marxist-feminist have a different view on this to, say, a radical feminist?'

If the PPPB approach can be used to get students thinking, it is now worth considering how we can use questioning to develop students higher order thinking skills more generally. Some closed answer questions could address simple knowledge, comprehension and application skills, but if we really want to develop students' skills of analysis and evaluation, it is worth considering how we ask questions in the first place. For example, Table 6.1 gives some ideas on how we can distinguish

Table 6.1   Higher order and lower order questions

Lower order questions: issues	Higher order questions: best practice
Any questions that require a 'yes' or 'no' response are lower order questions. Also, simply asking students to remember facts, figures, dates and names would be included here. For example, 'Who came up with the idea of strain theory?' Of course, these questions have their place, but they limit thinking.	Questions that include the commands 'explain', 'compare and contrast, 'analyse', 'assess' and 'evaluate' are clearly more complicated than 'yes' and 'no' answers and will develop students higher order thinking skills. For example, 'evaluate the view that Britain is a classless society? Can you think of a few points for and a few against?'
A hands-up approach where you ask individual students direct questions if they know the answer will inevitably lead to some students remaining silent and being passive in the classroom.	A hands down approach will engage all students in the class as it is up to you who you ask. You can also ask other students to nominate answerers, but this must only be done if you can trust the class to do it fairly.
Asking students straight away may be a good test of their immediate knowledge, but thinking takes time and it does not allow them to think through their answers.	As higher order thinking skills are more complicated than lower order skills, you need to give students thinking time before answering. It is often good to give them a timeframe for this.
Responding to wrong or poor answers negatively will obviously affect students' confidence. For example, 'No, you're wrong, class consciousness is not a functionalist idea; it's Marxist'.	It is more helpful to ask them why they answered the way they did or encourage them to think of alternatives. For example, 'Why did you think class consciousness was a functionalist idea?'
Focusing purely on students' immediate knowledge in answers will not allow students to think creatively or take them outside of their comfort zone through academic stretch and challenge.	You can ask more creative questions by asking, 'What if?' questions that involve a number of outcomes. You could challenge students by asking them to look for connections between different concepts, theories or studies. For example, 'How do modern socio-economic categories differ to traditional concepts of class?'
If you ask all the questions you will be in danger of teaching didactically as you will act as the 'agenda-setter' of the question and answer session. This also means that you will remain the centre of attention and will be using a 'teacher-centred' approach.	Give students the opportunity to ask questions. They could ask you, but an even better approach would be to get them to research similar topic areas and ask questions of each other. This would be a more 'student-centred' approach.

higher order questions from lower order questioning. The table is based on a similar table used to develop questioning skills for students in science, technology, engineering and mathematics (STEM) education (see Nondestructive Testing Resource Center, 2015).

Discussion

Although questioning and discussion often go hand-in-hand, it is the latter that fully develops students' argumentation skills as they need to continue thinking about their points as others analyse, evaluate and assess them. Moreover, it can be essential to students finding their 'voice' in the classroom as they give and subsequently defend their points of view. Nevertheless, it is still up to the teacher to get discussion going and this is best done through posing challenging and controversial questions; and this is key to sociology as so much of its content, from violence in the media to the legalisation of gay marriage, is controversial.

The Socratic approach

Perhaps a good place to start a review of discussion techniques is with the so-called *Socratic approach*, which is named after the ancient Greek philosopher Socrates. This approach to discussion rests on the teacher's ability to facilitate challenging, rigorous and insightful dialogue amongst students.[1] The idea is that the teacher sets up or manipulates a discussion that encourages the students to challenge and evaluate either the teacher's or each other's views in the same way that the ancient Greek philosophers challenged and debated each other. The latter can be developed into a student-centred approach to learning, especially if the students get into the habit of discussing issues this way. To this end, Socratic questioning and discussion is often referred to as a *dialectical approach* in that students identify and correct the misconceptions and misunderstandings of their peers, even if these misconceptions and misunderstandings will be disputed by others.

The Socratic approach can be used as a starter by asking questions based on the yet-to-be-learnt lesson objective. For example, 'Why do you think divorce rates have increased in the last 60 years?' Despite not having studied divorce, most students will have some knowledge of divorce from elsewhere and they may also have developed some sociological knowledge of societal change from other topic areas. They should be able to give a variety of opinions on this to get each other thinking. Here, not only are they building upon their knowledge and understanding, but they are also starting to analyse why they and others have interpreted things the way they have.

Whether the student is correct or incorrect is not important during the discussion as they will need to formulate their responses to each other throughout and can only do that by picking up on the strengths and weaknesses of each other's arguments. Of course, you will need to prep them to think critically about each other's comments and encourage them to challenge things they do not agree with; in essence, they are now evaluating the arguments aired. Encourage them to ask further questions of each other, too. For example, you can get students to try and defend the basic concepts behind their statements. Here, simple 'tell me more' questions can be used to facilitate deeper thinking.[2] Table 6.2 gives examples on how these types of questions can be formulated and then applied in sociology lessons. The ideas are adapted from Paul and Elder's (2006) six types of Socratic questions.[3]

Importantly, Socratic questioning can start to probe the students' initial assumptions about sociological concepts or research, especially if they have slightly misunderstood, understated or poorly defended a concept or study. This type of questioning can also try to unearth their own biases and prejudices. For example, you could challenge students by asking these types of questions:

- What else could we assume about your view given your own experiences?
- You seem to be assuming that all immigrants are so called 'health tourists'. Why is this?
- Please explain why you think the digital divide may be overlooked by policy makers in the developed world?
- What might a sociologist research to verify or disprove that idea, especially as you think it is so sound?
- What could the consequences be of re-introducing married couples' tax allowance (as you suggest) on cohabitating couples?
- How could your views on child poverty be used to defend child tax credits?

Table 6.2   Types of Socratic questions

Type of Socratic question	General phrasing/use	Possible sociological phrasing/use
Clarifying	• Why do you say that? • What do you mean by that?	• Why do you think that about middle-class people? • What exactly does 'embourgisement' mean?
Probing assumptions	• What else could we assume instead? • How can you verify or falsify that assumption?	• Do people really just believe what they see and hear in the media? • To prove your point, can you name any famous business people that come from working class backgrounds?
Probing reasons and evidence	• What would be an example? • What do you think causes this to happen?	• Can you give me an example of material deprivation? • Why do the public perceive crime as rising?
Thinking about viewpoints and perspectives	• What would be an alternative point of view? • What are the strengths and weaknesses of this view?	• Why might feminists disagree with Talcott Parsons' view of the nuclear family? • What are the strengths and weaknesses of quota sampling?
Probing implications and consequences	• How does this idea/evidence affect what we are studying? • How does this idea/evidence relate to what we learned before?	• What do these statistics on stop and search tell us about the relationship between police and ethnic minorities? • How does Young and Willmott's study compare or contrast to Elizabeth Bott's?
Probing the actual question	• What was the point of this question? • Why do you think I asked this question?	• What was the point of asking you questions about the head teacher in the context of the correspondence principle? • Why do you think I asked this question about video games if we are looking at violence in the media?

Task 6.2 Modelling questioning techniques

To better understand the processes of Socratic questioning and discussion, practice it yourself with your colleagues. This may be embarrassing in front of other staff at lunch time, but there is no reason why you cannot practice Socratic questioning and other methods, such as PPPB, in department meetings and INSET or in-school CPD sessions. I have modelled PPPB at Newly Qualified Teacher (NQT) training sessions with a member of the history department. Modelling questioning and discussion techniques with colleagues really helps those new to the methods to 'see them in action' as well as giving you an opportunity to practice and improve your skills.

It may be a good idea to record some of the students' key points here in order to further the discussion once the class starts lagging. For instance, if someone suggests secularisation as a reason for increased divorce and someone else suggests the lack of social stigma, you could ask them if the two are connected.

What role should teachers play in questioning and discussion?

It is apparent from the above that the role of the teacher is essential in questioning and discussion. Does the teacher simply ask the questions and discuss them with the students? Should the students be asking the teacher questions to start discussions? Should the students be asking each other? Of course, all of this depends on what the aim of your questioning is: is it part of a brief recap or a longer student-centred activity? However, it is important to think about the role you play when questioning. Here, Gershon (2015) amongst others has identified a number of different roles the teacher can consciously adopt whilst asking questions (pp. 30–31). Although he applies these roles to history, they can easily be adapted to sociology. They include:

- **Facilitator:** this is a student-centred approach where the teacher provides the students with a series of questions and then lets them formulate answers amongst themselves. It is the dialogue between the students that generates answers. However, it is still monitored by the teacher who may step in to guide or re-direct the students if they go off on a tangent, off task or are in need of help. This is often useful if the students have already learnt some key sociological theories or studies as they will not need to ask the facilitator to keep intervening when they run out of things to say.
- **Neutral judge:** this is a common approach to sociological questioning and discussion that many teachers adopt naturally. The idea is that the teacher is an objective manager of the discussion that ensues from the question they posed. For example, the teacher may ask whether welfare benefits encourage dependency before simply controlling who speaks and ensuring that both sides get a chance to air their opinions. Of course, the teacher will also police the discussion to make sure the rules are respected. In some ways, this is similar to the chair on question and answer programmes like the BBC's *Question Time*.
- **Committed participant (personal):** this is basically where the teacher joins in the discussion, perhaps after letting students answer the question posed, with their own personal opinions or experiences. I have often done this as students often respect the fact that I have experienced something they are learning about. For example, I used to have a job working for a market research organisation phoning people up whilst they were eating their dinner to ask closed questions about anything from car tyres to ice cream. As some of the responses were quite humorous or, more often than not, rude, I will use this to point out some weaknesses of large scale surveys. Moreover, this role is useful if you are needing to confront challenging opinions, perhaps xenophobic, or if the class is largely against the position you are taking.
- **Committed participant (in role):** this is very much like the above role, but here the teacher will act the part of a committed participant if needed. For example, if no one in the class has put forward the views of radical feminism in a debate on gender equality, you could state the argument of a radical feminist. You would need to model the answer as if you were a committed feminist by adopting the critical stance they may have towards gender equality in society.

- **Devil's advocate:** again, this may seem very similar to the above role, but it is slightly different as you would not just be adopting a view or perspective that has not been aired, but would be deliberately juxtapositioning your views to that of the class or, at least the majority. Although you may not like the position you adopt, it will be a way of getting the students to fully evaluate their own views, prejudices or biases. I have often done this when discussing the views of the new right who argue that the welfare state has created an 'underclass' of ill-educated work shy social security dependent people who are often lone parents (Murray, 1999, pp. 2–3). The latter point can cause students to fundamentally disagree and it is left to me to defend the perspective's contribution to sociology even if I disagree with some of its assumptions.

Card sorts

Although card sorts will be mentioned in the next chapter in more detail, they are an excellent way to check knowledge and understanding as well as getting students to analyse and assess. Card sorts, therefore, can be many things from simple matching exercises to more elaborate flow charts. The only difficulty is having the time to make them. However, once you have got the hang of making various types of card sort, creating them becomes straightforward.

The simplest card sorts will inevitability test knowledge and understanding. An example of this is a *keyword definition card sort*. Here, a key word will simply have to be matched to a definition (see Figure 6.3 for an example using family types). The great thing about these is their simplicity to produce. You literally use a template and add your words and definitions. It can be used for any topic area.

Of course, the above only deals with knowledge and understanding and we really want to get students interpreting, analysing and evaluating. In order to do this, we need to create card sorts that literally live up to their name; in that they 'sort' information. One way of getting students to interpret the importance of information and analyse its significance is to get them ranking ideas. Ranking exercises of this kind not only develop higher order thinking skills as per Bloom's cognitive domain, but they also apply to the affective domain, which focuses on students' values, motivations and attitudes (Krathwohl, Bloom & Masia, 1964; also see Figure 5.1 in the previous chapter).

The reason this plays out so well in ranking card sorts is that it gets students to think about how they perceive the value of certain issues; for example, although the affective domain's levelling starts with *receiving* (which is simply an awareness of the information), the higher order levels really impact the sociological imagination as students start attaching *value* to phenomena as they begin recognising the importance of various sociological issues. After the valuing level we have *organising* whereby students organise the different values, information, and ideas through a process of comparing, contrasting, and connecting what has been learned or what they already know from sociology or elsewhere. This is clearly a process of interpretation, analysis and evaluation that leads to the final level of *characterisation*, which means students can start conceptualising the characteristics of affective issues in a systematic way; in other words, they have a recognisable value system that guides their views. By way of example, I use a diamond card sort to get students thinking about crimes at GCSE (see Figure 6.4). They have to discuss the relative 'immorality' of crimes *vis-à-vis* other crimes and rank them in order of severity. It is used in an introductory lesson on crime. Interestingly, the emerging value system (characterisation) evident in most students' responses is that violent crimes are worse than non-violent.

Nuclear family	This is often seen as the traditional type of family. It usually consists of two parents and their children.
Single/lone parent family	This family consists of one parent raising one or more children by themselves.
Extended family	This family includes many relatives living within the household and working toward common goals, such as raising children and completing household duties.
Reconstituted family	As many marriages now end in divorce, divorcees may choose to get remarried; this may involve two separate families merging into one new family unit.
Beanpole family	The idea that the family is becoming much taller and skinnier as generations live longer, but families have fewer children.
Negotiated family	A family that does not conform to society's view of the traditional family. This family will adapt to the wishes and expectations of its members, especially as society changes over time.
Neo-conventional family	This family is similar to the nuclear family as there are two parents and their children. However, it acknowledges that the woman has more independence than in the traditional family.

Figure 6.3 A keyword definition card sort on family types (AS Level)

		Murder		
	Rape	Child abuse	Domestic violence	
Shoplifting	Pickpocketing	Burglary	Car theft	Fraud (affecting the public)
	Tax evasion	Health and safety violations	Insider trading	
		Downloading music illegally		

Figure 6.4   A diamond ranking crime card sort used at GCSE level

Group work

Group work is a great way to bring together the students' knowledge and understanding, get them analysing ideas together and then evaluating collaboratively. Again, examples of group work and collaboration will be used in the next chapters, but a simple activity that demonstrates their use for developing analytical and evaluative skills is through making posters to advocate sociological positions. The process is straightforward:

1   Get students into opposing groups/teams;
2   Get them to read through some key ideas about a sociological perspective/argument;
3   Get them to design a powerful poster advocating that point of view. Ensure it summarises key theoretical or empirical points;
4   Halfway through, let them see each other's posters to engage their competitiveness;
5   When finished, get them to swap and then verbally defend the opposing team's poster; give them time to prepare this;
6   Set an evaluative piece of writing summing up the exercise.

How this works in relation to developing sociological skills is also relatively simple: firstly, students are tasked with creating a poster that has the key points from a sociological argument, such as arguments saying that globalisation is leading to cultural imperialism or 'Disneyfication' versus the cultural flow argument. This builds their knowledge and understanding. Secondly, students will then interpret, analyse and apply the argument by choosing and agreeing on which parts are most important. This can also include turning the main focus of the argument into jingles etc. as well as the use of relevant pictures or symbols. However, in order to further the skills of analysis, students should be allowed to view opposing teams designs halfway through so they can add to, develop and adapt their arguments in view of the opposition's efforts so far. Lastly, students should then swap posters and be asked to defend the opposing team's points; in this sense they will 'put themselves in someone else's shoes' and be better placed to write up the activity as an objective evaluation. Furthermore, going back to PLTS and BLP, this also builds up team working skills and reciprocity.

Role plays and drama

According to Fairbrass, role plays 'can ensure that every viewpoint in debates about complex controversial issues is considered. Careful allocation of players to roles can ensure that students are obliged to express opinions that are not their own, and can help to develop skills of empathy' (Ofsted, 2006 as cited in Brown & Fairbrass, 2009, p. 42). In many ways this relates to the sociological pedagogies discussed in Chapter 3 as it engages the sociological imagination, can encourage a Weberian sense of empathetic understanding and be used to unpack Goffman's ideas on dramaturgical analysis with the class. Moreover, it can also develop higher order thinking skills through an evaluative exploration of the issues involved in the topic area being studied. If a role play is set up well and two or more perspectives are covered in the play, then students can reflect on it, watch it if recorded and discuss it to further analyse and evaluate the issues involved.

An example of a sociological role play I use is the 'Chivalric Court'. In this activity the students start by watching a music video called *Testify* by Common, which is about a female criminal, before reading various texts on the *Chivalry Thesis*. The thesis, formulated by Pollak (1961), argues that the prosecution and court systems are more lenient towards female offenders than male offenders. It takes its name from the idea of chivalry whereby male knights exhibited courteous behaviour, especially towards women. In this role play students have to act out either an arrest, cross examination or sentencing. The roles, perhaps unfortunately, have to be allocated so that boys (or girls acting as boys) are either police, lawyers or magistrates/judges. Obviously, the offenders are to be female (or boys playing girls). It is up to you how serious you want to make this activity; it can be a simple dialogue or a mock trial with props and costumes etc.

Although role plays can be fun and engaging, you would have to consider whether it will work with your students. Despite the need to take students out of their comfort zone, small classes of particularly quiet students could make this activity embarrassingly difficult for all involved; perhaps consider their learning styles. If, however, these activities work, they can be used all over the syllabus, such as mock interviews with 'lads learning to labour' in *sociology of education* units (see Willis, 2000) or setting up news programmes when discussing news values and the presentation of the news in *sociology of the media* units.

Kinaesthetic activities

Although kinaesthetic activities may seem conducive to lower order thinking skills, they can in fact be used as ways to promote interpretation, application and evaluation in the classroom. Firstly, very basic activities like *stand on the line* (Brown & Fairbrass, 2009, p. 39) are useful here. By simply clearing the classroom and giving the students a statement, such as 'all politicians come from higher social classes', you can get them to stand in position along a line from totally agree at one end to totally disagree at another. Once in place, use PPPB to give them time to think through their responses for standing there. You can than add to it, for example, 'all politicians are from higher social classes and are male', to see if there is any further movement or change. Thinking about where to stand will involve analysis and evaluation on the part of the students.

There are plenty of other activities that get students moving around. A popular strategy here involves *marketplace* activities where students circulate the room listening to sales pitches from other students – this can be on anything from the main sociological perspectives to championing different health policies (see the next chapter for similar ideas to this).

Another useful activity is *speed-dating* where students take sides on a particular issue. They will need to be given time to plan their defence or attack of the issue. Then pair them up with opposites and give one side a minute to get their points/argument across before allowing them to discuss openly with each other. Give them, perhaps, two or three minutes in total before getting them to swap partners. At the end the students have to 'fall in love' with the person who gave the best answer. If you want this to be very active, you could shorten the timings to get them moving around more.

Task 6.3 Share fair

Ask the colleagues in your school who are responsible for teaching and learning and/or whole school training and CPD to organise a 'share fair' as part of the school's In-Service Training of Teachers (INSET) provision. This would involve each department in the school setting up a number of tried and tested learning activities on a 'market stall' or in their classrooms. Only one or two teachers will stay on the stall or in the classroom as the others will visit the other stalls or classrooms to pick up new ideas for learning activities from other departments. This is a great way to pick up new and often original ideas. You can even have 'secret shoppers' to see which departments have the best ideas; this adds an element of competition.

Writing essays

Essays are an essential part of any sociological exam. Whether this involves sort evaluative essays at GCSE or longer answers at AS/A Level, they are arguably the activity students need to perfect the most. Unfortunately, it is also – for many students – the hardest to perfect. Nevertheless, there are plenty of strategies to help students through this and as a sociology teacher it is important to get five key things conveyed to students. These include:

1   Ensuring they fully understand command words, such as 'identify', 'explain' and 'assess';
2   Ensuring they are 'fluent' in sociological key words and terms;
3   Following on from above, ensuring they know what an 'outline', 'analyse' or 'evaluate' essay actually looks like;
4   Making sure they briefly plan their key paragraphs before writing the essay;
5   Ensuring they have plenty of practice, which includes scaffolded activities and then timed practice in exam conditions.

In order to get students to better understand command words, it is advisable to use plenty of short recap activities to reinforce any explanations you have given. Key command words common to all exam boards include: identify, describe, explain, outline, analyse, examine and assess. For example, I use matching keyword/definition card sorts, keyword bingo and cryptic crosswords to teach this. This would need to be followed by modelling answers based on these command words in pairs, groups or as a class as well as getting students to assess model answers themselves. In relation to sociological skills, these activities are the basic building blocks of getting the students to apply their knowledge and understanding in addition to their interpretation, application, analysis and evaluation skills as the command words literally specify the skill required in the answer.

In addition to command words, a general sociological fluency or literacy is central to student success in assessments and exams. Key words and terms from *socialisation* to *simulacra* may be needed depending on the level of qualification. All of the activities listed above, especially the starters, are useful here as are the ideas in the games section. It is also imperative to constantly use these words yourself – as teachers should in modern foreign languages – so that students use them automatically like you do.

It is also worth bearing in mind that examiners now award additional marks for spelling, punctuation and grammar (SPaG) explicitly at GCSE and implicitly at AS/A Level (where it is often called quality of written communication (QWC)). Therefore, there is no reason to not use *spelling bee* competitions at GCSE and get students to look out for SPaG in peer assessment.

One of the biggest issues, though, is getting students to conceptualise how to apply key words and terms in written answers as well as what the command words are requesting; this can only be done by showing them what model answers look like. However, merely showing an answer to students is not good enough. Prior to getting students practising model answers, perhaps after learning how a mark scheme works, it is essential to scaffold their understanding using various activities. Again, I use card sorts that are essentially 'chopped up' and 'muddled up' model answers and ask students, in pairs, to re-arrange the cards into an order that they think the essay should be in. This activity can be extended into longer kinaesthetic activities. For example, one of my colleagues likes to post paragraphs from model essays around the school. In groups students then have to go 'on a treasure hunt' to find the paragraphs and then put them in the right order; to make it harder, though, he includes other essays or essays of different grades so that the students can debate and finally see the differences between good and not so good answers.

Another key idea for scaffolding written answers is to give students a writing frame. A very simple writing frame for a 12 mark GCSE question could look like Table 6.3 below – remember, you can differentiate it and adapt it to the actual mark scheme if based on previous exam questions. Moreover, the better your students get, the less help you can give them by suggesting less or getting them to write their own templates. Of course, if this was for an AS/A Level question it would be more detailed and, perhaps, be more theoretical.

A good way to teach the higher order learning skills needed in analysis and evaluation answers is to get students to write their view of a sociological issue or perspective, such as media ownership or Marxism, and then get another student to annotate it with additional issues or strengths and weaknesses. Although this can be messy, the student who writes their initial thoughts on media ownership or Marxism then has to re-write the text as an essay incorporating the annotations. This can also be done in analyse, examine or evaluate essays where students have to look at various arguments for, say, the increase in life expectancy over the last hundred years. As these are not simple 'for and against' essays (in that they do not pit feminism versus other theories etc.), it is good to get the students to annotate their initial essay plans to see what they have missed out or could elaborate on.

Table 6.3   Exam question writing frame

Essay title	Assess how far students' social class affects their educational achievement (12 marks)
Introduction	• Write a brief outline of what you think the issue is about. • Say that there are various reasons for and against and your answer will evaluate these different views.
Part 1: arguments for	• Give some arguments that suggest students' backgrounds do influence their educational attainment. • You could identify three key pieces of evidence and briefly explain how they apply to the question. • Perhaps mention things like private education, university/Oxbridge degrees; parents understanding school league tables. You can also use concepts like the 'old boy network'. • To get As or an A* include another point that explains how a key theory applies to the question.
Part 2: arguments against	• Give some arguments that suggest students' backgrounds do not influence their educational attainment. • You could identify three key pieces of evidence and briefly explain how they go against the points made in part 1. • Perhaps mention things like 'hard work', 'achieved status' and 'meritocracy'. • To get As or an A* include another point that explains how a key theory applies to the question and goes against the theory in part 1.
Conclusion	• Sum up the point above. • You do not need to give your opinion, but you can suggest which set of evidence you think is stronger.

If the essay is a straightforward for and against answer, such as 'Examine the strengths and limitations of large scale surveys', I get a student to write out an introduction and then explain the strengths before asking them to swap with a classmate who will then counter the first students' explanations with opposing points. The essay is then given back to the first student who will re-read their work and then their peer's before writing up a brief conclusion. This exercise is often timed.

On the theme of collaboration, peer assessment is a very useful activity for getting students to understand what identify, explain, outline, analyse or evaluation answers look like. It is important, however, to give students plenty of model answers before they mark each other's. It is also important to get them to mark in a different colour and give written feedback on strengths and weaknesses as well as grades (see Chapter 10).

Another key tip for getting students exam ready, especially for essay questions, is ensuring they briefly plan at the start. Of course, in an exam time is limited, so my colleagues and I encourage students to briefly mind map or list key points they think are relevant to the question. This need not be a comprehensive mind map or long list, but the key ideas would be essential. We recommend students spend no more than two minutes doing this so long as the question is 20 minutes long or more. For example, a 20-mark question at AS Level on why the birth rate is decreasing could include the following brief bullet points (this was written on an actual mock in which the student gained 21 out of 24 marks):

• Improved IMR
• Improved health

- Improved education
- Social welfare
- Nuclear Family
- Industrialisation
- Cost
- Cult of childhood
- Contraception and abortion
- Feminism
- Improved career prospects for women

Lastly, it is so important to practise timed essays under exam conditions. Granted, this cannot take place straight away and, also, that it will not go down well with most students, but exam practice is a key procedural process, like learning to drive, where students start making connections in their heads and learn how to think through essays in the stressful situation of a timed examination. For AS/A Level, it is also worth giving students copies of mark schemes (which you may want to re-write in student friendly language) and examiner reports that are available from the exam boards. Moreover, at both GCSE and AS/A Level, ensure your students have access to up-to-date past paper packs, especially as the exam paper formats are often changed.

Further reading

Ginis, P. (2002). *The teacher's toolkit: Raise classroom achievement with strategies for every learner*. Bancyfelin: Crown House Publishing.

> This is a really useful treasure trove of general teaching ideas. Paul Ginis explains how these activities should be set up and used and they are by and large applicable to sociology.

Hodgson, D. (2009). *The little book of inspirational teaching activities: Bringing NLP into the classroom*. Bancyfelin: Crown House Publishing.

> This 'little book' has various activities that are split into 4 sections corresponding to the suits of playing cards, which include: believe in yourself; know yourself; have a plan; and go for it. Within each section there are 13 activities with instructions as well as possible follow up activities that can be used in most classrooms, including sociology classes.

Redfern, A. (2015). *The essential guide to classroom practice*. London: Routledge.

> A fantastic book that is full of activity ideas. The chapters are based on general themes such as planning and engagement, which is useful, but also includes 200 useful strategies that can be used for teaching sociology.

www.tes.com and www.resourcd.com

> Both these websites have downloadable resources that have been created by teachers. Some are specifically for sociology, but there are plenty of generic teaching resources too. www.tes. com is the website of the *Times Educational Supplement* and www.resourcd.com was formally called *Sociology Exchange*.

Notes

1   There are lots of introductions on using the Socratic method on the internet. A useful, but untitled, introduction can be downloaded from the University of the Western Cape, which is available at: file:/// home/chronos/u-9264b63aa2f5ba9278938e458ddc6ab8c952ce4f/Downloads/Socratic%20 Method%20(1).pdf

2   For a really good and extensive list of Socratic questioning techniques, see the 'Socratic Question' section of *Changing Minds* website, which is available at: http://changingminds.org/techniques/questioning/ socratic_questions.htm

3   Paul and Elder's six types of Socratic questions, which have been expanded to nine, can be found on numerous websites, including this one hosted by the University of Michigan: www.umich.edu/~elements/ probsolv/strategy/cthinking.htm. However, for more detail and a better understanding, please see Paul, R. and Elder, L. (2006), *The thinker's guide to the art of Socratic questioning*, Tomales: Foundation for Critical Thinking.

Bibliography

Brown, K. & Fairbrass, F. (2009). *The citizenship teacher's handbook*. London: Continuum.

Brualdi, A. C. (1998). *Classroom questions* (ERIC/AE Digest). Retrieved from http://files.eric.ed.gov/fulltext/ ED422407.pdf

Gershon, M. (2015). *Teach now! History: Becoming a great history teacher*. London: Routledge.

Ginis, P. (2002). *The teacher's toolkit: Raise classroom achievement with strategies for every learner.* Bancyfelin: Crown House Publishing.

Hockey, J. & James, A. (2002). *Social identities across the life course*. London: Palgrave Macmillan.

Hodgson, D. (2009). *The little book of inspirational teaching activities: Bringing NLP into the classroom.* Bancyfelin: Crown House Publishing.

Krathwohl, D. R., Bloom, B. S. & Masia, B. B. (1964). *Taxonomy of educational objectives: The classification of educational goals* (Handbook II: Affective Domain). New York: McKay.

Leven, T. & Long, R. (1981). *Effective instruction*. Washington, DC: Association for Supervision and Curriculum Development.

McGill, R. M. (2011, November 17). How to move your lessons from good to outstanding. *The Guardian Teacher Network*. Retrieved from www.theguardian.com/teacher-network/2011/nov/17/ lessons-good-to-outstanding-afl-questioning

Murray, C. (1999). *The underclass revisited*. Washington, DC: AEI Press.

Nondestructive Testing Resource Center. (2015). *Practice effective questioning*. Retrieved from www.nde-ed. org/TeachingResources/ClassroomTips/Effective_Questioning.htm

Ofsted (2006). *Towards a consensus? Citizenship in secondary schools*. London: Ofsted.

Paul, R. & Elder, L. (2006). *The thinker's guide to the art of Socratic questioning*. Tomales: Foundation for Critical Thinking.

Pollak, O. (1961). *The criminality of women*. New York: A.S. Barnes.

Redfern, A. (2015). *The essential guide to classroom practice*. London: Routledge.

Simpson, E. (1972). *The classification of educational objectives in the psychomotor domain: The psychomotor domain* (Vol. 3). Washington, DC: Gryphon House.

Willis, P. (2000). *Learning to labour* (2nd ed.). Farnham: Ashgate.

7 Teaching sociological concepts and theories

This chapter includes:

- A brief discussion on the complexities of teaching sociological concepts and theories.
- An example of how teachers can create card sorts of differing complexities to get students thinking about abstract ideas.
- Examples of representing information in pyramid diagrams and charts and how these can aid students' understanding of the development and evolution of theoretical perspectives.
- An explanation of how mind maps, spider-diagrams and concept maps differ and an evaluation of their uses.
- An explanation on the importance of using case studies to illustrate theoretical positions or arguments.
- A discussion on how narratives can make abstract theories 'more real' to students.
- An argument that Play-Doh, Lego and loo rolls can have a serious role to play in teaching sociological concepts and theories.
- An outline of how learning marketplaces can be used to engage students to learn and understand that concepts and theoretical perspectives compete with each other.
- An overview of SOLO taxonomy and how it can be used to guide students through the bewildering process of understanding what can initially be seen as incomprehensible conceptual and theoretical mumbo-jumbo.

Sociology is full of abstract concepts and theories. From key terms like *proletariat*, to concepts such as *religious pluralism* and then theoretical perspectives, such as postmodernism, sociology is laden with complex and often bewildering ideas. Therefore, an outstanding and successful sociology teacher needs to be able to communicate abstract concepts and theories in ways that students comprehend. Moreover, to enable students' comprehension of these abstract ideas, we must ensure we have an arsenal of appropriate teaching methods to aid us. Nonetheless, perhaps the most challenging aspect of teaching abstract conceptual and theoretical ideas is that they often have no absolute agreed upon interpretation, which muddies the waters of any straightforward explanation, and makes finding the right methodology or activities to teach them all the more difficult.

How, for example, do we adequately explain ideas associated with *social structure*? There is another concept we can employ to explain this – namely *social class* – but even that is a controversial abstract term without any agreed upon interpretation of what it actually is. For instance, is social class empirically related to income or a reflection of *cultural status* (perhaps both). Subsequently, if we set out explaining social class, are we sure students understand what income and cultural status refer to. Even more troublesome is the fact that sociologists can have massively divergent views on what these individual terms mean; does cultural status refer to someone's relative social standing in a given community or social group or does it refer to their rank or position in society as a whole? Thus, teaching sociological concepts and theories involves the double whammy of trying to make contestable ideas more convergent despite them not arguably being objectively provable one way or the other.

Another problematic example of an abstract concept is Weber's (1958) *Protestant work ethic*. Not only does this concept involve at least two abstract terms – *Protestant* and *ethic* – that students may not be familiar with, it also rests on the assertion that Calvinist beliefs lead to a greater devotion to work. Here, we have the added problem of explaining and teaching what Calvinists are prior to any explanation of what the Protestant ethic means in relation to American capitalism; this assumes some basic assumptions about the students' existing knowledge of Christian and European history.

Nevertheless, concepts and theories are integral to sociological language, which the students must master if they are to be successful. Furthermore, if they are to develop a sociological imagination they must be fluent when participating in a sociological discourse in order to understand, interpret and apply the sociological ideas studied. Importantly, if we quickly re-cap on Durkheim's view that education should incorporate specialist skills, we can see a thorough understanding of sociological concepts and theories as *conceptual tools* for interpreting, applying, analysing and evaluating social issues and problems. In this Durkheimian vein, we could even go as far as arguing that a sound understanding of theoretical perspectives can lead to greater solidarity with concerned schools of thought or social movements that students may not have been fully aware of; for example, a male student may become both aware and concerned about *age patriarchy* and how the domination of women can adversely affect childhood (Gittins, 1998). Of course, they may not identify as a feminist, but they could be more sympathetic to their cause.

Therefore, this chapter will go through some practical ideas for teaching sociological concepts and theories before venturing into more, ironically theoretical, ideas on how to set up learning activities and processes to help students fully comprehend the complexities of sociological theories. This latter part will employ the ideas of SOLO taxonomy to give an alternative structure to developing higher order learning skills than discussed previously in Chapter 4 in relation to Bloom's taxonomy.

Card sorts

Although highlighted as a general way to develop sociological skills in the previous chapter, card sorts can be very effective for developing deeper comprehension of sociological ideas. An example of using card sorts to develop more complex conceptual and theoretical knowledge and understanding of sociology can be broken down into simple stages:

1 Divide students into pairs, threes or small groups;
2 Provide each group with a set of cards that include different concepts written on some cards and their definitions written on others;
3 Ask the students to match the concepts with the correct definitions;
4 Sort the concepts into groups, such as functionalist concepts or Marxist concepts;
5 Rank the concepts according to a set of specific criteria (for example, the concepts that are most evident in society and those they think are not);
6 And, lastly, provide some blank cards so that students can write their own arguments for or against the concepts to demonstrate some original evaluation.

Using card sorts allows for some kinaesthetic learning in an otherwise very academic learning environment. Moreover, the fact that cards can be moved around allows students to make mistakes, change their minds and think creatively. Of course, as students' progress from GCSE to AS/A Level, teachers can adapt the card sorts to the content studied by making the information in them more in-depth, the arrangements more complicated and the justifications more numerous. It is always essential that any thorough card sort is followed up by a good discussion where students will be expected to defend, justify and revisit or evaluate their decisions. To top the activity off, it can then lead into a more mundane piece of written work or a practice exam question. For an example of a complex and theoretical card sort based on abstract concepts see Figure 7.1, which is a template for a card sort linking audience theories to their definitions. It also has a third column that incorporates relevant examples or studies that back the theories up. The template is already in order and is used as part of a lesson linking the audience theories to violence in the media.

Pyramid diagrams and charts

We discussed the importance of using diagrams for visual learning in Chapter 4. However, it is worth revisiting the methods we can employ to visually represent abstract information, especially as diagrams can become more complex as the concepts and theories they depict become more complicated. A very simple way to visually represent concepts and theories is through *pyramid diagrams* and charts.

For example, one basic activity I use to teach Marxist perspectives on social class is through the use of a three-tiered pyramid. In this activity, students have to assign various professions or occupations to the relevant tier, or strata, they think people carrying out those jobs would belong to (see Figure 7.2). Of course, this is extremely simplistic, but it would be a good way of getting students to consider where certain professionals, skilled and manual workers fit into the classical Marxist class structure. There are more working class jobs to signify that the few rule the many. The exercise can also be complicated by including more detailed strata found in units of study focused on stratification and socio-economics. For instance, it could include Goldthorpe and McKnight's (2004) class schema.

Another way to represent ideas in triangular or pyramid form is through a simple flowchart that starts from one central point and branches downwards; these are often referred to as *pyramid charts*. They are hierarchical visual depictions, in many ways similar to mind maps and spider diagrams (discussed below), that cascade ideas, studies, key sociologists or keywords from a central concept or theory at the top of the page. They can be particularly useful when highlighting

Theory	Description	Example/Study
Hypodermic syringe model	This model suggests that when people see violence they will copy the violence. This could be seen as 'copy-cat' as the passive-observer sees the violent behaviour as normal.	An example would be children copying the example of Chucky in the *Child's Play* films.
Uses and gratifications model	This suggests that not everyone sees violence in the same way. Some will see violent films as pure entertainment or escapism. Others will watch violence on news reports as information. Each type of violence is seen in a different way by the viewer.	Anderson and Bushman argued that people get aroused by violence in different ways. Excitement when playing video games is not the same as being horrified by war crimes on the news.
Two-step flow model	People will see the violence as good or bad depending on how it is discussed by opinion leaders. For example, boxing may be seen as good by opinion leaders, but bare knuckle boxing will be seen as bad.	Many people vote in elections because they have agreed with an argument from friends or family. Katz and Lazarsfeld did similar research on this model.
Cultural effects model	Although no one really watches violence and just goes and copies it, over time there may be a gradual influence. For example, if a child grows up watching violent movies, they will be desensitised to violence.	Newson found that modern children witness so many forms of violence on TV that they come to see it as a social norm and culturally acceptable.
The selective filter model	This model argues that individuals actively select and choose what is acceptable violence or unacceptable. For example, *Kung Fu Panda* may be OK, but mindless violence and graphic rape scenes may not.	Klapper did research on people's selection of media. For example, selective exposure means a person who is pro fox hunting will not watch media that sees fox hunting as violent, backwards and privileged.
Reception theory	People read into the theories what they want to. Some will see violence as harmless fun whereas others will not. A kickboxing match may be sport to martial artists, but awful cruelty to someone else.	Morley found that people received information from the news show *Nationwide* in their own way. Some found it supported their views, and others found it supported theirs.

Figure 7.1 A template for a card sort on audience theories that combines three things: the theory's name, a definition/description and a relevant example/study

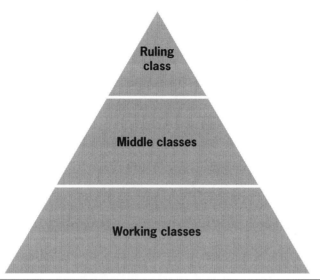

Write these jobs and professions next to the class that you think they belong to: *Plumber, landowner, shop-assistant, road-sweeper, merchant banker, joiner, police officer, painter and decorator, teacher, small-business owner, politician, army officer, secretary, bus driver, labourer, fruit picker, media tycoon, vicar, welder, fisherman, nurse, merchant sailor, gardener.*

Figure 7.2   A tiered pyramid that semi-depicts the Marxist class structure

how key theoretical thinkers have influenced various sociologists or how sub-perspectives or different takes on the original theories have evolved. For example, it can depict how feminism has led to liberal, Marxist, radical and black feminism (see Figure 7.3).

Mind mapping, spider-diagrams and concept mapping

Mind maps, spider-diagrams and concept maps are diagrams that visually represent, organise and order information that would otherwise be written as text. Mind maps are a common feature of most lessons and can be used in almost any subject. The general concept of a mind map is often credited to Tony Buzan, who has trademarked the term, and has written some useful rules to follow when creating them (see Buzan, 2002). However, they are very straightforward. Firstly, a mind map centres on a single concept or theory, which is written in the centre of an empty piece of paper (the concept can also be represented by an image or symbol). Secondly, the student creating the mind map then makes links to associated words, concepts or examples by simply writing them down and connecting them with simple lines. Buzan has emphasised the importance of making these links hierarchical in that each addition to the mind map is of lesser importance than the previous one. He also suggests that the thickness of each line should represent the importance of the idea branching away from the previous idea and that colour and images should be used to stimulate interest in the mind map. One of the key benefits here is getting the students to actually see how theories can link to key concepts and then link to actual situations or research studies that exemplify the said theory or concepts. For example, Figure 7.4 mind maps some basic

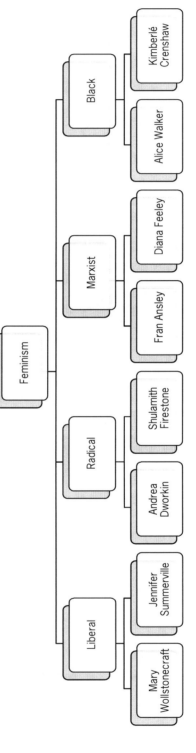

Figure 7.3 A pyramid chart showing different branches of feminism

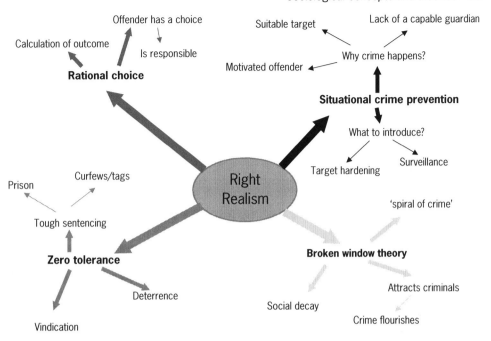

Figure 7.4 A simple mind map on right-realist views of crime

ideas of right-realism. Although it does not include names or studies, it does map key ideas and then brief examples from those ideas.

Similarly, spider-diagrams start with a single word, concept or theory in the centre of the page. However, whereas Buzan says that mind maps should stick to single words as ideas branch out across the page, a spider-diagram will incorporate more information, perhaps in sentences or even short paragraphs, and will have *nodes* coming off of each hierarchical line, which in turn will have its own sub-branches. When mind mapping in class and for revision, students do normally complete finished work that more closely resemble spider-diagrams than mind maps. This is simply because they use far more text than is recommended for a spontaneous mind map (see Figure 7.5).

Unlike mind maps and spider-diagrams, concept maps connect multiple concepts or theories as opposed to connecting lots of simple ideas to one central concept. In essence, a concept map is far more complex than mind maps and spider-diagrams, as in a concept map the student will endeavour to connect each term, concept or theory to another and eventually back to the original concepts or theories used instead of merely branching away from the main concept with associated ideas. This is particularly useful for sociology as by making connections between individual agents, such as individuals in society or interactions between people and social groups, students can start to make connections between smaller acts and the wider structures or processes of society. Importantly, they can start to see how individual actions form part of a larger whole. An example of this is using concept maps to visually represent how the sociological perspectives of functionalism, Marxism and social action theory all have different explanations on what leads to success and failure in school (see Figure 7.6).

Importantly, a very well-made concept map can be developed within a specific *context frame* in order to unpack a *focus question*, which can constitute an exam question in the context of teaching

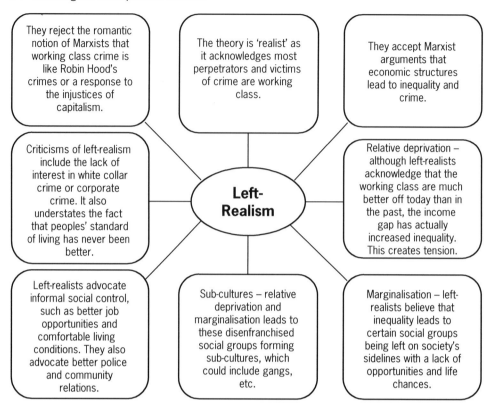

They reject the romantic notion of Marxists that working class crime is like Robin Hood's crimes or a response to the injustices of capitalism.

The theory is 'realist' as it acknowledges most perpetrators and victims of crime are working class.

They accept Marxist arguments that economic structures lead to inequality and crime.

Criticisms of left-realism include the lack of interest in white collar crime or corporate crime. It also understates the fact that peoples' standard of living has never been better.

Left-Realism

Relative deprivation – although left-realists acknowledge that the working class are much better off today than in the past, the income gap has actually increased inequality. This creates tension.

Left-realists advocate informal social control, such as better job opportunities and comfortable living conditions. They also advocate better police and community relations.

Sub-cultures – relative deprivation and marginalisation leads to these disenfranchised social groups forming sub-cultures, which could include gangs, etc.

Marginalisation – left-realists believe that inequality leads to certain social groups being left on society's sidelines with a lack of opportunities and life chances.

Figure 7.5   A spider-diagram of left-realist views of crime. Please note that these nodes have no sub-branches, but there is no reason why they cannot be added.

Task 7.1 Using mind maps, spider-diagrams and concept mapping in department meetings

In order to better understand the differences between mind maps, spider-diagrams and concept mapping, use them in department meetings to plan lessons, schemes/units of work and other resources. It is worth pooling you and your colleagues' knowledge in planning sessions as specifications, mark schemes and other materials available from exam boards are quite sparse. For example, if planning a unit of work on health you may want to read the relevant chapters from different textbooks before completing a mind map. Start by branching off 'health' into the subsections of the specification and then branching off from those with your own further ideas related to those subsections; this will include key ideas not specifically mentioned in the specification itself. It will deepen your awareness of what needs covering in the unit.

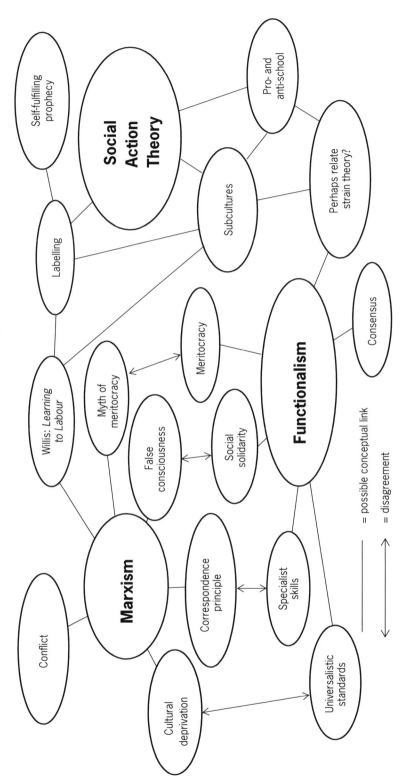

Figure 7.6 A concept map linking some key theories and perspectives on education

Contents of the concept map:

- Self-fulfilling prophecy
- Social Action Theory
- Pro- and anti-school
- Labelling
- Subcultures
- Perhaps relate strain theory?
- Willis: *Learning to Labour*
- Myth of meritocracy
- Meritocracy
- Consensus
- Functionalism
- False consciousness
- Social solidarity
- Marxism
- Conflict
- Correspondence principle
- Specialist skills
- Cultural deprivation
- Universalistic standards

___ = possible conceptual link

⟷ = disagreement

sociology. Whereas a mind map or spider-diagram's branches do not fully relate back to the central concept or theory other than by back tracking or thinking abstractly, a concept map can visually represent all the key features needed for an essay question before explicitly relating the final ideas back to the exam question or concept/theory. This mirrors the skills needed in evaluative essays, especially if we are to get the students referring back to the question and summarising their points in relation to the question asked by way of a conclusion.

Moreover, as teachers, we can always scaffold complicated concept maps by using concept cards (de A'Echevarria & Patience, 2008). These cards will already have the key ideas to be mapped written on them; the cards can also be photocopied and then cut out by the students so that they can stick them on a large piece of A3 paper. This allows them to re-arrange the ideas as they think through how to map and connect the cards and saves them laboriously copying up the ideas. In fact, this is very useful for scaffolding GCSE students whose intellectual skills are, obviously, not as developed as students studying at AS/A Level; it can also be used to help less able students – by way of differentiating resources – and prompt lethargic thinkers at AS/A Level.

Case studies

Case studies give in-depth insights into individual people, groups, or situations that have been studied over time. Importantly, well-chosen case studies can engage students by linking the in-depth study taught to wider sociological concepts and theories. Not only will the case study illustrate the concept or theory taught with a real life example, but they will allow the students' sociological imagination to contextualise an isolated 'biography' – as Mills (1959) would put it – with society at large, which fits into the idea of transposing 'personal troubles to public issues'.

Case studies can be simple or complex in order to fit the complexity of the topic taught. A simple case study, for example, could include brief summaries of two primary school students that illustrate how one has access to a wide range of *cultural capital* and another is arguably *culturally deprived* (see Figure 7.7). In this example, the very brief description of the two students can act as a conduit for a wider discussion on their backgrounds, privileges and subsequent life chances. More complex case studies can bring together the various real life experiences of individuals or groups in relation to larger scale social policies, social structures and processes. For instance, we may prepare and create resources explaining the impact of falling cocoa prices on farmers in Ghana (see Swift, 1998 as cited in Browne et al., 2009, p. 134), which could be used for topics on *global development* or *world poverty*. This could involve studying various articles or other texts on how decisions made by the International Monetary Fund and World Bank arguably forced the Ghanaian government to cut subsidies, which coupled with the fall in global cocoa prices, lead to farmers switching to crops they could sell locally. This story could be told through written explanations of the institutions' decisions, testimonies from farmers and their families, graphs showing the fall in prices and timelines on the chronology of the events studied. Other methods, such as card sorts, can be used to piece these events together. Here, writer and history teacher Mike Gershon (2013) suggests case studies serve two purposes. Firstly, and in relation to the idea of cocoa farmers, they provide students with a means of contextualising the concepts of price fluctuations, structural adjustment programmes and conditionality as well as how these abstract concepts impact on real people. Secondly, the case study contains a wide range of primary and secondary data that can be pulled together in order to see how lots of individual agents and interactions impact on society as a whole.

Alexandra Jameson – 7 Years Old

- Lives in a spacious semi-detached house with a large garden.
- Discusses her day with her family as they have dinner together every evening.
- Her parents have bought her lots of books and educational toys.
- Her parents spend at least 15 minutes reading with her every night.
- She is limited to watching one hour of TV a day.
- Her parents go to all her parent evenings at school etc.
- Goes to the library every week.
- Goes to swimming, karate and badminton lessons.
- Most weekends the family go on walks in local woods and parks.
- The family visit lots of cultural and historical attractions when on holiday.
- The family recently went to Paris and Alexandra saw the Mona Lisa in the Louvre.

Claire Jolly – 7 Years Old

- Lives in a small terraced house with a small paved back yard.
- Often has a sandwich and crisps for dinner whilst watching TV.
- Often watches TV or DVDs or plays games on her mum's old phone.
- She spends most of her time watching cartoons on TV until her parents get home from work and change the channel.
- The family do not read or have many books.
- Her parents like to watch reality TV and soap operas.
- Mum goes to some parents evenings.
- Occasionally goes to the cinema.
- Goes to the park with her older brothers.
- Has not been to many museums, but the family do go on trips to theme parks.
- The family go on holidays to self-contained holiday parks.
- The family did go on a foreign holiday and spent the week in an all-inclusive hotel 3 miles along the coast from Malaga in Spain.

Figure 7.7 Two PowerPoint slides used to present very basic case studies on two students' cultural capital/deprivation

Case studies are also beneficial to teaching sociological concepts and theories as, quite simply, this is exactly what many sociologists do themselves. For example, lessons on labelling theory or school subcultures could include Mac an Ghaill's (1988) ethnographic case study of African and Asian students in a state secondary school; where he found that the students' reaction to racism, especially from teachers, did not necessitate an anti-school culture, but actually lead to a 'resistance culture'. Therefore, Mac an Ghaill's case study can be used to relate the students' experiences (in the study) to the wider conceptual and theoretical issues of labelling theory and school subcultures. This may seem self-evident to any experienced sociology teacher, especially as these types of case studies are part of most syllabuses, but making the most of a case study by using various activities, such as card sorts, storyboards, readings and, of course, games based on them, can really embed both the study (including the research methods used) and the concepts and theories they illustrate.

Gershon also advocates the use of narratives as an aid to grappling with conceptually challenging ideas in class. For example, postmodernist ideas often frighten students immensely, especially as everything they have been taught is labelled as almost redundant, but well-constructed and relevant narratives can help shed light on the postmodernist point of view. Like teaching the concept of *life course analysis* (Hareven, 1999), which is often used as an example of how a narrative of someone's *postmodern life* (from being born to dying) can be compared to someone with a more *modern/ modernist life* course. These simple and brief narratives can help students make sense of the differences of people's life courses in the two eras. I teach this by using a straightforward card sort that students have to compare and contrast and see if they can arrange in the right chronological order; once they finally put the two sequences in order they should be able to see the difference between a 'modern life course' and 'postmodern life course'.

Another example of a narrative that highlights a concept in sociology is the story behind the bomb planted on Greenpeace's *Rainbow Warrior* flagship. I use this to teach Stanley Cohen's (1993) three-staged concept of state crime denial, sometimes referred to as the *spiral of denial*. By merging the three stages of 'it didn't happen', to 'it is something else' and, finally, 'it was justified' with the French government's denial of its attack on *Rainbow Warrior*, its subsequent suggestions to the contrary and its final acknowledgement that it did happen and why, students can see how the three stages follow the narrative of actual events and place them in a chronological order that relates to real people and places.

In order to find real life narratives, especially those that are not necessarily based on actual sociological studies, Gershon (2013) suggests using non-governmental organisations such as Amnesty International and Oxfam, which offer resources – often for free – that are really useful for teaching about development issues and human rights abuses; these, in turn, fit into sociology as not only are they related to topics on *global development*, but also sub-topics like state crime in units on *crime and deviance*. The resources often centre on individuals' stories, which make for useful narratives for students to follow. Other charities or interest groups offering useful resources include Greenpeace (green crime) and Shelter (stratification/poverty).

Play-Doh, Lego and loo rolls

Play-Doh, Lego, loo rolls and glue are not just for the primary school classroom. As sociology is full of different perspectives on the structure of society, there is no harm in having some fun by trying to create those structures in class. I have already mentioned that Lego can be used in lessons on childhood; where students will construct their idea of childhood, but Play-Doh and Lego bricks can be used to construct so much more. For example, I have challenged students to depict Charles Horton Cooley's (1992) *looking-glass self*, which is a concept covered when studying units of work on social action theory and/or identity and culture, in Play-Doh. Cooley's basic idea is that a person's self grows out of their interpersonal interactions with other members of society and, therefore, from their perceptions of others' views of them. Here, I ask students to recreate in Play-Doh how they imagine they must appear to others. They are then asked to reflect on why they feel their appearance is like it is (as expressed by the Play-Doh model). Lastly, the students are asked to make another Play-Doh model of their partner in class and then to compare models to see if their modelled 'self' is similar to others' model of them. If you use this idea, you would obviously need to be wary of any overly self-conscious students or those with confidence issues.

Lego, on the other hand, is fantastic for building and depicting macro structural theories. I have challenged my Year 13s to construct classical Marxist views of society's structure, particularly the economic base and superstructure, out of Technical Lego. This can be made even more difficult for able or very creative students if you ask them to re-design classical Marxist structures to represent neo-Marxist ideas, such as Louis Althusser's (2001) clarification that the structure has a political and ideological superstructure as well as an economic base.

Of course, many of the concepts and theories we teach can be made out of old loo rolls, cereal boxes and other empty packaging. Whether it is hypodermic syringes made from loo rolls in order to represent the *hypodermic syringe model* in 3D or using cereal boxes to depict television channels with channel buttons for 'information', 'personal identity', 'socialising' and 'escapism' as per the *uses and gratifications* theory of active audiences (McQuail, 1987), almost any concept or theory can be depicted in some way out of usable household junk.

Task 7.2 Visit a primary school

It is quite common for schools to allow teachers to visit other schools as part of their CPD (see Task 2.1 in Chapter 2). This facilitates the sharing of best practice and is especially helpful if you are starting out as a sociology teacher.

However, if you are looking for ideas that are both imaginative and unusual in a secondary setting, do not rule out visiting primary schools. Some of the learning activities in primary schools, such as playing with Play-Doh and making things creatively, can be adapted for secondary students with a bit of bravery, imaginative thinking and experimentation by the secondary teacher.

Marketplace

So called marketplace activities place the responsibility for planning, developing and teaching a concept or theory with the students themselves. These activities essentially get small groups of students to 'sell' a concept or theory to the rest of the class through a competitive market or trading floor where the students not doing the selling will have to 'buy' or vote on which group of students selling concepts and theories have the best pitch. This is a great way of getting the students to see how sociologists come up with competing theoretical perspectives on various social issues from health to political power. These activities are relatively easy to set up. For example:

- Divide the class into small groups and give each group a competing theoretical perspective or concept; for example, you could give each group a perspective on 'power and the state' in a unit on *power and politics*. This would include Weberian views of the state, pluralist views, Marxist views, neo-Marxist views and the views of the new right. Then, each group should produce promotional materials including posters, flyers and a quick presentation or pitch. Students can use their notes for this, especially if this is part of a revision lesson, or they can be set a research task to find out about their allocated perspective. Alternatively, this can be scaffolded with materials and resources provided by the teacher.
- Once the groups are well versed on the content of their allocated perspective and have produced their presentations, they are ready to start selling or pitching their ideas. However, only one student is left to 'sell' and present on the group's stall as the other students go out to view, hear and potentially 'buy' (rank, vote or rate) the other groups pitches. More importantly, for the students 'buying', their real task is to gain knowledge of the other perspectives. If they do this separately, then they will need to reconfigure the ideas in their heads and explain them to the rest of the group when they feedback on what they have learned.
- Subsequently, once the students have visited the other presentations, they will need to brief each other on what they found out and share the knowledge learnt. Each group can evaluate the perspectives from their fact finding missions and decide – after debate – which perspectives most appeal to them. Again, they can then 'buy' or vote on the best one or rank them in order of how convincing they are.
- In time, this knowledge can be debated through class discussion (see the previous chapter on how to facilitate this) or the students can complete a basic pro-forma with columns of boxes for summaries, positives and negatives for each theory.

Marketplace activities are ideal for developing students' interpersonal intelligence or team working skills (see Chapter 4). Moreover, if we are to again consider Durkheim's specialist skills, marketplaces not only get students cooperating, researching and evaluating, but they can also see the importance of categorising key concepts into the relevant theoretical perspectives as well as building a sense of social solidarity with their peers in their groups. We could also argue that the marketplace of competing ideas in the classroom is a microcosm of the wider sociological and political worlds of competing theoretical perspectives and political ideologies.

Task 7.3 Teach-meet marketplace

If you have time, organise a 'teach-meet' for local sociology teachers. As many schools now offer sociology at GCSE and AS/A Level, it may be worth contacting colleagues in other schools and meeting to share best practice. If there are enough of you, why not organise a marketplace activity in order to sell your best ideas? To make up the numbers, you could include other social science subjects, like psychology, or even other humanities subjects.

Deeper learning: Using SOLO taxonomy

In a similar vein to Bloom's taxonomy (see Chapters 4 and 6), the Structure of Observed Learning Outcomes (SOLO) taxonomy, which was developed by educational psychologists Biggs and Collis (1982), provides a structured framework for developing deeper thinking and learning skills. However, whereas Bloom's ranks thinking skills by difficulty, SOLO taxonomy sets up a process through which students explicitly develop their thinking and learning skills. Importantly, SOLO taxonomy encourages stretch and challenge in learning as students are expected to be baffled, confused and bewildered by the ideas presented to them at the start of a lesson or learning activity or a series of lessons or learning activities on a particularly difficult issue. However, as students progress through SOLO taxonomy's five main stages, they gradually grapple with, start to comprehend, understand and then master the ideas being taught. In this way, the taxonomy is ideal for teaching complex sociological concepts and theories successfully.

Biggs and Collis' original formulation of the taxonomy labelled the five main stages as follows:

- **Pre-structural:** At this stage, the learning activity is not attacked nor understood appropriately; the students do not understand the point of the learning activity and tackle the activity in a simplistic and inappropriate way. They fail to understand what they are learning about, especially if this is a multi-faceted concept or theory.
- **Uni-structural:** In this second stage, the students start to respond to the learning activity, but they understand only one relevant aspect or part of the learning activity. Thus, they do not understand the full complexity of the concept or theory being taught, but do start to recognise a relevant aspect or part of the abstract idea or ideas involved.
- **Multistructural:** The students move on from understanding one aspect of the learning activity (and/or concepts and theories being taught) and start to understand various relevant aspects.
- **Relational:** This is an essential part of their learning; the students start to see how different aspects of the activity (as well as ideas being taught) are integrated into a coherent whole, which may also involve them in understanding how the learning activity has been set up the way it has. In other words, everything begins to make sense.
- **Extended abstract:** This is true stretch and challenge; here, the integrated and coherent whole that was conceptualised previously, is further analysed, tested and evaluated so that a far higher level of abstract complexity is understood by the students. Moreover, they can start to place the concept or theory they have just learnt alongside other theories, perhaps through the application of the same learning activity.

However, advocates of SOLO taxonomy argue that teachers need to embed the processes of the taxonomy through its regular use and through explicitly teaching its procedures to the students. In many ways, this is similar to how some teachers approach PLTS and BLP skills (see Chapter 4), in that these learning skills must be shared and signposted to the students so that the students *learn to learn*. Hook and Mills (2011), for instance, state that making learning 'visible' to students not only improves their cognitive development, but also allows for the sharing of learning outcomes, especially if the content to be learnt is complex and gradual, and also allows for effective feedback (p. 10). The former is important as students will be aware that the outcomes may not seem apparent to them for some time and the latter is important as teachers and students will be aware of the stage of learning completed, which means feedback can be directed at the next stage. One thing I like about this idea is that it can aid students' resilience as they know that learning is not a straightforward process; in this sense SOLO taxonomy synergises nicely with the resilience emphasis of BLP and, sociologically, champions *deferred gratification* over *immediate gratification* when it comes to learning (see the 'education' section of any GCSE or AS/A Level sociology textbook to see what I mean by this).

Hook and Mills (2011) go on to say that teachers should embed SOLO taxonomy across the school community by creating a 'common language' centred on SOLO's learning outcomes, especially in terms of 'declarative knowledge', which is knowing about things learnt, and 'functioning knowledge', which is an awareness of how one is performing in their appropriation of the knowledge taught and learnt so far. One way to create this common language is to use regular verbs for approaching the different stages of SOLO taxonomy's learning framework (see Table 7.1). Another way is to use symbols to identify which stage of learning the student is currently focused on. If this all sounds too methodological, it is worth pointing out that this is to flag up to the students that the abstract concepts and theories they are learning about take time to both comprehend and cognitively master. It is through this process that students will learn to be resilient and be aware that learning takes time, patience and effort; there are, of course, no quick fixes to understanding the most complex of sociological concepts and theories.

Importantly, Hook and Mills argue that SOLO taxonomy works best when it is consistently used and is explicitly evident in the classroom. They go on to suggest that in addition to using the common learning verbs and the SOLO symbols (see Figure 7.8), teachers should design assessment for learning pro-forma that highlight SOLO, use SOLO centred learning logs, create SOLO learning maps and rubrics to visually aid students understanding of the taxonomy's stages and display the verbs and symbols throughout the classroom.

To illustrate SOLO taxonomy's potential use in sociology, I have applied the five stages to an activity that aims to get the students to fully understand the *marketisation of education* and *parentocracy* from a new right perspective. In order to break this down into each process of SOLO, I have written it in Table 7.2.

Table 7.1   SOLO taxonomy verbs. I have highlighted where key AO1, 2 and 3 skills and common exam command words overlap with the SOLO verbs and have added a few others

SOLO stage	Verbs and terms
Prestructural	Learning verbs are not used here as students are not expected to achieve the learning outcomes at this level. Of course, the prestructural level may merely be an implicit prelude to attempting the more concrete unistructural level.
Unstructural	find, **identify**, **define**, label, match,
Multistructural	**describe,** list, combine, give a basic **explanation** (of various components of the concept or theory)
Relational	**select** (relevant parts of the content taught), compare and contrast, **analyse** (aspects or the whole of the concept/theories), **explain** causes, **explain** effects, identify (and **interpret**) sequences, organise, distinguish, **apply** (or say how you could apply what you already know about sociological concepts/theories to the new knowledge learnt).
Extended abstract	**assess,** generalise, **judge**, predict, **evaluate,** theorise, prioritise, create, construct, justify, **argue**.

Adapted from Biggs and Tan (2007, p. 79) as well as Hook and Mills (2011, p. 13).

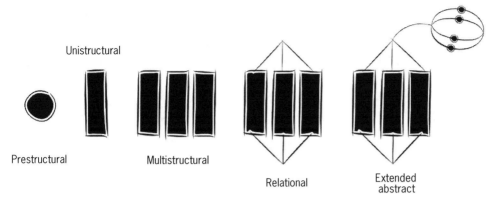

Unistructural

Prestructural   Multistructural

Relational   Extended
abstract

Figure 7.8   The SOLO taxonomy symbols (re-printed with the permission of Pam Hook and Essential Resources)

Table 7.2   Teaching the marketisation of education through SOLO taxonomy

SOLO stage	Applying SOLO to the 'marketisation of education' and 'parentocracy'
Prestructural	The idea of the marketisation of education is posed to the students; for many this will be extremely difficult to comprehend at all, especially as they have not received guidance on how to understand it.
Unistructural	Divide the students into two groups and then pairs within these groups. In one group, pairs are given profiles of Year 6 primary school students. The pairs with these profiles are tasked with thinking about the child's characteristics; they must decide which type of school is best for 'their child'. In the other group students are given a name of a school, information on the school's demographics, ethos, results, facilities and the expertise/interests of the staff. The common SOLO verbs used here could include 'identifying' what type of child or school they have, 'finding' positives and negatives in their characteristics and 'defining' the main characteristics of the school or the key characteristics of the child. At this stage the students are tasked with simply knowing what they have been given.
Multistructural	Here, the students need to think about the child's further needs or potential characteristics; they can 'list' them, 'combine' the given ideas with their own ideas and can briefly 'describe' or 'explain' the child's personality, needs and abilities. Exactly the same activity can be applied by the pairs with the schools. Then the students have to either think about their child's ideal school or, if the school, how they would 'sell' their school's attributes at an open evening. Importantly, most students move on from understanding the initial task (aspect) of the learning activity and start to understand how it fits in with this second task or 'aspect'. They are aware that both the activity and theory/concept involve various parts or aspects.
Relational	To move this on to the next stage and to get the students to see how what they learnt in their pairs in the previous stage relates to the other pairs, ask the pairs with profiles of the children (they are now the parents of this child in terms of role play) to visit the pairs with the schools (they are now the principal and vice principal of these schools). Quite simply, the parents need to select a school and the principals and vice principals need to try and convince them to select them. The role play activity will then be explained using the language of marketisation and parentocracy. Students can initially be exposed to this by the instructions for the activity, which will then be linked back to the sociological theory by a de-briefing discussion that relates the activity to a sociological explanation of the marketisation of education and of the concept of parentocracy. In terms of the SOLO verbs, not only would the students have 'compared and contrasted' the schools or 'applied' a school's attributes to the needs of their child, but they would have also 'explained the effects' of marketisation and parentocracy and 'identified' how the 'sequence' of the activity fitted in with the theoretical explanation.
Extended abstract	Once the above stages have been completed, the theoretical 'argument' for applying these concepts to education can be 'evaluated' and, of course, 'judged' by the students in relation to other theoretical perspectives, such as Functionalism and Marxism.

I have used this activity and have used SOLO taxonomy to teach it and other activities with a mixed ability group of Year 12s. The taxonomy does aid learning and can be used as an effective bulwark against students' complaints of 'it's too hard' or 'I don't get this'. One drawback, though, is that SOLO taxonomy is not widely used, or known, in UK schools and creating a common language and understanding of its processes will inevitably be hindered by the fact that other teachers are not using it. Of course, the teaching of abstract ideas is also central to Bloom's taxonomy, which is also relevant to teaching sociological concepts and theoretical perspectives, but is discussed in relation to general sociological skills in Chapter 6.

Further reading

Buzan, T. (2002). *How to mind map: The ultimate thinking tool that will change your life.* London: Thorsons.

Although mind maps might seem old-hat and straightforward, it is worth reading Buzan's books, including the above, if you get a chance. It is a method that can be habit-forming and useful if mind maps are not merely reproducing notes. Buzan's method can really help with 'quick revision', planning revision or as knowledge checks at the start of lessons.

Ginis, P. (2002). *The teacher's toolkit: Raise classroom achievement with strategies for every learner.* Bancyfelin: Crown House Publishing.

As recommended in the previous chapter, this is a really useful treasure trove of general teaching ideas. Paul Ginis explains how these activities should be set up and used and they are by and large applicable to teaching some of sociology's more complex issues.

Hook, P. & Mills, J. (2011). *SOLO taxonomy: A guide for schools.* Laughton: Essential Resources.

Hook and Mills' book is full of ideas on applying SOLO taxonomy to the classroom. It covers various aspects of teaching and learning, including displaying the symbols associated with the taxonomy around the school to fully embed its methodology amongst students.

Bibliography

Althusser, L. (2001). Ideology and ideological state apparatuses: Notes towards an investigation. In *Lenin and philosophy and other Essays* (pp. 85–126). New York: NYU Press.
Bandura, A. (1977). *Social learning theory.* Oxford: Prentice-Hall.
Biggs, J. B. & Collis, K. (1982). *Evaluating the quality of learning: The SOLO taxonomy.* New York: Academic Press.
Biggs, J. & Tang, C. (2007). *Teaching for quality learning at university: What the student does* (3rd ed.). Berkshire: Open University Press.
Browne, K. Blundell, J., Law, P. and Whalley, M. (2009) *Sociology for A2 AQA,* Cambridge: Polity.
Buzan, T. (2002). *How to mind map: The ultimate thinking tool that will change your life.* London: Thorsons.
Cohen, S. (1993). Human rights and crimes of the state: The culture of denial. *Australian and New Zealand Journal of Criminology, 26*(2), 97–115.
Cooley, C. H. (1992). *Human nature and the social order.* Piscataway: Transaction Publishers.
de A'Echevarria, A. & Patience, I. (2008). *Teaching thinking.* Alresford: Teachers' Pocketbooks.
Gershon, M. (2013, May 10). How to help your class grasp abstract concepts. *TES.* Retrieved from www.tes.com/article.aspx?storycode=6333650
Ginis, P. (2002). *The teacher's toolkit: Raise classroom achievement with strategies for every learner.* Bancyfelin: Crown House Publishing.

Gittins, D. (1998). *The child in question*. Basingstoke: Macmillan.

Goldthorpe, J. H. & McKnight, A. (2004). *The economic basis of social class*. Retrieved from http://eprints.lse.ac.uk/6312/1/The_Economic_Basis_of_Social_Class.pdf

Hareven, T. (1999). *Families, history and social change*. Boulder: Westview.

Hook, P. & Mills, J. (2011). *SOLO taxonomy: A guide for schools*. Laughton: Essential Resources.

Mac an Ghail, M. (1988). *Young, gifted, and black: Student-teacher relations in the schooling of black youth*. Buckingham: Open University Press.

McQuail, D. (1987). *Mass communication theory: An introduction* (2nd ed.). London: Sage.

Mills, C. Wright (1959). *The sociological imagination*. New York: Oxford University Press.

Swift, R. (1998, August 5). The cocoa chain: Conclusion. *The New Internationalist*. Retrieved from https://newint.org/features/1998/08/05/conclusion/

Webb, R., Westergaard, H., Trobe, K. & Steel, L. (2009). *A2 sociology*. Brentwood: Napier Press.

Weber, M. (1958). *The Protestant ethic and the spirit of Capitalism*. New York: Scribner.

8 Teaching sociological research methods

This chapter includes:

- An explanation as to why active learning is essential when teaching research methods.
- The importance of action research in facilitating the above, especially if students are to properly understand the processes of conducting research.
- Advice on how to get students started on their own research projects, including brief examples.
- Explanations on how to get students planning and designing their projects.
- A discussion on whether to get students to set straightforward research questions or challenge them to test more complicated hypotheses.
- Advice on how students should report and present their findings.
- An example of imitating an Ofsted inspection so the students experience research collaboration and the application of multiple strategies.
- How to help students interpret and analyse data, including secondary sources such as official statistics.
- Structuring an evaluation of the strengths and weaknesses of research methods through the P.E.T. and P.E.R.V.E.R.T. models.
- How to get students to structure evaluations.
- The importance of getting guest speakers and researchers in school to fully embed the relevance of research methods in both academia and the 'real world'.

Research methods can be as hard for the teacher to teach as they are for the students to learn. This is because, if taught poorly, the subject can be dry and uninspiring. However, like most things in sociology, research methods can be extremely engaging and rewarding if taught well and enthusiastically. Moreover, if we consider the rich, varied and seemingly infinite examples of sociological research that teachers can draw on to illustrate how methods are used, lessons on research methods will not only increase our students' specialist (sociological) skills and enhance their general subject knowledge, but will also further develop their sociological imagination as their eyes are opened to how sociologists go about making sense of the world around them.

Interestingly, there has been plenty of research on how teachers can effectively deliver research methods, especially in higher education. Any search of the American Sociological Association's

Teaching Sociology journal's back issues offers a host of theoretical ideas and empirical evidence for getting students engaged and, importantly, involved in sociological research. One such article by Pfeffer and Rogalin (2012) identifies three key approaches to learning that can be highly beneficial to students as they endeavour to make sense of research methods. These are: active learning assignments and discussion-based learning; guests who have participated in research themselves; and, thirdly, a focus on doing research in the 'real world'. The authors have come to this conclusion by reviewing the literature already available on teaching research methods as well as the impact of their own teaching. Although their research is in higher education, their approach to teaching research methods is easily transferable to the secondary classroom at both GCSE and A Level, albeit with slight differences due to the constraints of working with younger students in a school setting. Subsequently, my main focus in this chapter is on their first point, but I will briefly reference the last two points at the end of the chapter.

Active learning

As discussed at the start of Chapter 4, learning should be so much more than the simple acquisition of knowledge and skills by didactic instruction. Instead, learning should be *active* as students *learn by doing*. To quote Lowe (2013) for a second time, successful learning 'occurs when a learner takes some responsibility for the development of the activity' because 'emphasising a sense of ownership and personal involvement is the key' (p. 328). This is exactly the approach Pfeffer and Rogalin (2012) advocate for teaching research methods. They 'created "action learning" or "learning by doing" assignments to bring students into more active researcher roles', which allows students to actually experience the challenges and rewards of conducting research (p. 370). Similarly, in a study of leading sociology instructors at universities in the US, the factor that most distinguished these instructors as successful teachers was their ability to actively involve students in research and exposing them to empirical research in class (Persell, Pfeiffer & Syed, 2008). Indeed, it does not take a brain surgeon to figure out how conducive active learning is to research methods, especially because the methods themselves can be an active part of the learning. If this sounds too obvious to be stated, it may be worth considering your own sociology lessons or lectures. I never completed any of my own research for my A Level sociology classes (although some courses since have included research as part of coursework components) nor did I do anything of the kind in my master's degree that partially focused on research methods. Furthermore, it is only recently that the exam boards have included a requirement that students start referencing their *own* research in answers on research methods; this development, of course, is most welcome if we are to nurture the next generation of social scientists.

Nonetheless, getting students actively involved in research consists of more than simply doing a few surveys. I would suggest that there are three main ways to get students active when teaching research methods:

1   The first is to get students to prepare and conduct their own pieces of action research.
2   The second is to get students to interpret and explain data from various types of research.
3   The third is to get them evaluating sociologists or even their classmates' research and, importantly, being critical by using their own knowledge of the strengths and weaknesses of the various research methods studied, especially if this can be done without regurgitating the criticisms listed in their textbooks.

Task 8.1 Familiarise yourself with research methods

If you are to effectively teach research methods, you should familiarise yourself with them prior to delivering lessons on methodology in the classroom. Although you will need to learn about famous sociological studies (if new to sociology) or revisit them (if not), it may be worth looking at examples of educational research to see if the methods deployed convince you to improve or change your practice. In addition to conducting your own research (see Task 8.2 below), you can read and review research articles on pedagogy, assessment or other aspects of education from journals such as the *Online Educational Resource Journal* (visit www.oerj.org), which has a whole host of peer reviewed and interesting articles available for free download. By doing this, you are actually using social research methods to improve your day-to-day practice (this idea is adapted from Leask and Liversidge, 2013).

Students as researchers

There is a lot written on 'teachers as researchers' and the importance of social research in education by teachers in schools (Bell, 1993, pp. 6–8). However, there is no reason why students cannot conduct this type of research too. Of course, what we normally call *action research* is a study centred on the researcher's occupation that seeks to improve the practice of those involved. Therefore, in a similar vein, students can quite simply be given the opportunity to research the things that occupy them at school, during their leisure time or issues in the local community, in order to see if anything can improve these aspects of their lives. Essentially, action research is practical and aims to find feasible solutions to everyday problems and, if used by students in schools, will really make them see the relevance of research in finding answers to the social issues that most directly affect them. Although student research should focus on *safe topics* that will not put them in physical or emotional danger, by allowing them to investigate a topic that concerns their day-to-day lives they may find some purpose in the idea of research methods that would otherwise be lost to them, especially if their findings can be presented to peers, a school leadership team or local councillors. Moreover, if their research is focused on something directly relevant to them as well as others, it will arguably bridge what Mills (1959) referred to as 'personal troubles' and 'public troubles' as their research could have wider appeal for people in similar situations.

Task 8.2 Complete your own action research

In order to better understand the research process, especially if you are new to the social sciences or if your own social research skills are rusty, it is well worth finding the time to complete your own research project. Many teachers now do this as part of their CPD, particularly if they are enrolled on postgraduate courses in education. However, there are plenty of opportunities to conduct research with other organisations. One example is CamStar (Cambridge, Schools and Teacher Research), which is run by the University of Cambridge's Faculty of Education, but supports researchers in schools nationwide. Teachers completing action research on an aspect of teaching and learning in their own classroom can present their ideas to a conference, too. For more information, see www.camstar.org.uk.

Setting up action research projects in school does need some initial grounding in the classroom. Importantly, any unit on research methods would need to follow on from previous introductory units so that the students understand the purpose of sociological research in the wider context of the subject itself. Furthermore, if you have taught the key sociological terms, concepts, and perspectives as well as some topic areas, such as *culture and identity* and *families and households*, you will have reference points to relate back to when initially teaching about research methods.

Getting started

Once the students are reasonably well versed in the sociological vernacular, one way to set up the context of social research, especially at GCSE, is simply to ask the students how they would 'find out' something. At the very beginning of a research methods unit you could just let the students try to figure out the best way to find out information; this normally results in lots of very basic surveys. Nevertheless, as their learning progresses and they have been introduced to some research methods through general learning activities, such as those suggested in Chapter 6, student research will become more complicated and in-depth, especially as the students move up to AS/A Level.

Another way to use action research is to get the students completing quick, small-scale research activities as you go through the different methods throughout the unit on research methods. If you are doing this, it may be best to give the students a focus in order to save time. For example, after teaching a lesson on questionnaires you can simply get the students to write their own, which they will distribute and collect for homework. Table 8.1 lists a number of possible research activities related to schemes of work at GCSE and/or AS/A Level that the students may study. Of course, not all methods taught are feasible as small scale action research projects, but aspects of planning, conducting or collating the data that comprise larger studies can be taught in smaller chunks.

Table 8.1   School based activities focused on research methods

Research method	School based activity
Questionnaires	If students have previously studied a unit on *families and households*, they could set up a questionnaire to ascertain whether the nuclear family is still inevitable. This would include creating a series of closed questions asking if other students intend to get married, have children, think they will stay married, own their own home, etc. This will provide quantifiable data to give an overview of what type of family unit the students' peers think they will have.
Structured interviews	As the welfare state, especially the idea of 'social security scroungers', is often given a lot of airtime on TV and radio as well as column inches in the popular press, most students in schools will have an opinion on this. Therefore, students could canvas the views of other students through structured interviews if they have studied units on *wealth, poverty* and *work*. This could involve a series of closed or short open questions that allow interviewees to give their opinions during one-to-one interviews.
Unstructured interviews	If students have studied units on *culture and identity*, for example, they may ask each other what has the greater influence in the formation of their identity: gender, class, ethnicity, occupation, friends or the mass media? The keywords can be used as prompts and the interviewees encouraged to think aloud about which ones of these have the most influence on them.

Research method	School based activity
Observations (best to stick with non-participant and overt)	Students could ask permission to observe teachers in the staffroom or faculty offices etc. for short periods of time. They could look to see whether their subject teachers sit together or mix with other departments. This is tricky, but most colleagues seem to agree to these observations if short, unobtrusive and highly irregular. Alternatively, they could do something similar in the sixth form common room or school canteen and focus their observations on identifying whether there are groups representative of certain sub-cultures in these areas.
Content analysis	If the students have studied the *media*, content analysis is an ideal research tool to indirectly observe the presence of certain words, images or concepts within newspapers, magazines or websites. An example would be counting the number of loaded words used in articles on immigration. Of course, students would need to operationalise a working definition and criteria for identifying 'loaded words'.
Laboratory experiments	A difficult, but not impossible type of research method to use in school. For example, as this type of experiment is conducted in a well-controlled environment, the classroom is arguably ideal. A possible experiment could include seeing which type of music genre is most or least beneficial when working/revising with background music on; students simply see how much work they get done as various songs or tunes are played. The students can then debate how accurate and objective the measurements really were after the experiment.
Case studies	At A2 I have allowed students to compile case studies of famous people who have taken their own lives. Importantly, this was done with caution and care and my line manager was aware. Nonetheless, it allowed students to properly examine whether celebrities like grunge musician Kurt Cobain really fitted into Emile Durkheim's four types of suicide and whether it was because of too much or too little moral control or social integration (see Durkheim, 2013).
Analysis of official statistics	Almost every unit of study references official statistics, which means when you teach research methods you can easily find relevant statistics related to the topics that the students have looked at previously. The Office of National Statistics (ONS) allows you to download raw data as well as tables and graphs from its website, which your students can use to spot patterns, trends and correlations. This is discussed in more depth below under the heading 'interpreting and analysing data'.

Choosing research projects

If you are planning on getting the students to complete a more comprehensive piece of research, it may be an idea to allow them to decide what their research will focus on. If this is part of a general unit on research methods, then the options are obviously huge and the students may need help narrowing their areas of focus, but if it is part of a *methods in context* unit in relation to *education*, for example, then the students could think about an area of focus from what they have been studying. To facilitate this, Bell (1993) suggests using a 'first thoughts list' where students write down, mind map or even concept map all the possible areas they could look into and from that derive research objectives, questions and hypotheses (p. 17).

Developing a research strategy

Before getting the students to attempt their research method, they will need to set up a plan of action or a research strategy. For example, Cottrell (2008) says a good research strategy consists of:

- a plan;
- a search and review of relevant literature;
- the research hypothesis (or objectives and questions);
- a research design with a chosen methodology;
- the collection, correlation and an analysis of the data;
- drawing a conclusion;
- writing or presenting a report (p. 257).

If you are planning to regularly get students to conduct their own research then it is wise to get them into the habit of formulating a research strategy, especially as this can help them justify the research. However, as the basic strategy above is aimed at school leavers, university students and mature students studying courses in further or higher education, you will need to adapt this for secondary students. For instance, to save time and to focus the students, it may be wise to select the literature for review and ensure the students understand it as well as give them a selection of objectives, questions or hypotheses that could be used to scaffold their research (unless forming their own hypothesis is seen as stretch and challenge). Also, you would need to specify which methods are applicable and who the research sample can include. Depending on the needs of the students you are teaching, it is important to give them guidelines for conducting the research. These guidelines could also be differentiated.

Bryman (2004) argues that a research strategy is different to research design (discussed below) as it is when the researcher decides whether the general orientation of their research will be quantitative or qualitative in nature. This is an important foundation in research as it directly builds upon the researcher's theoretical views on the nature and philosophy of social sciences; this would include their epistemological view of social reality, their ontological perception of the social sciences and, if we are honest, where their abilities and preferences or biases fit into their understanding of social research. Although I completely agree with Bryman, any discussion on epistemology and ontology will be limited to the last year of A Level in most schools, especially as this is where the words appear on some syllabuses. At GCSE level, on the other hand, the quantitative versus qualitative debate will be more straightforward and explained as simply 'different' ways of conducting research – probably framed as a 'best fit' approach as opposed to being a prelude to a wider, deep and ultimately more complex philosophical debate. Perhaps one of the dilemmas here is whether to get AS Level students involved in this deeper debate when most AS syllabuses see the methodological differences as either a 'scientific' or 'non-scientific' approach to social research; at this level the content is devoid of the more philosophical vocabulary described above. It may be worth teaching the basic *'Is Sociology a Science?'* lessons prior to teaching the actual research methods, as it will allow AS students – and later on A2 students – to comprehend the importance of distinguishing between quantitative or qualitative research at an earlier stage. Of course, the same consideration would need to be applied when discussing Denzin's (1978) conceptualisations of triangulation – often covered at GCSE and AS – and Giddens' more complex ideas on structuration (Giddens & Pierson, 1998), which tend to be covered at A2. As I have reiterated previously, the depth you go into these theories and concepts probably depends upon the unique abilities and enthusiasms of you individual cohorts, which will vary year-on-year.

Research questions, hypotheses and objectives

It is also worth considering whether you want to ask students to use research questions or hypotheses in addition to outlining their research objectives (again, depending on the students' ages and abilities as well as time constraints, these can be set up by you to either save time or to scaffold the students' learning). This is an important point as hypotheses are far harder to grasp conceptually and are more complex than questions. As a rule of thumb, I would use research questions at GCSE level and aim to get students testing hypotheses by A2 (although there is no reason to hold back if you think your younger students can grapple with testing hypotheses). The key difference between the two is that a research question is the question (or questions) that the research simply sets out to answer. Subsequently, the research methods used and sample selected for the study depend on the questions asked. For example, students studying the *sociology of religion* could simply ask whether their classmates are religious believers or not to ascertain how religious or secular their class is. The question could be 'Is my class religious or secular?' and consist of a straightforward 'yes' or 'no' closed answer survey. This could then be developed further by using the word 'how' to ascertain 'how religious' the class is, which would mean codifying 'how religious' or 'how secular' a classmate is on a scale of 1 to 5. Of course, the simple survey question is now emerging into a basic closed answer questionnaire with quantifiable data. However, if this class were an A2 class looking at secularisation, they may want to see if their initial views can be turned into hypotheses. A hypothesis is not testing a question, but is testing an assumption about the relationship between two or more variables. Here, the first question above could become a hypothesis by asking whether students are secular because their own parents are secular or religious because their parents are religious. Importantly, a hypothesis will need three elements: two or more variables, a sample population and an identifiable relationship between the variables. A hypothesis is a great way to get students thinking about codifying, quantifying and looking for patterns or correlations in data for positivistic studies, such as structured interviews, but is harder for more interpretivist research methods, such as unstructured interviews, due to practical constraints and questions over the codification of variables.

Additionally, any questions or hypotheses will have to aid the objectives of the research. In many ways, the research objectives outline the purpose of the study and will also seek to justify the need for the study, particularly what the researchers aim to improve or tell us about the topic they are looking at.

Research design

In his book on research design for social scientists, Gorard (2013) argues that research design has too often been ignored in the teaching and development of new researchers, especially as courses have tended to focus on methods of data collection and analysis. However, research design has long been part of the AS and A2 Level syllabuses and now that students are required to conduct their own research projects, it has added importance as a tangible part of the actual research process. Moreover, GCSE syllabuses also require students to design their own research project. For example, the AQA (2012) specification states students should 'plan a simple research project', which would inevitably include research design once the students have decided on their objectives, questions and, perhaps, hypotheses to be tested (p. 5). Therefore, research design is basically a framework that comprises the methods the researchers will employ to conduct the research, collect and analyse their data. According to Bryman (2004), research design must reflect the importance the researchers attach to:

- demonstrating the causal connections between variables;
- generalising this to larger groups of individuals than those investigated in the study;
- understanding the behaviour garnered from the above points and what this means in the specific social context under investigation;
- realising the temporal (over time) dimension of the social phenomena and interconnections included in their study (p. 27).

Although research design is only one aspect of the students' overall plan or strategy, which will include their initial thoughts and objectives as discussed above as well as ethical considerations and how the data will be reported or presented, it is arguably the most important aspect of their overall strategy as it centres on how the research is actually gathered. Subsequently, in order to make students research work in practice, a simple school-based research design will include:

- an operationalised concept that constitutes the information needed to answer the research question or hypotheses;
- the methods that will be used to collect this, such as questionnaires, observations, analysing official statistics etc.;
- if the students are using questionnaires or interview questions they will need to design these so they are not ambiguous, but are easily understandable;
- if the students are observing, setting up unstructured interviews or semi-structured observations, such as focus groups, they will need to factor in practical constraints and permissions;
- if the students are using secondary data, such as official statistics, they will need to be able to locate and request a dataset;
- a sample group that will be both relevant and feasible to contact and interview or observe etc.;
- if the students have time, they may also design a small pilot study as well.

In addition to giving the students instructions or guidelines to help them formulate the above, Bell (1993) recommends using a checklist in order to ensure the project is both feasible and relevant. This is a particularly useful tool for A Level students attempting to complete a more substantive research project than at GCSE level. It is also essential if you are not giving the students research questions, objectives or hypotheses, as they will need to narrow their choice of topic area and focus their actual data collection. In addition, Bryman (2012) states that any research design should include considering the reliability, replication and validity of the research as part of the checklist (p. 28). This is to ensure that the quality of the research is factored into the research design. Therefore, it may be wise to get students evaluating some simple studies by established sociologists before setting up the students' own action research projects; this could involve the application of P.E.T. or P.E.R.V.E.R.T. (discussed below).

Reports and presentations

Although your students are not expecting to get their research published in an academic journal, if they have completed a more comprehensive piece of research you could get them to write up their findings formally. For example:

- Firstly, they should outline the objectives of the research in relation to the topic area studied and why they perceived a need to look at this issue and any problems associated with it. This can go on to explain why they then asked the questions or tested the hypothesis needed to fulfil the objectives.
- Secondly, they should outline their methods for collecting data, which would include justifying the research design, the sources of data and the chosen sample group. Moreover, this would also address issues such as response rates and any problems they may face when analysing secondary data.
- Thirdly, the students should summarise their results to explain, illustrate and justify any conclusions drawn. They could also discuss how this furthers their understanding of the topic area and sociological methods.

It may be a nice idea to have students present their ideas to the class who can act as 'critical friends' by giving constructive feedback or asking challenging questions; they could use the P.E.T. or P.E.R.V.E.R.T techniques to guide this (see below). It is also very rewarding for students to present ideas to senior teachers or school leaders. They may pretend not to like this, but it does give them a sense that their ideas are being heard (for example, see 'OFinSTED' below).

Case study: OFinSTED

One way to develop an in-depth comprehensive study within a school setting is to mimic the work of Ofsted inspectors. Although Ofsted often focus on the core subject areas within schools and pay little heed to sociology save for checking on teaching and learning, the inspectors are, in many ways, social scientists. Moreover, an Ofsted inspection includes the following research methods:

- an analysis of the school's data, especially the official statistics of GCSE and A Level results;
- non-participant overt observations of learners and teachers in lessons;
- semi-structured observation and interviews with students, especially through focus groups;
- interviews with various staff;
- and surveys of parental views via questionnaires.

Using all of these methods in one big student project facilitates collaborative group work amongst the class as various groups can be given different areas to work on. For example, one group can be given the job of trailing through the school's public results and spotting trends and comparing them to other groups (they can use RAISE Online or the Ofsted Dashboard for this). Another group can be tasked with seeking permission from willing teachers to perhaps observe a lesson – this is very conducive to AS/A Level as most students have 'frees' on their timetables. Another group can organise a focus group, perhaps centred on a lower year group, and some other class members can seek yet more willing teachers for interviews. Lastly, another set of students can prepare a question for parents, which, if their own, can easily be contacted. Ideally, all of this research can be planned in class, collected as homework and then collated and reported in the next lesson.

Again, as stressed above, it may be worth inviting senior school leaders to any presentation on reports or selected students could attend a senior leadership team meeting to give a more formal report just like Ofsted inspectors do.

Once the exercise is over, the students can discuss whether they feel the data they have collected actually reflects the school and their day-to-day experiences. Moreover, they can then start to evaluate the usefulness of the methods used in relation to the ideas on understanding and analysing data (discussed below). Of course, prior to any of these being completed, students must set themselves clear ethical guidelines for the activity and also ensure they have the consent of all those involved, including the leadership team, before commencing on the research.

This exercise is also a good way to teach the concepts of multi-strategy research, triangulation and, at A Level, even structuration. The first refers to any research that combines qualitative and quantitative research, the second includes using more than one method in the study so that any results can be corroborated or cross checked and the third includes combining micro and macro approaches to studying society as neither individuals nor social structures shape society alone (see Bryman, 2012; Denzin, 1978 and Giddens & Pierson, 1998 respectively).

Task 8.3 Review the research methods used by Ofsted inspectors

To prepare for the above activity, sit down with your departmental colleagues and pick through the methods and data used to create your own school's Ofsted report. Although it is up to your Senior Leadership Team (SLT) to challenge its outcomes, there is nothing wrong with privately evaluating the inspectors' use of research methods, especially if this makes you feel better about the strengths or weaknesses of the actual inspection itself.

Interpreting and analysing data from research

It is important to get students into the habit of interpreting and analysing both their own research data as well as the data used by other sociologists. Moreover, it is also good to give them a sense of how sociologists use data to justify their conclusions and theoretical perspectives. This is not just to better understand the methods used, but also to become more critical of the studies and perspectives they are looking at. Understanding how sociologists analyse their data is essential in order to see whether the arguments of the sociologists stand up to scrutiny. For example, students will not only be able to identify relationships between variables, but will be able to see if these relationships are strong enough to demonstrate a pattern of cause and effect if the researcher is claiming there is one.

If we are to consider quantitative and statistical data, it may be wise to always ask the students to consider:

- Who designed the research and, therefore, created the data?
- How reliable and valid are the statistics?
- Are the statistics merely descriptive or do they give an indication of what is causing or helping a social problem?

By way of example, the simple graph in Figure 8.1 can be used at both GCSE and A Level when discussing trends in crime, especially the role of the Crime Survey of England and Wales (CSEW), which is conducted by a private market research company for the Home Office.

Firstly, if we question who designed and researched this data, students can identify that a private company has a contract from the government to carry out the research. This can create a lot of general questions that students are quick to comprehend, such as: do the researchers want to please the government? This can then be counteracted and evaluated with a brief examination of the various codes of conduct covering market research organisations and the Office of National Statistics (ONS), which publishes the results.

Secondly, we can ask whether the statistics are reliable and valid. Key here is examining the research methods, which in the case of the CSEW involves yearly face-to-face interviews with 35,000 adults and 3,000 children aged 10 to 15 years old. Importantly, it can include looking at what crimes were included; some crimes, such as murder, are excluded. Moreover, if you are looking at theoretical perspectives, especially Marxism, many white collar and corporate crimes are not accounted for.

Thirdly, the descriptiveness of this survey will be clear for the students to see and they should comprehend the trend that crime is currently decreasing in general. However, despite more complex evidence available from the CSEW and ONS, this particular data set does not really tell us

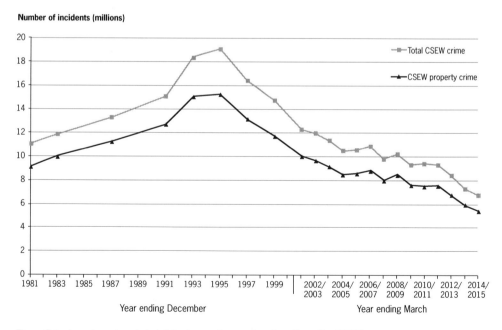

Figure 8.1   Long-term trends in total crime and property crime (from the CSEW)
Source: ONS and reprinted under the Open Government Licence v3.0.

what is causing the crime, which raises questions about the actual usefulness of the data. Of course, students can then be introduced to scatter diagrams and examples of regression analysis to analyse how the relationships and potential correlations between different variables play out. This last activity is largely confined to A Level, but simple scatter diagrams are still useful at GCSE and allow for students to see cross-curricular links to mathematics.

Importantly, students need to explain quantitative data and statistics in words and once they have got the hang of doing this, they can litter their explanations of sociological theories and concepts with statistical examples gleaned from various sources of social research, such as ONS data, and not just textbooks. For example, if we get them to understand Figure 8.2, the students will need to translate the numbers into a sentence that makes sociological sense. One simple way to do this is to teach a concept, such as the *march of progress* that claims childhood is constantly improving, and relating it to the empirical evidence found in quantitative research or official statistics. In this example, a student may articulate that 'childhood is still improving as the infant mortality rate has gone from 11 deaths per 1,000 per population in 1981 to 4 in 2011'. In similar activities, you can give out a variety of graphs or charts representing quantitative data and ask students to respond to it in prose as evidence backing up the concept taught. This type of activity also aids visual learners who can ultimately see how the numbers pan out across a graph or chart. To take this further and introduce numeracy, which is now a teacher standard, into your sociology lessons, you can get students to take raw data from tables and put them into charts, graphs and diagrams.

Of course, once students have analysed the data they will need to further evaluate the methods used to gain it and how trustworthy it is in more depth; this is discussed in relation to P.E.T. and P.E.R.V.E.R.T. below. However, it is important that students first understand how numbers are being used to defend arguments and, importantly, represent information. This is essential as sometimes a basic understanding of the mathematics used to defend an argument comprises the actual basis of the claim, especially if the sociologist is giving percentages or creating charts and graphs based on small samples of population or unrepresentative groups. A sound understanding of mathematics can also be used to defend the use of statistics, if the statistics are representative

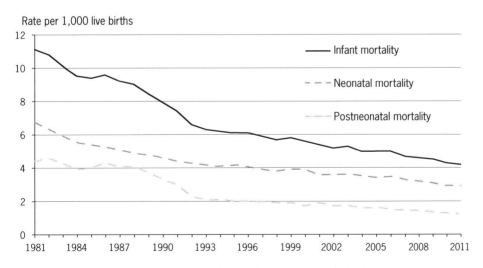

Figure 8.2   Infant, neonatal and postnatal mortality rates between 1981 and 2011
Source: ONS and reprinted under the Open Government Licence v3.0.

and reliable and if charts and graphs represent this data honestly. If you have enough time on your course or in your scheme of work, it is worth completing a couple of lessons on how statistics are represented in tables, graphs and charts, which may mean having a 'maths' lesson or two. I feel this is essential in sociology, as to quote Darrell Huff (1991, pp. 122–123), author of the entertaining *How to Lie With Statistics*:

> The fact is that, despite its mathematical base, statistics is as much an art as it is a science. A great many manipulations and even distortions are possible within the bounds of propriety. Often the statistician must choose among methods, a subjective process, and find the one that he will use to represent the facts. This suggests giving statistical material, the facts and figures in newspapers and books, and magazines and advertising, a very sharp second look before accepting any of them.

It is worth noting that a fear of using mathematics has been identified as one of the main reasons why research methods are unpopular amongst sociology undergraduates in the UK (Williams et al., 2008; Hodgen & Pepper, 2010 as cited in Brown, 2013). In response to this Brown (2013) argues that this perception by students in higher education is an over-reaction as the mathematical skills needed for social research, particularly on undergraduate and postgraduate master's degree courses, are no more advanced than those in GCSE mathematics exams. Not only does this defensive reaction affect students' confidence when considering using quantitative research methods, but it can also lead to disengagement and a lack of motivation. It is self-evident, then,

---

Task 8.4 Review the data used by your school's management to measure performance

As above, you could – with colleagues – sit down and analyse the methods used to set targets, track progress and manage performance in your school. Ideas could include:

- Assessing whether prior attainment data is better or worse depending on the feeder primary schools the students come from (this would really challenge Fischer Family Trust (FFT) data if it is found wanting).
- Whether your department (and others) internal marking/tracking data and predictions actually correspond to end results, such as final GCSE and AS/A Level grades (this could question the effectiveness of assessment in your school).
- Whether lesson observations are adequately standardised to make comparisons between teachers reliable (this questions whether observation grades for staff should be trusted).

Of course, some of this could land you in trouble with SLT, but there is nothing wrong with analysing the methods used to collect this data if you are informally reviewing this with trusted colleagues. You could also seek the leadership's permission to review this as part of a sanctioned action research project; but that depends on the openness and confidence of your SLT.

---

that as secondary school teachers we have a responsibility to start addressing these fears early on in order to demonstrate to the students that quantitative research methods can be used by those with even the most rudimentary numeracy skills.

Getting students to analyse qualitative data is essential, too. Although the data is very different to quantitative data, there are some similarities in how we would analyse it. For example, if students were shifting through their write ups of unstructured interviews or uncodified observations, they will need to look for recurring patterns or themes related to the topic studied. If the responses or actions of their sample seem to offer similar answers to the research question or fulfil the objectives, then the students will need to categorise these responses in order to make justifications in their findings and to evaluate whether the data is not just valid, but representative of the small sample population used for the study.

It is worth reading widely to find good examples of resources for teaching qualitative data. Aside from getting students to attempt unstructured interviews as homework with their friends or observations of colleagues' classes if allowed, it is worth finding interesting interview transcripts, diaries and case studies that will engage students. I have used prison diaries for this as they really seem to interest students. There are, of course, textbooks available with examples of qualitative data that students can analyse. These books often have commentaries. Two good, but dated, examples include *How to Do Social Research* (Dunsmuir and Williams, 1991) and *Sociology: Dealing with Data* (Marsh et al., 1999).

Brett (2012) recommends using the UK Data Service's online data catalogue, which holds over 250 qualitative data collections. These include various interview methods, focus groups, examples of studies based on diaries and case studies. Some of the data available is not only relevant to units of study at GCSE, AS and A Level, but include famous studies, such as Peter Townsend's (1979) *Poverty in the United Kingdom: A Survey of Household Resources and Standards of Living, 1967-1969*. Moreover, the website also offers free and open access teaching resources that may be of use to sociology teachers in schools. Brett argues that by engaging with these research collections students will learn how real data is conceived, collected and analysed by researchers as well as critically engaging with the research under scrutiny by evaluating the strengths and weaknesses of particular methodologies.

Using P.E.T. or P.E.R.V.E.R.T. for analysis and evaluation

Analysis and evaluation, as mentioned in Chapters 2 and 6, are both key assessment objectives and key skills (or even specialist skills) in sociology. They are also essential skills for assessing the strengths and weaknesses of research methods. Importantly, as an analysis is a detailed examination of the key elements or structure of a piece of research and an evaluation allows us to make judgements about the advantages and disadvantages of the actual methods used, it is ideal if you can formulate a systematic way of analysing and evaluating research that is both easy to remember and easy to use. One way to do this is to use the P.E.T. acronym, which stands for *practical, ethical* and *theoretical* issues (I would use this at GCSE level as the more thorough P.E.R.V.E.R.T. acronym is not appropriate for KS4). Here:

- The P is essential as students need to consider all the practical issues associated with the methodologies studied at GCSE. This would include the cost and time it takes to produce the research as well as the general feasibility of the study. For example, would it be wise for a university sociology lecturer to take two years off work to study criminal networks in a foreign country? The cost and time would be a factor in this type of study as would linguistic issues and whether the researcher could gain access to the network.

- The E part of the acronym stands for the ethical approach of the researchers. This includes issues such as gaining informed consent, ensuring that vulnerable groups receive appropriate care and consideration and that participants and researchers do not suffer any physical or psychological harm during the research.

- Lastly, the T aspect would include evaluating the strengths and weaknesses of the type of evidence that the researcher finds. For instance, this could include looking at the positives and negatives of using evidence collected from surveys, observations or experiments. Here, issues such as validity, reliability and representation would need to be considered. Additionally, underlying theoretical issues, such as the use of quantifiable methods versus qualitative methods and, perhaps, the deeper issues of whether sociology is a science, which covers positivism and interpretism, would also be included.

Alternatively, you could teach the P.E.R.V.E.R.T. acronym (see Table 8.2). Obviously, the word is easy to remember as it is a little edgy for the classroom and will, rightly or wrongly, amuse the students. It is also quite thorough and covers some of the key aspects of any good evaluation of sociological research methods. However, it should only really be used at KS5 and you should check that your senior leadership team are happy for you to use it. Of course, it should be explained to students that it is merely an acronym to remember the key elements of evaluation and is not used because it is meant to be funny in any way. Although P.E.R.V.E.R.T. is discussed in some AS and A Level textbooks (see, for example, Browne, 2015), if you think it is inappropriate for your school, college or students, then use P.E.T.

Using an evaluative structure

Marsh et al. (1999) in *Sociology: Dealing with Data* suggest students should also consider structuring their evaluative responses. This can be a useful way of getting them ready to answer research methods questions and can include an analysis of P.E.T. or P.E.R.V.E.R.T. I have adapted Marsh et al.'s (1999) original ideas for my own classes, but it still mirrors the four sections of their evaluative structure, albeit in a different order.

1. What are the researchers actually trying to find out?

This would include identifying the researchers' objectives, questions and hypotheses; identifying how these objectives, questions and hypotheses fit into the sociological topic area being studied; identifying what particular social problems or issues the researchers are attempting to address; identifying any evidence of ideological bias in the researchers stated positions or how they have defined the issues; identifying any weaknesses in the operationalised concepts being applied by the researchers.

Table 8.2 The P.E.R.V.E.R.T. method for evaluating research methods

Practical: practical issues could affect the methods chosen by sociologists. For example, time constraints, costs and feasibility all come into this. Students could be challenged to consider the practicality of using unstructured interviews to research the views of students truanting from school, for example. Practical questions could include: how do you find them? Would you have the time? Would they want to talk to the researchers?

Evidence: this refers to whether the research is primary or secondary evidence and the strengths and weaknesses of these types. For example, a strength of primary evidence is that researchers can design the research or choose their own questions whereas secondary evidence, such as official statistics, can be easier to get hold of, but will be designed by other people.

Representative: this is how typical the sample is compared to the target population as a whole. For example, would an observation of one Year 10 class show behaviour representative of the whole year group or even the school? Moreover, would a focus group on political voting preferences using semi-structured questions represent the population as whole?

Validity: this questions how insightful the research is in relation to the research question, hypothesis or objective. For example, do statistics really give a deep insight into how respondents of a questionnaire on satisfaction at work really feel about their positions and management, especially if the questionnaires are vetted by the management first?

Ethical: this questions whether the research is fair on respondents and whether ethical guidelines are in place and are being followed. For example, is there informed consent, protection from harm, confidentiality, anonymity etc. This is a very important issue and can be very useful if teaching things like *health, crime and deviance* and, in relation to child protection, *education.*

Reliability: this asks whether the research can be easily repeated in order to see if the results or findings are similar or coherent. This is essential if sociologists are going to make claims about the cause and effects of social phenomena. One area where this works well is with quick closed question questionnaires that are easily distributed amongst different groups.

T

Theoretical: this basically relates to whether the research methods are positivist or interpretivist. Students can then relate the research being evaluated to the strengths and limitations of both approaches. For example, they could argue that correlations from statistics are more objective, value free and scientific than assumptions drawn from a limited number of covert observations.

2. Is their choice of research method the right one? What are the strengths and weaknesses here?

This would include an analysis and evaluation of the research, perhaps using the P.E.T. or P.E.R.V.E.R.T. method of evaluation. Importantly, students need to assess how valid and reliable the data is, especially in giving a genuine insight into what is going on. Another key issue here is the theoretical aspect of the research. Students can weigh up the merits of using quantitative data versus qualitative data in relation to the objectives, questions and hypotheses identified above. In turn, this debate can then be related to the wider debates between positivism and interpretivism.

3. Are there other studies that agree or disagree with the researchers' findings?

This is, of course, the bread and butter of sociological argument: comparing theological perspectives and trying to unpick the research methods used to justify them. However, as it involves wider reading and knowledge, it is one area where the teacher may need to scaffold the evaluation activity by providing relevant readings or directions to particular studies. One example could be an analysis and evaluation of Willmott and Young's research on joint conjugal roles for their book *The Symmetrical Family* (1975), which can then be compared to Ann Oakley's studies on the same issues for her book *The Sociology of Housework* (1974). Oakley is useful here as her findings directly challenge not only Willmott and Young's findings, but their research methods, too.

4. Concluding the evaluation

Lastly, students will need to say whether point 1 was effectively answered; whether the research methods deployed were, in their view, the right ones and whether they were rigorous enough when tested against the P.E.T. or P.E.R.V.E.R.T. evaluation frameworks; they would then need to say whether the other studies they have looked at in relation to the topic area or social problems under scrutiny are more or less convincing; and, lastly, their overall view of the strengths and limitations of the research and whether it sheds any useful light on the topics or issues studied.

Importantly, getting the students into the habit of using an evaluative structure like this can help them plan essays and extended exam answers on research methods. Initially, these can take the form of formal reports, but then can be adapted and built into timed assessment exercises where the evaluative structure is applied (again, an AO2 skill) to particular exam questions.

Cross-discipline and cross-method guest discussion (in the real world)

At the start of this chapter I referenced an article by Pfeffer and Rogalin (2012) that identified three key approaches to sociological learning that I think can be highly beneficial to students learning about research methods in schools. These were: active learning assignments and discussion-based learning; cross-disciplinary and cross-method guest discussion facilitators (I called this 'guests who have participated in research themselves'); and a focus on doing research in the 'real world'. Although the authors are in higher education, their ideas can be adopted by school teachers, but the approach needs to be simpler and more general in its focus. We have indirectly looked at the first area throughout most of this chapter and it is clearly the most relevant aspect of their overall approach. However, the latter two points can also be useful.

For instance, the aim of 'cross-discipline and cross-method guest discussion facilitators' is getting in people that have used research methods as part of their job or role in a particular institution. This brings the research to life as students not only meet people who make a living or a viable use of research in their day-to-day lives, but it also allows the students to discuss the research with them. Although Pfeffer and Rogalin seem to focus on academic researchers, there is no reason why other professionals who use social research cannot be invited in to discuss their use of research; this can include civil servants, people employed in marketing or health professionals who record data to improve performance or even for publication. For example, my students have had the opportunity to meet with social workers from a non-governmental organisation working with victims of domestic violence. Despite the primary purpose of the visit being in relation to a sub-topic on *power-relations in the family*, students were encouraged to ask questions about research on domestic violence, especially the statistics released by Amnesty International, as the organisation represented compiled its own data and research on this as part of its advocacy work. Of course, finding guests can be difficult and time consuming, but be imaginative in thinking of who you could ask. For example, although Police Community Support Officers (who are regularly available to schools) are not social researchers *per se,* they do record crime and could be useful in quizzing over the reality and representativeness of crime statistics and whether they think evidence from the British Crime Survey or the CSEW is reflective of their actual experience. Finally, do not be hesitant to ask researchers at local universities – many are more than happy to come into schools and discuss their research; my local university sees this as part of its outreach and wider recruitment strategy.

Another reason Pfeffer and Rogalin suggested getting speakers in is that they wanted students to understand that research is never a perfect enterprise and, ironically, that imperfection may result in useful and unexpected insights and innovations. This is their third point: that research in the 'real world' throws up *potentiality* as well as difficulties. Of course, they centred this on guest speakers, but this aspect of teaching and learning about research methods applies to any research conducted by the students as much as it does professional sociologists and social scientists.

Importantly, the great thing about sociological research is that it is all based in the 'real world' (with the possible exception of postmodernism). Nevertheless, it is always wise to select studies that actually appeal to your students when illustrating how research methods work in context. As I have emphasised previously, you know your students better than any textbook writer or resource compiler and it is best to choose studies that you think will really engage and motivate them as opposed to bore them senseless and put them off research methods for life. Therefore, you will need to research the sociological studies out there and not simply rely on the textbooks, which – despite being very good overall – may have picked a rather dry example for the method under discussion. Teaching research methods is, consequently, a laborious task, but if done well, it can be very rewarding for yourself and extremely beneficial for your students.

Further reading

Bryman, A. (2015). *Social research methods* (5th ed.). Oxford: Oxford University Press.
Bryman's book is the 'go to' social research methods textbook for many undergraduate and postgraduate courses dealing with practical social research. It is useful, therefore, as a resource for your 'more able' AS or A Level students, but also as a reference book for yourself. It is far more comprehensive than any general A Level textbook could be.

Marsh, I. Trobe, K., Griffiths, J., Hope, T., Best, S. & Harris, G. (1999). *Sociology: Dealing with data*. Harlow: Longman.
Although dated, this book goes through all the key research methods and explains them with relevant examples in a clear and concise way. It is not particularly engaging for 'Generation Z' students, but is a helpful resource if you, the teacher, are new to sociological research or are teaching research methods for the first time in a long time.

Dunsmuir, A. & Williams, L. (1991). *How to do social research*. London: Collins Educational.

> As above, this book is a bit dated, but it does give useful case studies to introduce the key ideas found in sociological research methods. Moreover, it is designed for students and is accessible for AS, A Level and some GCSE students. It also uses some famous studies as examples.

The Sociology Teacher

This is a magazine available quarterly from the British Sociological Association's Teaching Group. The articles often cover issues associated with teaching research methods and the intended readership seems to include anyone interested in teaching sociology. A lot of articles may seem aimed at A Level or undergraduate level, but the ideas within can be altered to suit GCSE students. If your school gets an institutional membership of the BSA, *The Sociology Teacher* can be downloaded from www.britsoc.co.uk.

Teaching Sociology

Teaching Sociology is an academic journal concerned with how sociology is taught. Although focused on higher education and clearly North American in its approach to the social sciences, it is useful if you are completing an initial teacher training assignment based on teaching research methods or if you have an intrinsic interest in this subject. The journal is published by the American Sociological Association and Sage Publishing. It can be accessed online via www.uk.sagepub.com, but may be free if you have access to a higher education institution's library and electronic resources.

Bibliography

Assessment and Qualification Alliance. (2012). *GCSE specification sociology* (Version 1.0). Manchester: Assessment and Qualification Alliance.

Bell, J. (1993). *Doing your research project: A guide to first-time researchers in education and social science.* Buckingham: Open University Press.

Brett, B. M. (2012). Liven up your teaching: Teach using real-life data. *The Sociology Teacher, 2*(1), 16–17.

Brown, M. (2013). Engaging students in quantitative methods: It's all about the data. *The Sociology Teacher,3*(1), 14–19.

Browne, K. (2015). *Sociology for AQA* (Volume 1). Cambridge: Polity.

Bryman, A. (2015). *Social research methods* (5th ed.). Oxford: Oxford University Press.

Cottrell, S. (2008). *The study skills handbook* (3rd ed.). Basingstoke: Palgrave Macmillan.

Denzin, N. K. (1978). *The research act: A theoretical introduction to sociological methods.* New York: McGraw-Hill.

Dunsmuir, A. & Williams, L. (1991). *How to do social research*. London: Collins Educational.

Durkheim, E. (2002). *Suicide*. London: Routledge.

Giddens, A. & Pierson, C. (1998). *Conversations with Anthony Giddens: Making sense of modernity*. Palo Alto: Stanford University Press.

Gorard, S. (2013). *Research design: Creating robust approaches for the social sciences*. London: Sage.

Hodgen J. & Pepper, D. (2010). *Is the UK an outlier? An international comparison of upper secondary mathematics*. London: Nuffield Foundation.

Huff, D. (1991) *How to lie with statistics*. Harmondsworth: Penguin.

Leask, M. & Liversidge, T. (2013). An introduction to practitioner research, reflective practice and evidence informed practice. In Capek, S., Leask, M. & Turner, T. (Eds.), *Learning to teach in the secondary school* (6th ed.) (pp. 360–371). London: Routledge.

Lowe, M. (2013). Active Learning. In Capek, S., Leask, M. & Turner, T. (Eds.), *Learning to teach in the secondary school* (6th ed.) (pp. 325–344). Abingdon: Routledge.

Marsh, I. Trobe, K., Griffiths, J., Hope, T., Best, S. & Harris, G. (1999). *Sociology: Dealing with data.* Harlow: Longman.

Mills, C. Wright (1959). *The sociological imagination.* New York: Oxford University Press.

Oakley, A. (1974). *The sociology of housework.* New York: Random House.

Persell, C. H., Pfeiffer, K. M. & Syed, A. (2008). How sociological leaders teach: Some key principles. *Teaching Sociology, 36*(2), 108–24.

Pfeffer, C. A. & Rogalin, C. L. (2012). Three strategies for teaching research methods: A case study. *Teaching Sociology, 40*(4), 368–376.

Townsend, P. (1979). *Poverty in the United Kingdom: A survey of household resources and standards of living.* London: Allen Lane.

Williams, M., Payne, G., Hodgkinson, L. & Poole, D. (2008). Does British sociology count? Sociology students' attitudes toward quantitative methods. *Sociology, 42*(5), 1003–1021.

Young, M. D., & Willmott, P. (1975). *The symmetrical family: A study of work and leisure in the London region.* Harmondsworth: Penguin.

9 Planning sociology

> **This chapter includes:**
>
> - An overview of long-term planning, which includes examples of how to break syllabuses down in order to fit them into the academic year.
> - An overview of medium-term planning that pays particular attention to schemes of work.
> - An explanation as to why it is useful to adapt and share schemes of work with students.
> - An overview of short-term planning, which will focus on lesson plans.
> - A discussion on considering the context of the lesson in relation to the syllabus, objectives and outcomes as a key aspect of your planning process.
> - An explanation and examples of three and four-part lesson plans.
> - A discussion on the merits of using '5-minute lesson plans', which includes examples.
> - A discussion on using data to plan lessons, especially FFT at GCSE and ALPS or ALIS at A level.
> - How you can adapt predictions and differentiation centred on data by tracking current working grades (CWG).
> - A brief explanation of various differentiation strategies.

Planning is an essential component of teaching sociology. In fact, it is an essential part of any teachers' practice and has been recognised as such by Ofsted. In their 2015 *School Inspection Handbook*, the grade descriptors for outstanding teaching, learning and assessment highlight the importance of planning by stating that, 'Teachers plan lessons very effectively, making maximum use of lesson time and coordinating lesson resources well' (Ofsted, 2015a, p. 43). This makes clear that, whilst inspectors do not require an actual lesson plan if they rock up to one of your lessons unannounced, they do expect the lesson to be carefully thought through. Moreover, the handbook then goes on to acknowledge the importance of planning beyond individual lessons. Here, the guidance states that outstanding teachers 'provide adequate time for practice to embed the pupils' knowledge, understanding and skills securely.' This indicates that we should consider and factor in the various ideas and skills found in sociology into our overall planning so that we cover the syllabus comprehensively. Lastly, the guidance suggests that planning should account for personalised learning and differentiation as we should, 'introduce subject content progressively and constantly demand more of pupils,' which also suggests stretch and challenge, whilst at the same time insisting that we, 'Identify and support any pupil who is falling behind, and enable almost all to catch up'. This may seem a tall order, but Ofsted are right to say that if you plan well, you will end up having more success when actually teaching.

Stages of planning

Most books on teaching and learning split planning into three very simple stages (see, for example, Gershon, 2014 and Holt, 2015). These are:

- Long-term planning
- Medium-term planning
- Short-term planning

Although many books start with lesson planning, which denotes short-term planning, it probably makes more sense to start with long-term planning. This is because you will need an overview of the year ahead in order to literally fit the syllabus into the school calendar. Quite simply, if you do not manage to teach all of the content and skills and allow for exam practice, your students will be unprepared.

Long-term planning in sociology

In sociology, long-term planning is essential as there is so much on both the GCSE, AS and A Level curriculums. I have lost count of the times I have sat in meetings with other staff members, particularly senior leaders and heads of sixth form, and have had to explain that, unlike other subjects, my students will not have finished 'learning all the content by Easter'. As made clear in Chapter 2, sociology syllabuses are content heavy and can overwhelm teachers as much as students. Of course, your planning should start as I have already suggested in Chapter 2, by canvassing your future students on what topics they would prefer to study and considering which topics are your stronger areas in terms of knowledge. This will make your planning easier as you will be more aware of the difficulties ahead.

Another issue that will crop up when planning is 'who will teach what?' This is inevitable as most schools will assign at least two teachers to sociology. This is normally one specialist with a non-specialist, but can often be two non-specialists if a sociology teacher leaves. Unless you are lucky enough to have additional sociologists at school, leadership of the department will fall, obviously, to the specialist even if they have not formally been appointed as a head of department. Here, planning is fundamental in guiding your non-specialist colleagues, who may be quite needy even if they seem confident, especially when they browse through a textbook for the first time. In order to lead them through the syllabus and, by default, the year and their week-by-week teaching, it is important to sit down with them, go through the specification and assign topic areas and give a rough indication of when these topic areas will be taught. For example, the initial plan could be as straightforward as Table 9.1.

However, once you have decided on the topic areas to be taught, you need to align the syllabuses with the school calendar. This exercise is not to be underestimated as the school year is mined with INSET days, off-timetable days, occasional days, extra-curricular visits, extended assemblies and mock exam weeks, which excludes the actual holidays and the silly season close to exams where students, especially at GCSE level, are off doing intervention and coursework catch up left, right and centre. Therefore, one very simple way to do this is to break the syllabus you are planning to get through down into subtopics and map them against the weeks that fall within each term. For this to be effective and account for all the time that will be missed through the activities mentioned above, it is worth leaving 2 weeks spare at the end of each term. For example, see a simple AS plan for Year 12 in Table 9.2.

This type of brief table would be repeated for the Spring Term and the first part of the Summer Term. The content of each week would be marked off on the exam specification and vice versa to ensure the whole of the course is delivered in good time.

Table 9.1 Initial long-term planning

Term	Andrew	Tom
Autumn Term	Introduction to theory; education and theoretical perspectives; start educational social policies.	Research methods; P.E.R.V.E.R.T; quantitative methods; qualitative methods.
Spring Term	Finish educational social policies; theoretical perspectives on the family; start childhood.	Ethnicity, gender and class in education; student teacher relationships; school subcultures; family types; power relations in the family; start demographics.
Summer Term	Finish childhood; start revision. After exams, look at postmodernism.	Finish demographics; start revision. After exams, look at stereotypes in the media.

Table 9.2 Week-by-week long-term planning

Week	Andrew	Tom
Week 1	Introduction to sociological theories (Functionalism, Marxism)	Introduction to research methods (using P.E.R.V.E.R.T)
Week 2	Introduction to sociological theories (Feminism, Social Action)	Quantitative methods (surveys)
Week 3	Introduction to sociological theories (New Right, Postmodernism)	Quantitative methods (structured interviews, coding)
Week 4	Practice exam question (scaffolded)	Quantitative methods (official statistics)
Week 5	Education: functionalist perspectives	Qualitative methods (participant observations)
Week 6	Education: Marxist perspectives	Qualitative methods (non-participant observations, overt and covert)
Week 7 Half-term	Education: feminist perspectives	Practice exam question (scaffolded)
Week 8	Education: new right perspectives	Qualitative methods (unstructured interviews)
Week 9	Education: social action theories (including labelling)	Qualitative/Quantitative methods (case studies, experiments)
Week 10	Summary and exam practice (seen)	Methods: Positivism vs. Interpretivism
Week 11	Education social policy: introduction	Is sociology value free/science?
Week 12	Education social policy: historical context	Practice exam question (seen)
Week 13	Buffer week	Buffer week
Week 14	Buffer week (Christmas)	Buffer week (Christmas)

Medium-term planning

Medium-term planning could, in terms of classroom practice, just be another way of saying *schemes of work* or *units of work*. Put simply, a scheme of work is a plan that outlines what work needs to be done in the classroom over a given timeframe. In many ways, a scheme of work is intrinsically linked to medium-term planning as each scheme will normally take between 6 weeks to a term to work through. However, many teachers seem to limit schemes of work to at most 6-week or half-termly units. In sociology, this may mean teaching the topic areas of a syllabus within 6-week periods or breaking down the syllabus into smaller topic areas. For example, an AS Level topic area such as *families and households* can be broken down into sub-topics, which would include *childhood, family types, power relationships, changing family patterns, demographics* and *social policy*. Each of these sub-topics would constitute a separate scheme of work.

Before embarking on designing a scheme of work, it is a good idea to read or re-read the exam board's specification to fully understand what is required in that area of study or from the syllabus you have chosen to follow. It is also worth asking yourself a number of key questions as well. This is to ensure your attention is directed towards the key issues outlined in the specification. For example, you could ask:

- What are the overall objectives of the scheme of work?
- How long is it going to take? Here, it is important to refer back to your long-term plans in order to make sure everything fits into the academic year.
- What activities will you be using throughout the scheme of work? Do they offer diversity for different types of learners?
- How will students' progress be measured? Is there a final goal, such as a completed mock exam on the area of study or a project that needs completing?
- What resources need to be prepared, especially any that need to be shared?
- Does the scheme of work overlap with others? Could this reinforce the knowledge to be learnt or simply overload and bore the students by going over the same old ground?

As stated above, it is essential that the scheme of work includes a variety of learning activities so that students are fully engaged. Revisiting the learning styles and skills section of this book (Chapter 4) as well as the more practical ideas listed in Chapters 6 to 8 would be beneficial as most students will want lessons to be different and the tasks to be as diverse as the topic issues. Some topics in the scheme may be better suited to certain types of activity than others. For example, with demographics you can plan in plenty of games and numeracy-based learning that would be less easily applied to social policy, which may focus on activities that involve debate and reading through, comparing and contrasting policy briefings or newspaper articles on changes to government policy (although numeracy is also ever-present in this unit). Of course, if you know your class well from previous years, it is always important to adapt and change schemes of work to personalise learning to particular groups and cohorts.

When creating a scheme of work, you will need to devise a pro forma that maps out how learning activities, resources and assessment strategies fit together throughout the timeframe decided on. This is to ensure that the objectives of the overall scheme of work are achieved in line with the specification. Therefore, a scheme will not only include the order of lessons, types of activities and strategies of assessment, but they will also briefly list generic needs for delivering the content, such as how to access videos and other resources that may be stored centrally within the department or elsewhere in the school. However, these lists or overviews can be kept short as the lesson plans will provide more detailed information. See Table 9.3, which is an example of a scheme of work pro forma used for a GCSE scheme of work on basic sociological knowledge; it is partly an introductory unit and partly a unit looking at sociological processes, structures and key themes that is centred on an exam syllabus. In the further reading section for this chapter you will also find links to the key exam boards offering sociology as they all provide downloadable schemes of work.

It is important that you share your planning with students. This is quite straightforward with long-term planning as it can involve a very brief overview of the topics to be taught throughout the year at the start of the course. Moreover, it is also self-evident with short-term planning as it will be clear to the students in the objectives and outcomes shared with them at the start of the lesson. However, with medium-term planning, it is a good idea to give the students a breakdown of the topic areas and what will be covered lesson by lesson. This will allow them to read ahead, plan in advance for homework assignments and annotate as they go along to triage areas for intensive revision. I share these plans in unit booklets that basically correspond to the scheme of work. For example, see Table 9.4 that sets out the areas to be studied in a unit on the *mass media*. These plans are often given out in booklets with glossaries of key words and concepts, key sociologists and selected readings. The plan also includes recommended readings for students.

Short-term planning

In the same way that medium-term plans are often referred to as schemes of work, short-term planning often simply denotes lesson planning. A lesson plan is a detailed account of what will happen in a lesson in order to guide the teacher or teachers through the various activities and assessments that are needed to ensure that the students achieve the stated learning objectives and learning outcomes of the lesson. There is no one way of planning a lesson and, as stated earlier, actual lesson plans are not required by Ofsted inspectors. Since September 2015, Ofsted's advice has been widely circulated and championed by teachers:

> Ofsted does not require schools to provide individual lesson plans to inspectors. Equally, Ofsted does not require schools to provide previous lesson plans.
> Ofsted does not specify how planning should be set out, the length of time it should take or the amount of detail it should contain. Inspectors are interested in the effectiveness of planning rather than the form it takes.
>
> *(Ofsted, 2015b, par. 3)*

It is clear that inspectors are not looking for any uniform way of planning a lesson. However, you would be silly not to plan your lessons; not least if Ofsted were visiting. Therefore, despite the devaluation of actual physical lesson plans, lesson planning is still a major aspect of your job and you need to consider very carefully how you intend to do it.

Table 9.3   Scheme of work for an introduction to GCSE sociology

Lesson no.	Topic area	Learning objectives and outcomes	Learning activities	Assessment for learning	Resources and materials
Lesson 1	Introduction to sociology	Main objective: to understand some basic key words and the course content. Main outcomes include describing what sociology is and being able to contrast the sociological approach to understanding the social world to other academic subjects, such as the natural sciences approach to understanding the natural world.	Explanations, pair work, card sort, short videos and written exercises. See lesson plan for more detail.	Hands down/targeted Q&A. The plenary will include a short written response to a GCSE question (scaffolded). If TA is available, ask to circulate amongst least able.	Course booklets, PowerPoint, card sorts, text from textbook and videos (available on YouTube). There are also newspaper articles on various sociological issues, especially teenage crime, to foster discussion on social norms and values, as well as the nature versus nurture debate. These are in the filing cabinet. Homework is written on PowerPoint.
Lesson 2	Processes of socialisation	Main objective: to understand the idea of socialisation. Main outcomes: students will be able to explain the basic concept of socialisation, especially the difference between primary and secondary socialisation.	Explanations, mind mapping on past experience, short videos (see PowerPoint), structured debate and written responses. See lesson plan for more detail.	Use RAG cards and mini-whiteboards to check initial responses to class Q&A. The plenary will include a short written response to a GCSE question (scaffolded). If TA is available, ask to circulate amongst least able.	Course booklets, PowerPoint, mini-whiteboards, RAG cards, A3 paper, coloured pens, text from textbook and video clips from Super Nanny and Nanny 911 (available on YouTube: see lesson plan). Homework is written on PowerPoint.
Lesson 3	Gender socialisation	Main objective: to gain a solid understanding of gender socialisation. Main outcome: students will be able to explain gender socialisation and evaluate whether these processes are a result of nurture or nature.	Explanations, class mind mapping on the main board, use of images and videos (see PowerPoint) and a structured debate. See lesson plan for more detail.	Use mini-white boards to check initial responses to class Q&A. If TA is available, ask to circulate amongst least able.	Course booklets, PowerPoint, mini-whiteboards, board pens, text from textbook and videos clips from The Harry Enfield Show (on YouTube: see lesson plan). There are also laminated pictures to emphasise different aspects of gender socialisation. These are in the filing cabinet. Homework is written on PowerPoint.
Lesson 4	Social structures in the UK	Main objective: students will have a basic understanding of the class system in the UK. Main outcomes: students will be able to describe the key features of the social structure of modern society.	Short video, card sorts involving jobs and social status, explanations, drawing diagrams and the use of Lego to create these class structures. See lesson plan for more detail.	Targeted Q & A. The main activities and plenary will include short creative activities that will indicate basic understanding. If TA is available, ask to circulate least able.	Course booklets, card sorts, worksheets, text from textbook and PowerPoint. See the PowerPoint hyperlink to the John Cleese/Two Ronnies sketch. Please use the Lego (blue box in the office) for the last activity (see lesson plan), but put it back. Homework is written on PowerPoint.

Table 9.3 Continued

Lesson no.	Topic area	Learning objectives and outcomes	Learning activities	Assessment for learning	Resources and materials
Lesson 5	Culture and class	Main objective: to understand that different classes are often seen to have different cultural attributes. Main outcome: students will be able to explain cultural and linguistic deprivation and compare these to material deprivation. An additional outcome will be the ability to write a short evaluation on whether class stereotypes are justified.	Explanations, pair work through mind mapping, use of images and videos (see PowerPoint) and a structured answer to a made up GCSE style question. See lesson plan for more detail.	Targeted Q & A. White boards and RAG cards. The plenary will include a short written response to a GCSE question (scaffolded). If TA is available, ask to circulate amongst least able.	Course booklets, PowerPoint, mini-whiteboards, board pens, text from textbook and videos clips from *EastEnders* and *Downton Abbey* (on YouTube: see lesson plan). There are also laminated pictures linking stereotypes to certain activities (these can be used as card sorts as well as discussion cards). These are in the filing cabinet. Homework is written on PowerPoint.
Lesson 6	Subcultures and cultural diversity	Main objective: to understand the concepts of subculture and cultural diversity and how they relate to each other. Main outcomes: students will be able to explain both concepts and apply various examples to further illustrate them.	Explanations, 'spot the subculture' game, short videos, music clips and a small written task. See lesson plan for more detail.	Targeted Q & A. The plenary will include a short written response to a 4 mark GCSE question (scaffolded). If TA is available, ask to circulate amongst least able.	Course booklets, PowerPoint, game (in cabinet), text from textbook, a video clip from Benjamin Zephaniah and music clips from Kanye West, The Levellers, The Cure and Baharon Phool Barsao from the Bollywood film *Suraj* (available on YouTube: see lesson plan). Homework is written on PowerPoint.
Lesson 7	Social control	Main objective: students understand what is meant by social control and how state agencies control individuals in society. Main outcomes: students will be able to differentiate how formal and informal agencies of social control operate in the UK. An additional outcome will be their ability to describe how individuals are controlled in society.	Explanations, keyword game, group work through mind mapping, textbook activity, and a structured answer to a made up GCSE style question. See lesson plans for more detail.	Targeted Q & A. Whiteboards and RAG cards. The plenary will include a short written response to a GCSE question (scaffolded). If TA is available, ask to circulate amongst least able.	Course booklets, PowerPoint, A3 paper, pens, laminated photocopies of 'Activity 4' on p. 23 of the GCSE textbook. There is also a keyword game in the cabinet, but the sheets will need photocopying. They correspond to the images on the PowerPoint (focused on Key agencies of social control). Homework is written on PowerPoint.
Lesson 8	Social status, power and authority	Main objective: students will know the key concepts of 'status', 'power' and 'authority' in relation to social structures in the UK. Main outcome: students will be able to define the words 'status', 'power' and 'authority' in a written response. An additional outcome will involve students relating the three key words to gender, social class, ethnicity and age and comment on how this can result in inequality.	Explanations, a short video, card sorts involving social groups and social status (these are to be ranked as a 'diamond 9'), worksheet with word fill and a series of possible short answer GCSE questions. See lesson plan for more detail.	Targeted Q & A. The plenary will include a short written response to a series of short answer GCSE questions. If TA is available, ask to circulate amongst least able.	Course booklets, card sorts, worksheets, text from textbook and PowerPoint. See the PowerPoint hyperlink to the 2 clips from BBC news. Homework is written on PowerPoint. Extended homework: ask students to watch videos on BBC Bitesize Sociology pages on social processes, especially power and participation.

Lesson no.	Topic area	Learning objectives and outcomes	Learning activities	Assessment for learning	Resources and materials
Lesson 9	Social issues: poverty	Main objective: students will know what a 'social issue' is and why poverty is an example of this. Students will also discuss the contrasting definitions of absolute and relative poverty. Main outcome: students will be able to explain in writing different definitions of poverty and assess the difficulties of measuring these definitions. They will be able to reference Peter Townsend, too.	Brief clips from YouTube, lists of objectives (for 'need vs. want' activity), readings and worksheet on Peter Townsend. See lesson plan for more detail.	Use mini-whiteboards to check initial responses to class Q&A. You can also check written answers on the Peter Townsend worksheet. If TA is available, ask to circulate amongst least able.	Course booklets, object lists, 3 types of worksheet, abridged extracts from Townsend's *Poverty in the United Kingdom* and PowerPoint. See the PowerPoint hyperlink to the 2 clips from BBC3's *Poor Kids*. Homework is written on PowerPoint. Useful websites for homework: https://www.jrf.org.uk/ http://poverty.ac.uk/
Lesson 10	Recap and revision session	Main objective: to guide students' revision and complete a brief exposition of the unit so far. Main outcome: completed glossaries in unit booklets and revision cards/mind maps created.	Completed exercises in booklets, use of mobile phones for definitions and mind mapping. See lesson plan for more detail.	Students can work at their own pace; phones are allowed if used sensibly. If TA is available, ask to circulate amongst least able.	Course booklets, coloured card, coloured pens/pencils and a variety of textbooks. Homework is written on PowerPoint; revision.
Lesson 11	End of unit test	Main objective: to assess the students' knowledge. Main outcome: successful completion (by ability) of a variety of AO1, AO2 and AO3 questions.	Test papers	N/A	Test papers are on the shared area (school ICT system).

Table 9.4 A scheme of work written for students

Unit Topic Areas

Topic	Content	Reading	Understood?
Different sociological theories of crime and deviance, social order and social control	We will study how sociologists theorise about crime and deviance and how the two terms are differentiated. This will cover the functionalist, Marxist, social action, feminist and postmodern perspectives as well as right and left realism.	Moore, S. et al. (2009) *Sociology for A2*, pp. 330–337 Cameron, J. et al. (2008) *AQA Sociology* (A2), pp. 244–268 Webb, R. (2009) A2 Sociology AQA, pp. 72–100	☺☺☺☹
The social distribution and patterns of crime and deviance by locality, social class, age, ethnicity and gender	We will study whether there is a link between particular social groups and certain crimes and whether there are any causes or reasons for this. This will include ethnicity, gender, class and age. A key element will be recent trends.	Moore, S. et al. (2009) *Sociology for A2*, pp. 372–377 & 386–391 Cameron, J. et al. (2008) *AQA Sociology* (A2), pp. 269–278 Webb, R. (2009) A2 Sociology AQA, pp. 100–117	☺☺☺☹
The globalisation of crime in contemporary society	This aspect of the unit will look at how crime is increasingly global and affected by the media. It will also define and explain state, green and human rights crimes.	Moore, S. et al. (2009) *Sociology for A2*, pp. 366–371 & 378–385 Cameron, J. et al. (2008) *AQA Sociology* (A2), pp. 279–384 Webb, R. (2009) A2 Sociology AQA, pp. 126–135	☺☺☺☹
Crime control, prevention and punishment and the role of the criminal justice system and other agencies	We will study the police, Crown Prosecution Service (CPS), the court system, sentencing and prison as well as probation services. This will be in relation to each particular theory. Another key area in this sub-topic is victim studies and how crime affects victims.	Moore, S. et al. (2009) *Sociology for A2*, pp. 392–398 Cameron, J. et al. (2008) *AQA Sociology* (A2), pp. 285–290 Webb, R. (2009) A2 Sociology AQA, pp. 136–145	☺☺☺☹
The sociological study of suicide and theoretical and methodological issues that arise from it	We will learn about suicide, why it is/was seen as deviant and why Emile Durkheim thought it could be studied scientifically. This topic will, therefore, look at the methodological clash between positivism and interpretism. For example, it will look at the use of official statistics versus case studies in understanding suicide.	Moore, S. et al. (2009) *Sociology for A2*, p. 399 Cameron, J. et al. (2008) *AQA Sociology* (A2), pp. 291–196 Webb, R. (2009) A2 Sociology AQA, pp. 146–153	☺☺☺☹
The links between sociological theory and methods in relation to the study of crime and deviance	We will study what secondary and primary data show us about patterns of crime, how they are collected and their strengths and weaknesses. This will build into other areas of methodology. A lot of this will look at evaluating various methods through P.E.R.V.E.R.T.	Moore, S. et al. (2009) *Sociology for A2*, pp. 254–321 Cameron, J. et al. (2008) *AQA Sociology* (A2), pp. 297–305 Webb, R. (2009) A2 Sociology AQA, pp. 160–165	☺☺☺☹
Essay practice	You will practice various essays as well as complete a mock exam.	Re-read hand-outs! Webb, et al. (2008) *AS Level Sociology* (AQA), p. 488	☺☺☺☹

Context, objectives and activities

Before writing your lesson plan it is important to consider the context of the lesson, especially how it fits in with your chosen syllabus and what parts of the specification it covers. As sociology is not part of the national curriculum, you need not worry about how your lesson fits in here – although it may have some relevance to other national curriculum subjects that you could think about cross referencing if you eventually write up your lesson plans as a formal document. In addition to considering the syllabus of study, it is important that you link each lesson plan to a section of your scheme of work so that the whole scheme is covered comprehensively. When (and if) your lesson is written up, it may also be worthwhile labelling all these links (to the syllabus and scheme of work) so that other teachers can use your plans 'off the shelf' if you are to move on, change topic areas or collaborate (see Figure 9.2 for an example). If you choose to plan by mind mapping, PowerPoint or even the '5-Minute Lesson Plan' (see below), it is still worth indicating that you have considered these links and share them with both colleagues and students.

Another key consideration that you should address before thinking about what activities you will use, is the lesson's objectives and outcomes. Although some teachers only use one or the other, objectives and outcomes are often both included on lesson plans as they are technically different. You will, however, come across plenty of teachers who combine them, mix them up or misunderstand the subtle differences between them. Atherton (2013) states that 'objectives are statements of what you are setting out to teach, although expressed as if the students were going to learn it' whereas 'outcomes (more accurately "desired outcomes") are statements of what you might (in principle) assess.' Importantly, although you probably will not be able to get all students to access all of the learning outcomes, they should be statements of what a student will know or be able to do towards the end, at the end or even after the learning has been completed, such as a homework task. For example, a sociology objective could state, 'By the end of the lesson you will understand the importance of meritocracy as a sociological concept', whereas the outcome could state, 'By the end of the lesson you will be able to write a written explanation of the concept of meritocracy'. The demarcation between objectives and outcomes fits in with the discussion on assessment objectives in Chapter 2, especially the idea that AO1 corresponds to the objectives and AO2 and AO3 correspond to outcomes.

When planning objectives, it is a good idea to split them to allow for better differentiation and stretch and challenge. For example, Figure 9.1 shows an objective used in a lesson on the impact of globalisation on education policy. Here the objectives are split into three and link to the AO1 knowledge and understanding aspects whereas the outcomes are also split into three, but say what the students will have done by the end of the lesson and what skills are needed. The outcomes are differentiated by grades in that *all* students will be able to complete the basics (grades C3–C1), *most* will complete the majority of the work (grades B3–B1) and *some* will be able to attempt some very challenging activities (grades A3–A*).

The next thing to consider is the activities for your lessons. Key areas for consideration include how many activities you will include: for example, do you want the students to focus on a large research activity that will build on the skills of resilience and/or collaboration or would you like a lot of small engaging activities that all add up to achieve both the lesson's objective(s) and the main outcome(s)? Here, you will need to factor in timings and how each activity links to the next without confusing the students. Another important issue to factor in is how your activities will link to the students' ability (see differentiation, below), learning styles and skills (see Chapter 4) and, of course, the topic area. As stated above in relation to medium-term planning, it is also essential to have a variety of diverse activities, such as games, card sorts and written activities, in order to maintain students' interest, avoid repetitiveness and fatigue from overdoing certain types of activities. The amount of activities you use will be affected by your overall approach to lesson planning.

Lesson 14: The Globalisation of Education Policy	**Lesson Objectives:** **Grades C3–C1:** to know how education policy in the UK has responded to increased globalisation; **Grades B3–B1:** to understand how this has impacted on schools, especially the curriculum; **Grades A3–A*:** to know some of the theoretical responses to these policies. **Lesson Outcomes:** **Grades C3–C1:** to complete a 6 mark question identifying 3 education policies that are a response to increased globalisation; **Grades B3–B1:** to mind map all the curriculum changes and statutory requirements that could be linked to globalisation; **Grades A3–A*:** to write a 10 mark answer explaining both functionalist and new right views on the policies and changes studied above.

Figure 9.1 Graded lesson objectives

Three- and four-part lesson plans

Traditionally, most teachers have been taught to plan three- or four-part lessons. Three-part lessons are relatively straight forward: they will include a starter to engage students, a main activity or set of activities, often referred to as the *main body* of the lesson, to allow students to learn the key content and, lastly, a plenary, which will ideally check the students learning. A four-part lesson plan is basically the same, but includes a 'part' for introducing the topic or explaining the main aspects of the content being studied in between the starter and main activities. There is, of course, absolutely nothing wrong with these types of lessons and they are used day-in, day-out by teachers everywhere. For example, see Figure 9.2; although it does not have four exact parts, it does include a starter, main activities and a plenary.

As mentioned in Chapter 6, starters are needed to engage students and hook them into the lesson. This is best summed up by Beere (2012) who states 'a starter should stimulate curiosity and open-mindedness and prepare the brain for learning. These can be random or linked to the subject' (p. 11). In sociology there are no end of stimulating starters based on topical issues that can excite and prepare students for the lesson ahead. For instance, a good example could be using a controversial and recent music video that, if age appropriate, gets the students discussing a key area of study. Here, the students will be curious that you have used a seemingly unrelated video in a sociology lesson and this will then further their interest in what the video says about society. If you get a video that is popular amongst students, you are arguably quids in, so to speak; they will be hooked. You could alternatively get students to read short passages and answer quick questions on them. However, to add an element of surprise, especially if students are unaware of the main topic of that lesson, you could trick them into making stereotypical assumptions about social issues. A good example is a text with stereotypes based on jobs, such as nurses, soldiers and builders, which do not specify gender. When students are asked whether 'a man was

Goffs School – Sociology Lesson Plan

| Year: 12 AS Sociology | Unit: Education | | Lesson: 12 – Admission Policies |

Links with ICT: (Lesson Plan, PowerPoint and most resources in 'Sociology area' on J – Drive shared area)

Lesson Objective: students will understand how admissions policies work in practice (**grades C3–B3**) and they will also know some differing sociological arguments on the fairness of these policies (**grades B2–A1**). **BLP Skills Objective:** students will use their collaboration and questioning skills.

Learning Outcomes: all students will know some basic admissions policies centred on the key criteria of faith, ability and catchment area; **most** students will be able to evaluate the pros and cons of each policy; **some** students will be able to apply the sociological perspectives referenced in previous lessons to their own evaluations of each admissions policy.

Progress: there will be opportunities to measure progress throughout the lesson, especially during activities 3 and 4 (see below). Progress can be checked verbally and through checking written work.

Resources/Preparation: PowerPoint, card sorts and worksheet

Teaching and Learning Activities	Timing	Key Words	BLP/PLTS	Differentiation
Starter: (See PowerPoint) Ask the students to discuss what they associate with the images/symbols on the PowerPoint. Nudge suggestions towards admissions policies before revealing that they represent faith, ability, catchment area, parentocracy and banding, which form the backbone to this lesson.	10 mins	Admissions Policies Faith	Imagining – students will be asked to consider what links these images/symbols to education policy.	Guided Q&A (partly hands down based on data context sheet).
Explain the five main types of education policy. Students should not take notes as the text on the PowerPoint is on the worksheet. Encourage students to highlight key ideas as they read through the sheet. Ask them NOT to complete the questions as they are intended for a later activity.	10 mins	Ability Catchment area Parentocracy Banding	Listening – although a brief activity, students will need to listen to the teacher. They are to make links between what's said and previous knowledge.	Check students' differing level of comprehension by targeted Q&A. Allow very brief discussion on each policy, but ensure seating allows for peer-to-peer support.
Give out the card sort. Explain that students should try to match each policy with the written argument defending or criticising it. After this is complete, get students to discuss these arguments. Students can fill in the accompanying sheets for their own reference.	15 mins	Marxism Functionalism New Right	Planning – students will be taught a method for answering an exam question that can be applied to similar questions in the AS exam.	Use the context sheet for guided Q&A. Help weaker students during written exercises. The lesson objective is differentiated by outcome (see

Activity	Time	Key concepts / Questioning	Differentiation
Progress Check: target Q&A. Link answers about the policies back to the second part of the learning objective **(grades B2–A1)**. Also, see if more able students are aware of sociological links to Marxism, functionalism etc.		Labelling Theory Interactionist	above). However, all students are encouraged and expected to try and attain grade B or A grade outcomes.
Get the students to re-read the worksheet and answer the questions. This will allow them to apply previous learning and refers to the latter part of the learning objective. They can refer to prompts on the PowerPoint. Encourage them also to add additional sociological theory where possible. **Progress Check:** if stuck, students should indicate with RAG cards placed on the table. Ask them to do this.	15 mins	Middle class Working class <u>Questioning and collaborating</u> – students are to question the policies and consider in pairs whether they are fair on children.	The most able should be able to link to sociological theory whereas the less able can identify arguments for and against the policies and link to the basic theories highlighted on the PowerPoint. Group students according to ability so that they can attain the higher outcomes.
Plenary: Students answer the question posed about the fairness of selective admissions policies on Post-It notes. Also refer to the learning objectives in any discussion on these topics.	10 mins	<u>Questioning</u> – referring back to the L/O and other aspects of BLP identified above.	As per outcomes

Homework: n/a – lesson on Thursday reserved for setting homework.

Figure 9.2   A lesson plan on admissions policies

wolf-whistling a nurse', the students ask in the affirmative despite the fact that the nurse's wolf-whistler could have been female and the nurse male (or even that both could have been male or female) (see, for example, Hayward, 2002, p. 47).

The lessons' main activity, main activities or main body is, inevitably, where the main learning takes place and, ideally, will expand the ideas in the starter (although many teachers use random starters to simply settle students). When planning your main activity or activities, you should ensure the subject knowledge outlined in the objectives is covered and is challenging. Moreover, as already discussed, the activities need to comprise various learning activities that allow active learning to take place. Here, you should think about learning styles and skills and offer a variety of activities that the students can get on with collaboratively or independently. Beere (2012) also recommends factoring in the use of visual aids and practical activities to promote differentiated learning through different activities. Lastly, you could even give students a choice of activities that all centre on the same learning objectives and result in similar, if not the same, outcomes (for more on the main activities or body of the lesson, see Award Scheme Development and Accreditation Network, n.d.).

In an educational setting, plenaries are activities that take place at the end of the lesson. Interestingly, the word derives from the late Latin words *plenarius, which means* 'complete', and *plenus, which means* 'full'. Therefore, a plenary should complete the students' learning; ensuring that the students are full of knowledge. Plenaries are often taught as straightforward activities that simply recap on the learning that has taken place in the lesson. For example, basic plenaries in sociology lessons can include:

- List 3 things you have learnt today about Neil Postman.
- Ask your neighbour to explain 3 things they have learnt today about stereotypes centred on disability.
- Read the 10 statements on divorce. Identify which ones best reflect feminist or new right views.
- Summarise Marxist explanations of poverty in 3 bullet points. Write full and complete sentences.
- Sum up the idea of the looking-glass self in 3 sentences; then reduce the sentences to 3 words; and then, finally, choose the one word that best sums up the concept.

However, plenaries do not need to be short activities that are the inverse of starters. They can be far more complex and rich in order to fully summarise and complete the learning that has gone on in the lesson. For example, at GCSE you can build actual exam questions into plenaries. These can be a series of 1 mark questions or slightly more detailed 4 or 6 mark questions. If you ask the students to answer, 'Describe how sociologists may approach the study of gender differently to biologists', which is a 4 mark GCSE question, you could time them and then get them to peer assess their answers. This is important to planning as you can then record the answers, even if the students simply hold up mini-white boards with their grades on (see checking learning in the next chapter), to measure how many students have completed the specified outcomes of the lesson and the more implicit objectives. By doing this, you will also have assessed whether your own planning has paid off. Here, we can see that plenaries are a useful tool for checking learning and measuring progress.

5-minute lesson plans

Of course, with all the pressures piled onto teachers as part of their day-to-day responsibilities, lesson planning can be seen as a bit of a burden, even a chore, especially if you are to write them up formally. However, many teachers now use PowerPoints to guide them through the lesson or plan ahead using adaptations of Ross Morrison McGill's '5-Minute Lesson Plans'. McGill (2012) developed the original template in recognition that teachers spend too much time planning and have to juggle multiple responsibilities; let alone keep a semblance of a life away from teaching. The idea is straightforward, in that a lesson can be planned on paper in 5 minutes, but the actual method and format of the plan is more visually stimulating and simple than a conventional lesson plan pro forma, particularly those foisted upon trainee teachers. For me, this form of planning works well as I find it far more akin to mind mapping than typing everything up on a dull pro forma (see Figure 9.3 for how this could be adapted for sociology).

McGill breaks the plan into 8 parts, which include shapes in which you briefly note down key aspects of the lesson. These key aspects are:

1 **The big picture:** in this first shape you link the actual lesson content to the wider scheme of work, syllabus or national curriculum as well as recognising prior learning; thus giving anyone reading the plan the wider context of the lesson or, rather, 'the big picture'. However, McGill says that this should be written quickly and not in too much depth, taking no more than 30 seconds.
2 **The success criteria:** this second shape will contain brief points on how you will meet your learning outcomes. It is worth noting that this should follow on from the 'big picture' as the criteria will inevitably be building upon the needs of the scheme of work or furthering prior learning. To symbolise this, they are connected by an arrow, which will be present between each of the shapes, just like a flow chart.
3 **Engagement:** this shape will include something extremely engaging to draw your students into the lesson and retain their interest throughout. Here, many of the starter activities discussed in Chapter 6 will be useful, but you could also look for topical news stories linked to the area of the syllabus being studied, especially if those news stories are controversial.
4 **'Stickability':** bearing in mind that students will have many of their lessons long before their exams and before they start their revision, it is self-evident that a lot of what we teach will be forgotten by the time the exams roll round. So, 'stickability' refers to the key ideas, concepts or arguments you want the students to remember. In other words, what will they remember from the lesson the next time they walk into your classroom.
5 **Assessment for learning:** this is where you will briefly state your assessment strategies. For instance, will you use self or peer assessment at any point to measure progress and check learning? You could also include strategies such as targeted Q&A, even McGill's own PPPB (see Chapter 6). Of course, you do not need to expand on these strategies, as the plan will only require you to indicate what strategies you will be deploying throughout the lesson.
6 **Key word(s):** this shape is for you to highlight the keyword or words, which aids the current focus on literacy and SPaG. Moreover, McGill suggests you can add numeracy here, which would be useful with research methods lessons. In the context of sociology, you could also include the key sociological concepts or perspectives covered in the lesson.

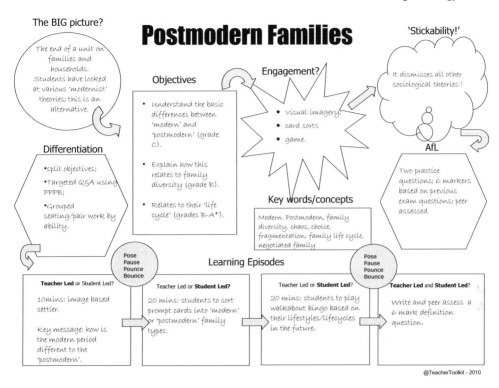

The BIG picture?

The end of a unit on families and households. Students have looked at various 'modernist' theories; this is an alternative.

Postmodern Families

'Stickability!'

It dismisses all other sociological theories !

Objectives

Engagement?

- Understand the basic differences between 'modern' and 'postmodern' (grade C).
- Explain how this relates to family diversity (grade B).
- Relates to their 'life cycle' (grades B-A*).

- Visual imagery;
- card sorts
- game.

AfL

Two practice questions; 6 markers based on previous exam questions; peer assessed.

Differentiation

- split objectives;
- Targeted Q&A using PPPB;
- Grouped seating/pair work by ability.

Key words/concepts

Modern. Postmodern, family diversity, chaos, choice, fragmentation, family life cycle, negotiated family

Pose Pause Pounce Bounce

Learning Episodes

Pose Pause Pounce Bounce

Teacher Led or Student Led?

10mins: image based settler.

Key message: how is the modern period different to the 'postmodern'.

Teacher Led or **Student Led?**

20 mins: students to sort prompt cards into 'modern' or 'postmodern' family types.

Teacher Led or **Student Led?**

20 mins: students to play walkabout bingo based on their lifestyles/lifecycles in the future.

Teacher Led and **Student Led?**

Write and peer assess a 6 mark definition question.

@TeacherToolkit - 2010

Figure 9.3 An example of a 5-minute lesson plan on postmodernism and the family

7 **Differentiation:** in this shape you can indicate whether you will alter seating plans or pupil groupings or use other strategies, such as differentiated tasks, complexity of texts and extension activities etc.

8 **Learning episodes:** these shapes will include what will happen throughout the lesson to further learning. They can include student-centred learning activities, teacher-led explanations, Q&A on videos etc. Of course, the episodes will be in chronological order. McGill emphasises that this does not signify four parts as found in the traditional plan, but a guide to what will be happening in the lesson.

McGill has developed this concept extensively in collaboration with colleagues. It is well worth visiting his website, www.teachertoolkit.me, which includes variations on the 5-minute plan pro forma as well as blogs on how it works. There is also a wealth of other useful teaching and learning ideas.[1]

Using data to inform planning

Another key aspect of planning is the use of data. Although data and its application to teaching sociology successfully will be discussed in the next chapter, it is worth mentioning it here as data is such an important element of life in modern secondary schools and FE colleges. Moreover, as sociology is mostly taught at GCSE and AS/A Level, there is plenty of prior attainment data available to inform your planning. This data is centred on *value-added* measures that compare students' levels of attainment at the end of a given timeframe with their levels of attainment at the start.

Firstly, at GCSE, many schools will be giving students targets based on their FFT estimated grade. As FFT estimations come from prior attainment data at KS3, KS2 and KS1 as well as other factors, they should first and foremost be used in assessing the possible needs of students. Not only is this useful for differentiation, but it can also inform your seating plans and whether to alter the general objectives and outcomes you set. For example, I sometimes place less able students with lower FFT estimated grades with more able students with higher estimates on the proviso that the more able student will be challenged by explaining concepts and theories to the weaker student and that the weaker student may benefit from a peer helping them as opposed to the teacher. Furthermore, depending on the size of your cohorts, your curriculum planner may decide to use the data to set, stream or band students into weaker or more able classes. Although this rarely happens in sociology, as the subject becomes more popular some schools may start separating classes by FFT estimates (in other words, academic ability).

Secondly, at AS/A Level, the vast majority of schools use one of two methods for setting targets via estimated grades. As with FFT at GCSE, the estimated grades will be a tool that you can use to think about when planning seating, setting up group work, differentiating and even setting or streaming at AS/A Level. Two very common methods are the A-level Information System (ALIS) and the A-level Performance System (ALPS); although there are other methods available.

With ALIS, which is an excellent example of the amplification of positivism in educational research (ALIS was developed by the Curriculum, Evaluation and Management (CEM) Centre at Durham University), students are estimated possible grades in each subject based on analysis of their GCSE grades (or other available baseline data). Essentially, the estimation is based on the mathematical probability of students attaining those grades in line with national averages as well as school-type comparisons. In a similar vein to ALIS, ALPS crunches the statistical differences between individuals, subjects and institutions to correlate the probability of students attaining certain grades (for a good discussion on ALIS and ALPS, see Jones, 2008 and Ofsted, 2009a).

As already suggested, you should use the data from ALPS, ALIS or other statistical models used by your school to plan seating, differentiation and identify the strengths of particular cohorts. The last point is important as you may find yourself differentiating for high achievers if the cohort has quite a low profile in terms of overall academic ability or planning differentiation for lower ability students if the cohort has a high academic profile. The pace, quantity of content and depth you cover in lessons should also be partially informed by this data when planning. Moreover, this data should inform the choice of texts you use, textbooks you encourage students to buy and your general choice of resources.

However, be prepared to adapt and change as students progress. I am a firm believer that students can change over time in terms of aptitude (see multiple intelligences in Chapter 4) and that intelligence is not fixed, especially by data. If students seem to suggest the data is limited, do not be afraid to change direction and go with your own data, such as the students grades from assessed work. Data is only a guide and many of my students have far exceeded their estimated grades.

Once you have started schemes of work and the students have started handing in essays and, more usefully, started completing timed assessments, you should also use their current working grades (CWG) to inform planning and change predictions. Although more will be said on this in the next chapter, it is worth considering the above advice on using prior attainment or baseline data, but in line with the changes recorded in your assessment trackers/mark sheets.

Task 9.1 **How reliable is FFT data?**

Interestingly, FFT data is essentially based on quantitative research methods, which would be agreeable to those social scientists that favour positivism over interpretivism. The data is produced from statistical models that input students' prior attainment data, if available, to produce estimated outcomes, or targets, for student attainment. Although FFT have overhauled the way they estimate grades, there used to be 3 main types of statistical models used by schools. These included:

- Type A, which estimated attainment outcomes from students' prior attainment, age and sex only. The estimations were based on an analysis of national averages. Importantly, this model did not take into account other factors, such as a contextual, albeit statistical, analysis of the school and its students.
- Type B, which is similar to type A, but accounted for contextual factors. This was still statistical as the context was limited to coded and quantifiable indicators; this includes FSM entitlement, average prior attainment and the distribution of prior attainment as well as a geo-demographic ranking of postcodes to give an additional, but nonetheless probable, indicator of students' socio-economic background. This allowed schools to compare their students' potential attainment to similar schools and cohorts.
- Type D, which was similar to A and B, but in this model potential attainment/student outcomes were adjusted to be comparable to schools in the top quartile (i.e. at the 25th percentile) nationally; this was deemed as more aspirational than the former two types. Obviously, student targets based on these estimations were higher than the former two.

To understand how valid and reliable these FFT data models were in terms of social science research methods, it is worth discussing this in the context of positivism versus interpretivism debate. For instance, was the statistical contextual analysis as valid as teachers' *Verstehen*, or empathetic understanding, of students' home life and aspirations? Even from a positivistic point of view, perhaps the statistical models ignored the benefits of cultural capital amongst middle class students *vis-à-vis* their actual intelligence and underestimated the intelligence of culturally deprived students.

Discuss with colleagues whether you think these targets are fair and whether they put some students under too much pressure or demotivate them by limiting their aspirations. These are sociological issues that are apparent in our day-to-day practice and many of us use FFT, ALPS and/or ALIS data without really considering the strengths and weaknesses of these approaches to estimating student outcomes. However, it is important to note that these models are no longer used and FFT have formulated new models, which could still be criticised in a similar way. Additionally, it may be best not to rock the boat with your opinions and I would recommend using FFT in planning as the consensus is that it is a sound statistical model.

For a more detailed analysis of the above, see Schagen (2008).

Differentiation

Obviously, as your data and your observations and interactions with students will give you a solid understanding of your students' ability, it is important to build differentiation into your lesson plans. This can be done in a number of ways:

- by setting differentiated objectives and outcomes;
- by resourcing;
- by targeted questions and dialogue;
- by grouping;
- by pace;
- through assessment.

Differentiated objectives and outcomes

Firstly, differentiation can be the result of students working on graded objectives and outcomes. There are two main ways of doing this. One is to explicitly tell them to attempt objectives and complete outcomes in line with their targets. Another is to give them some flexibility to choose which objectives and outcomes they wish to work towards; of course, they must be encouraged to aspire to the higher objectives and steered away from easy options. Graded objectives can simply reflect the depth you expect the students to understand, research or respond to the topic being learnt. As discussed above, they can be focused on GCSE or AS/A Level grades. For example,

- **Objective:** *by the end of the lesson you will have understood what is meant by exogenous and endogenous privatisation in education (grade C3–C1).* **Outcome:** *you will demonstrate this by comparing and contrasting the two terms in writing.*
- **Objective:** *by the end of the lesson you will have understood what is meant by exogenous and endogenous privatisation in education and how this has resulted from the social policies discussed in previous lessons (grade B3–B1).* **Outcome:** *you will demonstrate this by comparing and contrasting the two terms and evaluating the impact of the policies discussed.*
- **Objective:** *by the end of the lesson you will have understood what is meant by exogenous and endogenous privatisation in education, how this has resulted from social policies discussed in previous lessons and how this links to the debate on the marketisation of education (grade A3–A*).* **Outcome:** *you will demonstrate this by comparing and contrasting the two terms and evaluating the impact of the policies discussed in relation to the ideas of Chubb and Moe (1990) that education is best when fully privatised.*

Moreover, the objectives and outcomes can either simply reflect the level to which you expect students to progress despite using the same or similar resources or it can inform how you resource, question, group and assess students (see below).

Resourcing

In order to facilitate the above, it may be wise to give students different resources that are matched to their ability. This goes beyond mere extension activities in that all resources chosen, especially text, need to be carefully considered as to whether the students can comprehend the vocabulary, style and arguments put forward as well as, ironically, considering whether they fully stretch and challenge students. Not only will you need to evaluate this on a class-by-class basis, but you may well select different texts for students to read within the same class. You can either give students texts you think they will comprehend or be challenged by or, more discretely, give them a choice of texts. Additionally, you may have to adapt your own text or PowerPoint slides in a similar vein. The same process can be applied with instructions. Of course, extension tasks are not redundant and you could compile a few of these for quick learners.

Targeted questions and discussion

It is essential that you use language that the students can comprehend and enter a dialogue with. Therefore, it is worth being aware of their ability when you ask them questions and be mindful of how you are discussing concepts and research in class (this is discussed in relation to sociological perspectives in Chapter 3). Do not take for granted that the students have an elaborate vocabulary, let alone an elaborate sociological vocabulary, and do not make assumptions about their knowledge of political and social institutions. You may know what the DWP is and what *elite* means, but your students may not. Moreover, as discussed in Chapter 6, target questions and answers to ability by occasionally using a hands down approach so that you can aim easy and hard questions at certain students and employ the pose, pause, pounce, bounce approached developed by McGill (see Chapter 6). It is worth considering how you will approach questioning and discussion as part of planning, even if this is informal.

Grouping

As discussed above in relation to planning with data, you should plan your seating with ability in mind. Redfern (2015) calls this the 'information rich seating plan' as it will not only use baseline or prior attainment data from FFT, ALPS, ALIS or other models, but should also be informed by changes in the students' CWG and other needs, such as stress levels, throughout the year (p. 37). As mentioned already, you may plan to match low and high achievers together to facilitate peer help or group the students by ability if you think the most able will be hindered by the least able or the least able will feel uncomfortable around those with more ability. Importantly, this may need to be revisited lesson by lesson or even task by task. Often, general discussion is good between students of different abilities, but there may be a greater need to group by ability for research projects and peer assessment as students will need to be on the same wavelength to maximise learning and challenge each other.

Pace

Pace is important and the speed at which you progress is not limited to the students' ability, but also the depth to which you want to explore topic areas. On the one hand, high ability, or most able, students may feel pegged back by the time you spend going over key points for less able students and, on the other hand, less able students may be overwhelmed if you go through key ideas at lightning speed. Reversely, if you go in depth into an abstract topic area as a few of your most able are fascinated, your less able students may be bored senseless. Importantly, you should look at planning differentiated resources if you think pace could be an issue. By and large, all learners appreciate well-paced lessons where students move on once the subject has been understood or thoroughly discussed, but if you do need to linger on an issue, especially difficult conceptual ones, plan various tasks so that learners can move on if they need to or stay on the initial task if struggling (or vice versa if aiming for set objectives and outcomes); this still gives the lesson pace for those that need it.

Assessment

Although Talcott Parsons championed the idea of universalistic standards in education, in that all students sit the same test and can, therefore, be judged against one another, it might be worth considering building up the difficulty of class tests over time and giving less able students more time to get use to the easier types of question; this is in terms of how the questions are phrased as much as length. Moreover, it is essential that you fully comprehend exam structures and how marks are built up through AO1, AO2 and AO3 questions in exams (see Chapter 2). When assessing, it is important to include a variety of questions, especially in end of unit tests, which mirror the actual exams. For instance, if you only use harder evaluative questions in order to bypass the additional marking or simply focus on what is hardest, you may demoralise less able students who pick up marks from lower order questions. Also, it may be worth starting student assessments earlier in the topic with easier questions so that less able students build up confidence before attempting more challenging past papers.

As stated above, all of the above factors will need to be considered and you should make effective use of prior attainment data, CWGs, your interactions and feedback from students when planning for successful differentiation.

Further reading

Bassett, S., Bowler, M. & Newton, A. (2013). Schemes of work, units of work and lesson planning. In Capel, S., Leask, M. & Turner, T., *Learning to teach in the secondary school*. Abingdon: Routledge.

This is a good introduction for new teachers and those re-capping on how best to plan in the short and medium term. It is worth reading if you are mentoring trainees or NQTs as it has plenty of ideas that will be useful in mentor meetings.

Beere, J. (2012). *The perfect Ofsted lesson*. Bancyfelin: Independent Thinking Press.

A compact, but useful book that will help you plan the type of lesson Ofsted inspectors are looking for. The book factors in the key characteristics of an outstanding lesson and gives practical advice on planning, delivering and assessing.

Covington, P. & Piper, V. (2008). *Success in sociology: AS teacher's book for AQA*. Haddenham: Folens.

This guide for teachers is geared towards the AQA syllabus at AS, but the content does mirror other boards. If you are new to sociology, the pre-planned lessons and schemes of work may be useful.

McGill, R. M. (2015). *Teacher toolkit: Helping you survive your first five years*. London: Bloomsbury.

Although the title suggests this is for new teachers, the book does include planning 5-minute lessons as well as the 5-minute marking plan, the 5-minute teach meet plan and the 5-minute interview plan that might arouse the curiosity of experienced teachers.

Redfern, A. (2015). *The essential guide to classroom practice*. Abingdon: Routledge.

Redfern's book, recommended for further reading already, includes a chapter on planning that discusses five-part lesson plans, planning in practice and the use of data in the classroom.

Exam board schemes of work

AQA, OCR and WEJC/Eduqas all offer free schemes of work for the syllabuses they offer at GCSE and/or AS/A Level. These are obviously useful if you are following their specification, but you can also use them to inform your own, more bespoke, schemes of work. They can be found online at:

AQA: www.aqa.org.uk/subjects/sociology
OCR: www.ocr.org.uk/qualifications/by-subject/sociology/
WJEC (Wales): www.wjec.co.uk/qualifications/sociology/index.html
Eduqas: http://eduqas.co.uk/qualifications/sociology/

Note

1   McGill's ideas are expanded upon and developed on his website, see: www.teachertoolkit.me/the-5-minute-lesson-plan/5minplan-series/. In additional, the 5-Minute Lesson Plan is available in digital format from Teacher Toolkit and Angel Solutions, see: www.5minutelessonplan.co.uk/. He has also published a book, which is ideal for trainee teachers, NQTs and teachers generally, which covers the 5-minute plan as well as other quick planning strategies. See, McGill, R. M. (2015), Teacher toolkit: Helping you survive your first five years, London: Bloomsbury. He can also be followed on twitter at @TeacherToolkit.

Bibliography

Atherton, J. S. (2013) *Learning and teaching; Objectives*. Retrieved from www.learningandteaching.info/teaching/objectives.htm

Award Scheme Development and Accreditation Network. (n.d.). The perfect (Ofsted) lesson: Guidance and advice for teachers. Retrieved from www.asset.asdangroup.org.uk/56d57894575fa

Bassett, S., Bowler, M. & Newton, A. (2013). Schemes of work, units of work and lesson planning. In Capel, S., Leask, M. & Turner, T., *Learning to teach in the secondary school* (pp. 99–111). Abingdon: Routledge.

Beere, J. (2012). *The perfect Ofsted lesson*. Bancyfelin: Independent Thinking Press.

Chubb, J. E. & Moe, T. M. (1990). *Politics, markets and America's schools*. Washington, DC: The Brookings Institution.

Covington, P. & Piper, V. (2008). *Success in sociology: AS teacher's book for AQA*. Haddenham: Folens.

Gershon, M. (2014). *Teach now! History: Becoming a great history teacher*. London: Routledge.

Hayward, J. (2002). *WORKMATTERS: A Key Stage Four resource employment strand of citizenship*. London: Institute for Citizenship.

Holt, J. (2015). *Religious education in the secondary school*. London: Routledge.

Jones, S. (2008). Compare, contrast, congratulate. Retrieved from www.tes.com/article.aspx?story code=370525

McGill, R. M. (2012). Outstanding teaching using the new #Ofsted framework. Retrieved from www.teachertoolkit.me/2012/11/17/outstanding-teaching-ofsted-framework/

McGill, R. M. (2015). *Teacher toolkit: Helping you survive your first five years*. London: Bloomsbury.

Ofsted. (2009a). *Inspecting the sixth form: Supplementary guidance*. Manchester: Ofsted.

Ofsted. (2009b). *The learner achievement tracker: A report on the responses to consultation*. Manchester: Ofsted.

Ofsted. (2015a). *School inspection handbook*. Manchester: Ofsted.

Ofsted. (2015b). *School inspections: Myths*. Retrieved from www.gov.uk/government/publications/school-inspection-handbook-from-september-2015/ofsted-inspections-mythbusting

Redfern, A. (2015). *The essential guide to classroom practice*. Abingdon: Routledge.

Schagen, I. (2008). Understanding Fischer Family Trust output. *Practical Research for Education, 40*, 46–51.

10 Assessing sociology

This chapter includes:

- An overview of different ways of assessing, including:
  - Norm referencing;
  - Criterion-referencing;
  - Ipsative assessment.
- A discussion on how GCSE and AS/A Levels are marked and assessed.
- The difference between summative and formative assessments.
- Why it is important to fine grade assessments, especially at AS and A Level.
- The importance of using *assessment for learning* (AfL).
- How to use www, ebi and ntt as a framework for feeding back and getting students to act on their feedback.
- Why it is useful to get students self-assessing their own work and peer-assessing each other's work.
- How checking learning during the lesson can be seen as assessment.
- Why it is essential to properly record and track your assessments using datasheets.
- How to manage your workload in terms of marking assessments.

Assessment is a crucial part of learning. It is also a crucial part of performance management. However, we often get so obsessed and bogged down with ensuring we have completed all our assessments for performance management purposes that we forget just how important assessment is for guiding students through their studies, especially in evaluating their strengths and weaknesses and how to improve.

Ofsted, of course, highlights assessment as a key aspect of teaching and learning. As always, Ofsted makes us worry about ourselves and whether we are fulfilling the criteria needed to be outstanding, but as with lesson planning, their advice is arguably just emphasising the importance of *assessment for learning* as opposed to *assessment for performance management*. For instance:

> Ofsted does not expect to see a particular frequency or quantity of work in pupils' books or folders. Ofsted recognises that the amount of work in books and folders will depend on the

subject being studied and the age and ability of the pupils. Ofsted recognises that marking and feedback to pupils, both written and oral, are important aspects of assessment.

(Ofsted, 2015, p. 10)

To be fair, Ofsted (2015) argue that marking and feedback should be consistent with your school's own assessment policy. This is in recognition that assessment 'may cater for different subjects and different age groups of pupils in different ways, in order to be effective and efficient in promoting learning' (p. 10). However, this is where the focus on performance management comes in as schools often ask teachers to give in books for 'work scrutinies', 'to check the marking policy is being used' and to ensure books are marked within the correct timeframes or 'marking cycles'. Nevertheless, although this can put a lot of stress on teachers and eat into our time away from school, it is absolutely essential that we remain aware that the main reason we are spending so much time on assessment is simply to help our students.

Types of assessment

There are different ways of approaching assessment. For instance, most GCSE and AS/A Level exam bodies use *norm referencing* to actually award grades. However, the actual examiners will be awarding marks based on a *criterion-referenced* mark scheme. Moreover, you will probably be paying more attention to the idea of *assessment for learning* (AfL) in your day-to-day feedback.

Norm referencing

Norm-referenced assessments are setup to compare and rank students in relation to one another. Basically, students are compared to each other so that the top 5%, for example, attain A* grades whereas the bottom 5% attain E grades (see Table 10.1). This can be useful for assessing students of different abilities and for preparing differentiated materials.

   Ideally, these hypothetical grade boundaries will be based on baseline scores from previous cohorts' performances. This inevitably results in the bulk of students attaining B, C or D grades as they normally have the highest frequencies in mixed ability classes. Therefore, this distribution of grades creates a 'bell curve' as the frequency of grades, if plotted on a chart, will create a bell shape (see Figure 10.1). However, although norm referencing is used by exam boards, they are very problematic in the classroom. Firstly, they do not take into account the differing abilities of cohorts as a whole; for example, you may have a very able group one year and a weaker one the year after. Secondly, it suggests that student progress will be uniform and fixed. It does not account for students developing their knowledge and skills at different speeds. And, thirdly, it does

Table 10.1 Possible grade distribution for a norm-referenced assessment

A*	10%
A	15%
B	25%
C	25%
D	15%
E	10%

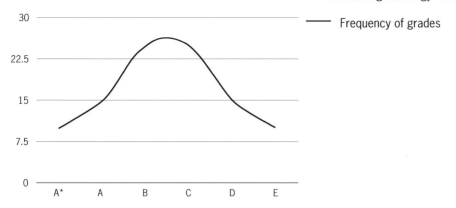

Figure 10.1 An example of a 'bell curve' from a norm-referenced assessment (based on Table 10.1)

not really tell you how students are progressing in terms of knowledge accumulated, just that in that test or exam the student was in the top, middle or bottom distribution of overall grades.

Brown and Fairbrass (2009) highlight the 11+ exam used to determine whether students go to grammar schools or comprehensive schools or, in the past, secondary moderns and technical colleges, as an example of norm referencing (p. 103). Although most local education authorities no longer use the 11+ to decide children's futures and have done away with grammar schools, in the past they would only be able to allocate the grammar school places they had the capacity for. This meant that the top students in a particular year group would be separated from the rest. However, if you had a particularly able year group followed by a lower ability year group the year after, it could well be the case that some able students in the year before would not get into the local grammar schools whereas students weaker than them the year after would. Of course, as a sociology teacher, you may cover the tripartite system and the 1944 Education Act as part of your course. It is also worth noting that some local authorities still have grammar schools.

Criterion-referencing

Criterion-referenced assessments do not take into account the students' position in relation to others. Therefore, it is obviously very different to norm referencing. Instead, the students' attainment or progress is checked against some criteria, which could be a checklist or a mark scheme, and the students are graded or awarded marks in relation to how many parts of the criteria they have fulfilled. For instance, a scout badge in first aid may require the scout to demonstrate knowledge of what to do if someone is not breathing, choking, has been burned or cut amongst other emergencies in order to be awarded the badge. It simply does not matter how many other people pass, fail, score high or low. A pass is a pass.

Although norm referencing is still used in public examinations, it is combined with criteria referencing as examiners use mark schemes. Importantly, as a sociology teacher you should be referencing the exam board mark schemes when marking your students' papers. For example, Figure 10.2 shows a typical GCSE mark scheme from WJEC for a 10-mark question.

When using this, you would quite simply need to cross reference what the student has written with the points made in Figure 10.2. AS/A Level papers have the same type of criteria, only in more

Question 7: Family

(a) Describe ways in which families have changed in recent years. [10]

The mark scheme is awarding marks for knowledge and understanding and the ability to apply this knowledge and understanding within sociological contexts. There should be sociological language applied to specific examples. The focus of the answer should be on description of changes to families.

Look for answers that may offer specific knowledge of the variety of family change. This could include mention of new family forms. To gain marks that are above level 1 and level 2, there should be additional information provided that is not drawn from information given on the paper and possibly rephrased. Answers should be sociological rather than personal in time.

Credit

- Accurate use of sociological language, concepts and theory, if relevant.
- Reference to clear understanding of differences in family structure and/or roles.
- Reference to changes in families drawn from British culture, but focussed on the terms of the question.
- Evidence of examples drawn from different cultures.

7	**Level 1 Limited (0–2 marks)**	5	AO 1
		5	AO 2
	Limited answers will offer responses that display little evidence of knowledge or understanding of traditional nuclear family. If some relevant factual material is used then up to 2 marks are available. The quality of written communication will be basic.		
	Level 2 Basic (3–5 marks)		
	Three marks are available for basic answers that may address the question but may be underdeveloped and vague. The information offered		

will be basic and sociological language will not be used accurately.

At the upper end of this mark band, there may be specific mention of roles and functions of family members. The quality of written communication will be acceptable, although there may be errors of spelling and punctuation.

Level 3 Breadth or Depth (6–8 marks)

Six marks are available for answers that offer a clear reference to the terms of the question, though description may be underdeveloped. There will be evidence of breadth or depth of knowledge and understanding.

The information offered will display accuracy and sociological language will be used. At the upper end of this mark band, there may be specific mention of family change and changes in the role and behaviour of children. The quality of written communication will be clear, with few errors of spelling, grammar and punctuation.

Level 4 Breadth and Depth (9–10 marks)

Nine marks are available for detailed answers that offer a specific and accurate knowledge and understanding of childhood and perhaps offer understanding that childhood is undergoing change or is perceived as threatened. The information offered will display accuracy and sociological language will be used.

At the upper end of this mark band, understanding may be displayed through contrasting and comparative descriptions of changes in childhood or reference to examples although this is not specified in the question and should not be used as a differentiator. At this level, there will be a balanced response, perhaps with reference to theory or research. Answers will demonstrate a good application of knowledge. The quality of written communication will be good, with few errors of spelling, grammar and punctuation.

Figure 10.2 A WJEC GCSE mark scheme
Source: Reproduced by permission of WJEC.

depth. Mark schemes for longer questions will include level descriptors based on AO1, AO2 and AO3 skills (see Chapter 2 if in need of a recap on what these assessment objectives are).

It is important to familiarise yourself with the mark schemes provided for past papers when you assess students' work as it is one way you can effectively measure, or check, how much knowledge they have and whether they are developing the required skills. Also, by regularly referring to the mark scheme, you will have the opportunity to see whether the students have improved and, therefore, progressed according to the criteria set out in the mark scheme. It is clear, then, that this sort of assessment is better than norm referencing when assessing students work as part of your day-to-day practice.

You can find the main exam boards' past-papers and mark schemes via these websites:

- AQA: www.aqa.org.uk/subjects/sociology
- OCR: www.ocr.org.uk/qualifications/by-subject/sociology
- WJEC (Wales): www.wjec.co.uk/qualifications/sociology/index.html
- Eduqas: http://eduqas.co.uk/qualifications/sociology

Ipsative assessment

Ipsative assessment compares the learner's current attainment or performance with their previous attainment or performance. This form of assessment literally seeks to see how the student has progressed regardless of anyone else's progress. In some ways it is similar to the concept of a *personal best* score in sports or games in that someone may have achieved their best ever score or result despite always winning, never winning or even playing alone. In education, it acknowledges that students' progress is an intrinsic measure of their own ability and learning. Here, ipsative assessment fits in very well with the idea of personalised learning as we should be interested in how an individual student has progressed from whatever starting point they had. For instance, it is all very well having a top set in a grammar school attaining 100% A*–A, but they may not have progressed as much as a less able student who left primary school with very low prior attainment, gained low levels at key stage 3 and started their GCSE course attaining G and F grades before eventually attaining an E or D grade in Year 11. Arguably, that student may have made more progress than the academic elite described above; perhaps their teacher was outstanding as opposed to lucky.

Interestingly, the government has acknowledged this with the creation of the *progress 8* measure at key stage 4; this seeks to compare a student's attainment at the end of key stage 4 with the students' prior attainment data from the end of key stage 2. The 8 comes from comparing the students' attainment in 8 of the various GCSE subjects recognised by the Department for Education (DfE); at the time of writing, this could include GCSE sociology in their 'open section' (DfE, 2014). However, it is not purely an ipsative assessment as the score will be calculated for individual students by comparing their attainment in the 8 recognised subjects with the average score of all students nationally who had a similar starting point in terms of prior attainment data (DfE, 2016). In this sense, you could call the assessment a hybrid of ipsative and norm referencing.

Summative and formative assessment

In your everyday practice, you are far more likely to refer to *summative* or *formative* assessment than norm-referencing, criterion-referencing or ipsative assessment. These two are often pitted against each other in books on teaching and learning and websites dealing with assessment, but they should really be used in conjunction in order to give your students as much information on their attainment and progress as possible.

Summative assessment simply measures the level of attainment that has been achieved in an end of unit test or exam. This would include a standard end of unit test, mock exam or even GCSE or AS/A Level exam. Of course, the test or exam may be norm-referenced, criterion-referenced or both.

Formative assessment, on the other hand, places greater emphasis on feedback that can be applied by the student to improve their learning (not simply their grade). For example, it could include the marker identifying the positives and negatives of the students' attitude to learning, effort and study skills in addition to what they did well and did badly. A key feature of formative assessment is its continuous use throughout a course or scheme of work so that the student has constant guidance on how to improve. It is worth stating, however, that both summative and formative assessment will be used together by outstanding practitioners. They are not really inseparable in academic subjects like sociology where regular testing is important preparation for exams (see assessment for learning below).

GCSE

Although you and your colleagues will obviously know what GCSEs are, it is worth briefly considering how they are assessed. Firstly, there are no exam boards offering coursework as part of the overall assessment anymore, which means that all GCSE assessments will be exam based. Secondly, these GCSEs will be a mix of norm referencing and criterion referencing as examiners will use mark schemes to give marks or levels before the exam boards adjust the scores through a somewhat complicated and convoluted norm-referencing process. Although the exam boards may approach this process in slightly different ways, senior examiners review the marked exams from the current year in comparison to the previous year and decide on the overall grade boundaries. The current year's marks will be compared, or rather norm-referenced, with the previous year in order to maintain a similar or equivalent standard on how grades are distributed. Moreover, these grade boundaries are then set against a uniform mark scale, or UMS, which standardise the grade boundaries so that comparisons can be made between years as well as students sitting in different exams with different boards. It is the mapping against UMS that secures the norm-referenced grades as they will have to fit into a patterned distribution. This process is, of course, all regulated as exam boards may use a different amount of unified marks on their particular scale (see, for more information, AQA 2015).

To ensure students following different GCSE sociology syllabuses study the same topic areas, the DfE (2016) sets out the content that will be assessed by the exam boards. It is also important to note that from 2017 the sociology GCSE will be assessed on a scale of 9–1 as opposed A*–G. This means students attaining top grades will receive a grade 9 and the lowest a grade 1. Furthermore, this is still norm-referenced, in that attaining a grade 4 or above will roughly be the same percentage that currently gain a grade C or above, the same applies to grade 7 or above in relation to the proportion of current students gaining grade A or above.

A Level

The sociology A Level, or rather General Certificate in Education (GCE) Advanced Level, generally requires students to study over a two-year period. Currently, the AS and A2 exams are being phased out and replaced by a stand-alone AS award and a separate award for the A Level. The former comprises roughly one year of full-time study and is often assessed with two 90-minute exams whereas the latter is studied over two years full-time and is normally assessed by three 90-minute exams (although exam boards do differ).

The grades for both AS and A Level range from A* to E, but do not run to F or G (or 2 and 1) as in the GCSE. As with the GCSE courses, there is no assessed coursework, although there has been in the past, and the process to award grades comprises both criterion-referencing from an examiner using a mark scheme as well as norm referencing when the marks are standardised against UMS. At AS, most exam boards include a two-module course that has a maximum of 200 UMS marks whereas the full A Level includes four modules and, by and large, a maximum UMS mark of 400. At the time of writing the typical UMS grade distribution at A Level for a course with a 400 UMS maximum was:

- 360 UMS for an A*, but this may require a higher percentage being attained on the A2 modules;
- 320 UMS for an A;
- 280 UMS for a B;
- 240 UMS for a C;
- 200 UMS for a D;
- 160 UMS for an E;
- Less than 160 UMS results in a U grade (see, for example, AQA, 2015 and OCR, 2015).

Please note that these are occasionally subject to change. You should check for changes to UMS by visiting the exam boards' websites. Please see the further reading section for links to these. You can also find information on the raw mark grade boundaries on these websites. The raw mark boundaries will tell you how much a particular mark on an actual paper is worth. For example, if the paper is out of 60 and a student gained 47, it will tell you what grade 47 marks is worth. Of course, these boundaries fluctuate year by year and are only published around the time of the results once they have been mapped against the UMS boundaries.

Fine grading

It is worth thinking about how you grade students, especially at AS/A Level since the GCSE exams will now start to be graded from 1 to 9. One of the problems with the current A*–E grades at AS/A Level is that a high B and a low B, for example, can be very different in terms of actual marks awarded. In fact, the banding of A*–E can often seem quite arbitrary, particularly if a student on 280 UMS at A Level gets a B and a student on 179 gets a C. It is imperative, then, that you give your students an indication of how strong or weak their grade is. One option is to abandon A*–E altogether and just use raw marks or the levels, or 'bands', used by some exam boards. Additionally, you could *fine grade* each grade into 3 parts; for example instead of A*–E, you have A*1–E3. In a timed assessment based on a question worth 33 marks, the grading could work as follows:

A*1 = 33 marks
A*2 = 32 marks
A*3 = 30 marks
A1 = 29 marks
A2 = 28 marks
A3 = 27 marks
B1 = 26 marks
B2 = 25 marks
B3 = 24 marks
C1 = 23 marks
C2 = 22 marks
C3 = 21 marks
D1 = 20 marks
D2 = 19 marks
D3 = 18 marks
E1 = 17 marks
E2 = 16 marks
E3 = 15 marks

The mark scheme here is not based on any exam marking criteria and accounts for the fact that the students have answered a stand-alone question as opposed to a whole paper, but a student on a C1, for instance, would know that they are close to that B they are working towards whereas a student on a C3 would understand that they need to get revising and working harder if they do not want to slip down to a D1 or below.

Assessment for learning

As both GCSE and AS/A Level courses are at least two years in duration, it is important to use both summative and formative assessment (as discussed earlier). Here, it is good to apply the ideas behind *assessment for learning* throughout the courses. The phrase assessment for learning (AfL) is one of the most used and emphasised in education today. It is primarily a form of formative assessment that advances students understanding of the subject taught by giving regular feedback that informs them on how to improve as much as their current attainment or levels. The current popularity of the phrase can be traced back to a paper by Black and Wiliam (2001, p. 2), who define assessment as:

> all those activities undertaken by teachers, and by their students in assessing themselves, which provide information to be used as feedback to modify the teaching and learning activities in which they are engaged. Such assessment becomes 'formative assessment' when the evidence is actually used to adapt the teaching work to meet the needs.

The key to understanding AfL is to see assessment as a tool for informing both the teacher and student. Here, the teacher will gain knowledge of the students' progress, their academic strengths and weaknesses and the enthusiasm or apathy they have for the subject. By the same measure, the teacher will also be able to gauge some measure of their own success in assisting the students in their learning. Their observations of the students' academic performance should include some reflection on how they delivered the particular part of the syllabus assessed; what teaching methods were used; and whether the planning involved proper consultation of the students preferred learning styles and needs etc. Moreover, the feedback given to the student must be useful; they must be able to comprehend any criticism given and understand how to improve. For example, Haydon (2013) suggests that AfL must incorporate these general principles:

- providing helpful and constructive feedback to students;
- an inclusion of self and/or peer-assessment at some stage in order to actively involve students in their learning;
- a willingness to adjust your teaching through reflection on the outcomes of the assessments;
- an awareness of student motivation and self-esteem in relation to assessment;
- and, lastly, sharing the success criteria with students (p. 418).

I have heard the word 'dialogue' used to describe the feedback that should be taking place between the teachers and students. This is apt as students need to have an ongoing conversation in terms of acting on comments made by teachers. In many schools, AfL is subsequently being codified in marking policies, including the idea of www, ebi and ntt (see below). This type of dialogue is essential for sociology students.

What went well (www), even better if (ebi) and now try this (ntt)

The idea behind *what went well* (www), *even better if* (ebi) and *now try this* (ntt) is straightforward and works well with the general principles of AfL. The www is basically praise; identify something the student did well and highlight this as a positive to move forward with. As referenced above, Haydon draws attention to students' self-esteem in relation to AfL and it is important to build up students' confidence and motivate them to not only improve, but carry on working hard. By identifying positives, even if their assessed work has major weaknesses, the student will be able to accept and arguably deal with the criticism much better as they will not be resigned to the idea of failure. The ebi, on the other hand, will deliver the areas identified for improvement. Here, it is important to actually think about the individual student rather than just giving a generic point; too many teachers use comment banks of prewritten criticisms that are either cut and pasted or highlighted on feedback sheets. The ebi should also be realistic and pick up on something that the student can literally avoid or add in their next assessment in order to improve their grade. Lastly, it is a nice idea to include an ntt, which requires the student then and there to act upon their feedback. The ntt can range from correcting spelling and grammar mistakes to adding sociologists' names. It could also ask the students to re-draft paragraphs to make more coherent sense or to be more evaluative etc. In my own practice, I get students to do this in green pen so that I, they and anyone else for that matter, can see their improvements over time. For example, in response to an AS Level answer to a question asking students to assess the changes in the status of children over the last 200 years, I have given this feedback.

WWW: *excellent use of abstract concepts, such as 'child-centred society' and the 'cult of childhood'. You also included the two competing theories of the 'march of progress' and 'conflict theory' very well. This made for a very good evaluation overall.*

EBI: *you added more empirical evidence or sociological studies to back up the competing perspectives. For example, although you discussed improvements in IMR etc., you could have mentioned changes in the law to protect children as well as greater awareness of child protection in order to support the 'march of progress' argument. Alternatively, you could have included the study of Bolivian childhood by Samantha Punch to suggest that the march of progress is not fixed across all cultures.*

NTT: *go through your essay with a green pen and annotate the text with facts and studies you could add. You'll find these facts and studies in your notes and the textbooks in class. As part of your revision, re-write this essay after looking at your annotations.*

Self and peer-assessment

It is a good idea to get students marking both their own work and their peers. Throughout this book there has been an emphasis on active learning and this also applies to assessment. If we are to involve students in their learning, then they need to go through the processes of marking to get a better understanding of what examiners are looking for in terms of AO1, AO2 and AO3 skills and how examiners award marks by using criterion-referencing centred on mark schemes. Of course, you are not going to explain criterion-referencing to your students, but you can get them going by adapting mark schemes into student friendly versions (and later on get them using actual mark schemes). Doing this regularly will turn the students' perceptions of mark schemes from abstract and quite alien guidelines into a way of thinking about planning and structuring certain questions. For example, during lessons I often use 4 or 6 mark questions as mini-plenaries. Here, the students will be given green pens and a simplified mark scheme; either handed out or put on a PowerPoint. This activity is useful as students often write too much in these types of questions, but by giving them time limits to answer the question and then getting them to assess that work, you can really iron out the temptation to write too much, too little or their assumption that they do not know what to do. I have included an adapted mark scheme for a made up 4-mark question below. Part of this exercise is to get the students to understand that examiners are looking for quite simple *developments* or *brief explanations* to the identified problems as opposed to detailed explanations that are redundant after the first 4 or 6 ticks. The mark scheme is not exhaustive, but is designed to give the students ideas about what could be marked positively.

Self and peer-assessment is also good AfL as it can develop into small activities where students discuss their work and identify the positives and negatives in pairs or groups after the initial marking to get a sense of common pitfalls. It may be worthwhile getting the students to use the www, ebi and ntt feedback criteria demonstrated earlier so that they become familiar with that criteria whilst actively thinking about what their peers are doing well, could improve and should do next. Hopefully, this will stick in their own minds so that they do not make the same mistakes.

Table 10.2 A mark scheme written for students

Identify and explain two problems with unstructured interviews [4 marks].

Potential problems	Possible developments
They are not practical...	... as they take too long. ... as interviewees may be put off by the idea of a long interview and refuse to be interviewed. ... as you may not be given permission if the interviewees are vulnerable or young.
They are not representative...	... due to limited time. Researchers cannot interview many people. ... due to limited time. Researchers may focus on a particular group that have similar views, which are different to the rest of society's. ... not many people will want to be interviewed if it is too long, so the research will be limited to interested people.
They are not reliable...	... as they are hard to reproduce due to time constraints. ... as you need structured questions to get relevant answers. ... as it is hard to repeat the interviews with different groups due to limited time.
They are not positivistic...	.... as you cannot quantify, compare and contrast data from them. .... as you cannot easily codify the answers in order to compare, contrast or correlate the causes and effects of social actions. ... as it is hard to find causes and effects as well as patterns in the data, which can then be seen as 'social facts'.
They are not objective...	... as the interview can be affected by interviewer bias. ... as the interviewer's body language or reactions may affect the interview. ... as the interviewer can interpret the answers subjectively.
They raise ethical issues...	... as the interviewee may disclose that they are harming others or themselves. ... as the interviewee may admit to committing crimes. ... as, if the interviewee is young, they may raise child protection issues.

Checking learning

Too many teachers assume that assessment only applies to substantial written work, such as exam answers or essays. Nevertheless, we should really be assessing the students all of the time. Here, it may be easier to refer to *checking learning*, which suggests we should be checking that students have understood what has been taught as much as possible – albeit through small activities, tasks or mini-plenaries. There are a number of ways of doing this in the lesson without rushing around marking all of the students' work. Below are some suggestions:

- **Circulation:** quite simply, you should get out of the chair and walk around the room talking to students about their learning and what they are doing. Granted, this will not involve all students if the class is large, but you can target who you talk to and which students you think you need to check up on.
- **Targeted Q&A:** this has been mentioned so much in this book, but by targeting questions, especially via PPPB (see Chapter 6), you can target a selection of students of differing abilities to quickly assess if they have understood the basics of what you have been teaching.

- **Mini-whiteboards:** you get students to respond to simple questions in short paragraphs or sentences. After responses have been written, you can ask for the boards to be held up so that you can read or get a sense of what the students have written; you do not need to check them all, but you can target which students you want to focus on. You can also get students to write their grades or levels to any self or peer-assessed work and get a quick measure of their basic attainment.
- **RAG cards:** many students, especially at key stage 4, have RAG cards in their planners. These are simple red, amber and green cards that students can hold up or leave on the table to indicate whether they are understanding the work. Here, green is 'understood' and red indicates they are struggling. I often use them to get a sense of whether the students comprehend the work set. Alternatively, you can use RAG cards or mini-whiteboards to get students' opinions or views in debates or on controversial issues. For example, green would be strongly agree, amber would be not sure and red would be strongly disagree. If the students do not have RAG cards in their planners, you can easily make them and fix them together with treasury tags.
- **Self or peer-assessment:** as discussed already, get the students to self- or peer-assess homework essays before they hand them in or assess smaller questions and answers as mini-plenaries or plenaries. Once these are assessed, marks can be written down on mini-whiteboards and held up, giving you a measure of how well the students did overall.
- **Games:** games can be a good way of checking the learning of key words or even concepts. Quite a few of the games suggested in Chapter 6 can be used as mini-plenaries that check students' learning throughout and at the end of lessons.

Recording and tracking assessments

In the previous chapter, a lot was said about using prior attainment data in your planning and how the students' current working grades (CWG) should inform how you use or adapt that data. Therefore, it is absolutely essential that you set up a sound system for recording students' attainment and tracking their progress. Not only should you record as much data as possible (despite being aware of how to manage your marking workload, see below), but this data should be used to compare and contrast scores in different units as well as work out average grades and predictions. If you can, or if you can find someone with excellent data management/spreadsheet skills, it is also worth using spreadsheets to calculate the students' current UMS and how many more UMS marks they need to gain certain grades etc. Figure 10.2 shows a spreadsheet, with made up names, used for an A Level class. The first columns give an overview of students' targets, CWGs and predictions before going through the *attained* grades unit by unit and finishing with the UMS scores *needed to attain* certain grades. This will help you advise the students on their areas of weakness when it comes to planning revision.

Managing marking

Marking work is, by and large, seen as a chore by most teachers. Despite the importance of assessing students' work, marking it often takes place after school or, especially if you have revision sessions after school or extracurricular activities, in your own time in the evenings and at the weekend. Although I generally take a positive approach to marking, literally looking forward to

Table 10.3 An A Level mark sheet used to track progress and attainment

Name	Target	Min Standard	SUMMARY CWG UMS	CWG Grade	CWG VA	Prediction UMS	Pred Grade	Pred VA	CWG Unit 1 UMS	U1 Grade	U1 VA	CWG Unit 2 UMS	U2 Grade	U2 VA	CWG Unit 3 UMS	U3 Grade	U3 VA	CWG Unit 4 UMS	U4 Grade	U4 VA	PRED Unit 1 UMS	U1 Grade	U1 VA	PRED Unit 2 UMS	U2 Grade	U2 VA	PRED Unit 3 UMS	U3 Grade	U3 VA	PRED Unit 4 UMS	U4 Grade	U4 VA	Add D (200)	Add C (240)	Add B (280)	Add A (320)	Add S (360)
STUDENT 1	B	C	247.8	C3	0	276	C1	0	52	C2	0	43	U1	-6	69	A2	+2	84	B3	0	52	C2	0	84	B3	+1	56	B3	+1	84	B3	+1		0	32	72	112
STUDENT 2	B	C	240	C3	0	259	C2	0	54	C1	0	62	D3	-1	44	D2	-1	80	C1	0	54	C1	0	79	C2	0	46	D1	-1	80	C1	0		0	40	80	120
STUDENT 3	A	B	325.3	A3	+1	306	B2	0	56	B3	0	90	B2	0	75	S2	+2	104	A1	+1	56	B3	0	90	B2	0	62	B1	0	98	A3	+1					35
STUDENT 4	A	B	281	B3	0	293	B2	0	50	C3	-1	79	C2	-1	72	S3	+2	80	C1	-1	59	B2	0	88	B2	0	62	B1	0	84	B3	0				39	79
STUDENT 5	A	B	303.2	B2	0	320	A3	+1	80	S1	+2	74	C3	0	59	B2	0	90	B2	0	80	S1	+2	88	B2	0	62	B1	0	90	B2	0				17	57
STUDENT 6	B	B	244	C3	0	255	C2	0	40	D3	-1	84	B3	+1	46	D1	-1	74	C3	0	49	C3	0	84	B3	0	48	C3	0	74	C3	0			36	76	116
STUDENT 7	A	B	318	B1	0	322	A3	+1	54	C1	-1	88	B2	0	76	S2	+2	100	A2	+1	68	A2	+1	88	B2	0	66	A3	+1	100	A2	+1				2	42
STUDENT 8	B	C	162	E3	-2	128	U1	-5	35	E2	-2	79	C2	0	48	C3	0	0	U3	-5	49	C3	0	79	C2	0	0	U3	-5	0	U3	-5	38	78	118	158	198
STUDENT 9	B	C	216.6	C3	-1	245	C3	0	52	C2	0	55	E2	-2	40	D3	-1	70	D1	+1	52	C2	0	77	C2	-1	46	D1	-1	70	D1	+1		23	63	103	143
STUDENT 10	A	B	186.7	E2	-3	234	D1	-2	48	C3	-1	53	E2	-3	44	D2	-2	42	U1	+8	48	C3	-1	77	C2	-1	42	D3	-2	67	D2	-2	13	53	93	133	173
STUDENT 11	A	B	263.6	C2	-1	286	B3	0	44	D2	+1	70	D1	-2	66	A3	+1	84	B3	0	44	D2	0	88	B2	0	62	B1	0	92	B1	0			16	56	96
STUDENT 12	A	B	238	D1	0	242	C3	-1	48	C3	-1	60	D3	-3	52	C2	-1	78	C2	-1	48	C3	-1	72	C3	-1	44	D2	-2	78	C2	-1		2	42	82	122
STUDENT 13	A	B	239.6	D1	0	283	B3	0	48	C3	-1	50	E2	-3	58	B3	0	84	B3	0	58	B3	0	85	B3	0	58	B3	0	82	C1	-1		0	40	80	120
STUDENT 14	A	B	304	B2	0	301	B2	0	62	B1	0	88	B2	0	64	A3	-1	90	B2	0	62	B1	0	88	B2	0	61	B2	0	90	B2	0				16	56
STUDENT 15	A	B	234	D1	-1	287	B3	0	44	D2	-2	58	E1	-1	54	C1	-1	78	C2	-1	58	B3	0	87	B3	0	58	B3	0	84	B3	0		6	46	86	126
STUDENT 16	A	B	203	D3	-1	253	C2	0	56	B3	+1	38	U1	-6	31	F2	-3	78	C2	0	56	B3	+1	77	C2	0	46	D1	-1	74	C3	0		37	77	117	157
STUDENT 17	A	B	316.8	B1	-1	295	B2	0	62	B1	0	82	C1	-1	69	A2	-1	78	C2	-1	62	B1	0	88	B2	0	64	A3	+1	90	B2	0				3	43
STUDENT 18	A	B	276.4	C1	-1	284	B3	0	54	C1	-1	82	C1	0	62	B1	0	98	A3	-1	54	C1	0	88	B2	0	64	A3	+1	78	C2	-1			4	44	84
STUDENT 19	A	B	282	B3	0	294	B3	0	54	C1	-1	82	C1	-1	54	C1	-1	92	B1	0	59	B2	0	82	C1	-1	61	B2	0	92	B1	0				38	78
STUDENT 20	A	B	353.8	A1	+1	347	A1	+1	68	A2	+1	102	A2	-1	75	S2	-1	108	S3	+2	68	A2	+1	102	A2	+1	69	A2	+1	108	S3	+2					6

	CWG	Prediction		
A*	0	0		
A	2	3		
B	6	9		
C	5	6		
D	5	1		
E	2	0		
F	0	0		
G	0	0		
U	0	1		
A*-C	65%	90%		
A*-A	10%	15%		

100%	0	
0%	14	
	6	
	0	
	0	
	0	
	0	

Average VA: -0.7   ###

what my students have produced, I would be lying if I did not admit to being a little annoyed at spending the whole of Sunday afternoon marking students work when I feel I should be spending time with my own family. It is important, therefore, that you plan your assessments in order to manage your marking workload. You can do this by setting work for different year groups on different weeks or ensuring that every other assessed piece of work is self or peer-assessed. For instance, if your school has a three-week marking cycle, perhaps set work on the first week that will be fully marked by you at GCSE level, self-assessed at AS Level and peer-assessed at A Level. On the second week you can change this to peer-assessed at GCSE, fully marked by you at AS and self-assessed at A Level. Then, inevitably, on third week you finally get the GCSE students to self-assess their work, get the AS students to peer-assess and fully mark the A Level assessments yourself. Another way to manage marking is to generally set smaller pieces or work throughout a unit and, if you forgive me for using this expression, binge on marking full assessments at the end of each unit. Of course, all this should be based on what works best for you and what suits your lifestyle.

Further reading

Black, P. & Wiliam, D. (2001). *Inside the black box: Raising standards through classroom assessment.* **London: BERA. Retrieved from https://weaeducation.typepad.co.uk/files/blackbox-1.pdf**

A concise introduction to assessment for learning and why it is important, works and can benefit teaching and learning. Although this is an academic paper, it is accessible for everyday practitioners and is essential reading for all teachers at every stage of their profession.

Capel, S., Leask, M. & Turner, T. (2013), *Learning to teach in the secondary school.* **London: Routledge.**

There is a whole section on assessment in this book that is ideal for both beginning teachers and those recapping on best practice. The chapters by Terry Hayden and Bernadette Youens cover the different types of assessment, GCSEs, A Levels, the vocabulary of assessment and external assessments.

Kyriacou, C. (2014). *Essential teaching skills.* **Oxford: Oxford University Press.**

Kyriacou has a detailed chapter on assessment that includes the purpose of assessment, types of assessment and assessment activities as well as recording and reporting on progress.

Exam board assessment materials

AQA, OCR and WEJC/Eduqas all offer downloadable assessment materials, such as past-papers, mark schemes, examiners' reports and occasionally examples of students' responses to exam questions. Moreover, you can also find information on grade boundaries and UMS on their websites. All this information is available online at:

AQA: www.aqa.org.uk/subjects/sociology
OCR: www.ocr.org.uk/qualifications/by-subject/sociology/
WJEC (Wales): www.wjec.co.uk/qualifications/sociology/index.html
Eduqas: http://eduqas.co.uk/qualifications/sociology/

Bibliography

Assessment and Qualifications Alliance. (2014). *AQA sociology mark scheme unit.* Manchester: Assessment and Qualifications Alliance.

Assessment and Qualifications Alliance. (2015). *Guide to the uniform mark scale (UMS): Uniform marks in A-level and GCSE exams.* Manchester: Assessment and Qualifications Alliance.

Black, P. & Wiliam, D. (2001). *Inside the black box: Raising standards through classroom assessment.* London: BERA. Retrieved from https://weaeducation.typepad.co.uk/files/blackbox-1.pdf

Brown, K. & Fairbrass, S. (2009). *The citizenship teacher's handbook.* London: Continuum.

Capel, S., Leask, M. & Turner, T. (2013). *Learning to teach in the secondary school.* London: Routledge.

Department for Education. (2014). *Factsheet: Progress 8 measure.* London: Department for Education.

Department for Education. (2016). *Progress 8 measure in 2016, 2017, and 2018: Guide for maintained secondary schools, academies and free schools.* London: Department for Education.

Haydon, T. (2013). First do no harm: Assessment, pupil motivation and learning. In Capel, S., Leask, M. & Turner, T., *Learning to teach in the secondary school* (pp. 417–438). London: Routledge.

Kyriacou, C. (2014). *Essential teaching skills.* Oxford: Oxford University Press.

Oxford Cambridge RSA. (2015). *Specification level UMS grade boundaries.* Retrieved from www.ocr.org.uk/Images/267743-specification-level-ums-grade-boundaries-november-2015-january-2016-and-june-2016.pdf

Ofsted. (2015). *School inspection handbook.* Manchester: Ofsted.

Welsh Joint Education Committee. (2015). *Sociology mark scheme.* Cardiff: Welsh Joint Education Committee. Retrieved from http://pastpapers.download.wjec.co.uk/s15-sociology-ms.pdf

11 Independent learning and revision

This chapter includes:

- An explanation of why independent learning is so important and how it aids revision.
- Using directed tasks to create independent learning and make independent learning a habit.
- How to flag up independent learning skills whilst teaching in the classroom.
- How to get students planning their independent study and revision.
- A defence of getting students to plan revision with revision timetables.
- Encouraging study groups and study buddies.
- And, lastly, using ICT and social networking for revision.

Teaching and learning in the classroom is just the tip of the iceberg when it comes to getting students through their GCSEs and A Levels. Most of the students' learning should really take place away from the classroom and away from their teachers. Whether in the school library, a quiet study area or at home, students will need to read up on an awful lot of sociological theories and studies if they want high grades and this will mean encouraging them to learn independently. Therefore, it is incumbent upon you, their teacher, to help nurture their independent learning skills and get them organised for revision. Although it might seem like an oxymoron to say we need to nurture and prepare these skills if they are supposedly independent, the reality is that many students have never had to take responsibility for their own learning; let alone make informed choices about what to study away from class. Moreover, this is even more apparent at AS/A Level as many teachers now feel schools 'spoon feed' students at GCSE level through intervention, after school revision sessions and even weekend and holiday revision sessions; this makes it harder for them to adapt to AS/A Level where there is less support. Subsequently, we have to find a middle way between helping them take responsibility for their own learning whilst ensuring they are not too dependent on us to do that.

What do we mean by independent learning and revision?

Put simply, independent learning is when an individual student has the ability and motivation to think about what they need to study away from the classroom and then put those thoughts into action.

They can do this by selecting and using the correct resources as well as using learning activities that improves their subject knowledge and skills without the help of the teacher. Researchers have found that independent learning benefits students in a number of ways. For example, Meyer, Haywood, Sachdev and Faraday (2008) pinpoint six key benefits in their literature review of research into independent learning (p. 1–2). The benefits for students include:

- improved overall academic performance;
- increased motivation and confidence;
- greater student awareness of their limitations and whether they can manage them;
- enabling teachers to provide differentiated tasks for students, especially as these can be completed over longer timeframes than lessons;
- and giving students a sense of social inclusion by countering a sense of alienation.

Thinking about the above, it would be an understatement to say that sound independent learning skills are transferable to revision, but I am going to make that point anyway. Basically, if you want your students to revise effectively, you must help them master the skills of autonomous study prior to the revision period in the run up to exams. Revision is literally going over everything the students have studied throughout their course of study, so it is self-evident that if your students can organise themselves and get studying without the help of a teacher, this process will be much easier and simpler for them; this is essential as you cannot possibly revise everything with your students, they will have to do most of it alone.

Task 11.1 How did you revise and learn independently?

As discussed before in this book, we have all been students and have a wealth of experience that we should not be afraid to explore, particularly as it may benefit our students.

Therefore, sit down with colleagues and reflect on how you studied independently for your GCSEs, A Levels and degrees. What methods and strategies worked for you? Did your teachers do anything that really helped? You may remember some useful ideas by discussing your own experiences.

Creating independent learners through scaffolding directed tasks

One of the easiest ways to get students to work away from class is simply to set plenty of homework. Students should be given directed tasks at least once a week in order to make homework a habit. By directing what they should do you are initially scaffolding their learning at home or elsewhere by setting specific readings, written requirements and timings. It is worth checking your school's policies here to defend the amount of work you set. Most schools specify at least three hours per subject per week. Furthermore, if you set reading or information finding tasks, be sure to factor in a piece of evidence so that the students can demonstrate they have done the work. For example, this can be annotating text, completing tables of information or writing up particular definitions from searching the internet. You should also sanction students for not doing this: detentions at GCSE level and requests to 'come back after school to complete work' at AS/A Level. This may not sound particularly independent, but you can always make clear that the work you set can be repeated by the students for any section of the syllabus regardless of whether you have set it or not.

Teach independent study skills

Although many schools try to teach study skills through form time and off-timetable days at KS4 and often through additional study lessons at KS5, you can still take time to teach independent study skills in class. However, you need not eat into valuable sociological teaching time as each time you get students to mind map, read, annotate and answer past exam questions, you can highlight how these can be used in independently. Moreover, you can suggest that pair and group work can easily be done away from class without the intervention of a teacher.

Another way to help students understand how to study independently is to identify different learning styles in class and suggest students use these at home if they feel they suit them best. Furthermore, many websites and self-help books on independent study argue that students must be 'motivated' to study, so they will need to find ways of studying that are conducive to their preferred learning styles. This can be done by varying your activities, as discussed in Chapters 6, 7 and 8, but also by pointing out what these activities are called and emphasising how students can use and adapt them at home. Another repeated word on the websites and in self-help books is 'resilience', which is discussed in relation to BLP in Chapter 4. Again, by varying activities and helping students find ways to learn that they feel are useful, you will indirectly give them the study skills to tackle difficult subjects in different ways; this also helps foster the social inclusion and counter the alienation highlighted by Meyer et al. (2008). For example, students can try reading texts, annotating texts, drawing spider-diagrams, making lists and debating sociological theories with friends in order to find a way of learning that genuinely helps them feel at ease with the sociological content in the syllabus.

Planning for independent study and revision

To help students plan their independent study or revision, use unit booklets with recommended reading lists and audit tools for analysing students' strengths and weaknesses. Chapter 9 had an example of a student-centred plan for a scheme of work on the *mass media*, which was part of a booklet with additional information, including the Tables 11.1, 11.2 and 11.3. These tables allow the students to check what they have learnt and where their weaknesses are in terms of subject knowledge. Encourage them to 'triage' or rank what they know most about and what they know least when using Table 11.1. You can also use this to get them planning how much revision time they will need for these areas. The booklet incorporating these tables also includes a glossary without definitions and a list of key sociologists without any information, see Tables 11.2 and 11.3. The point of this booklet is to get students finding information themselves as they go through the unit. You can give them websites in addition to further reading to help them with this. Importantly, if the students feel they are weak in a particular area of the syllabus or if they feel they have no clue what a keyword is or who a key sociologist is, then they are aware that they should basically knuckle down to some hard study and find out.

Table 11.1 Unit reflection audit

Topic	Exam confident?	Areas of strength and/or improvement
Ownership and control of the mass media	👍 👎	
New media, culture and globalisation	👍 👎	
The mass media and audiences	👍 👎	
Media representations of ethnicity, age, social class, gender and sexuality	👍 👎	
Exam practice	👍 👎	

Table 11.2 Keyword glossary for students to complete (the actual glossary is longer)

Look at the 'readings' suggested above to help you find these words.

Keyword, etc.	Your definition
Agenda setting	
Cross-media ownership	
Diversification	
Global conglomeration	
False-class consciousness	
Hegemony	
Horizontal integration	
Media concentration	
Media conglomerate	
Vertical integration	
Synergy	
Technological convergence	
Technological compression	
Collective intelligence	

Table 11.3 Key names list that students complete (the actual list is longer)

Along with the above, litter your essays with arguments from these people. Briefly say who they are and what they are associated with.

Louis Althusser

Herbert Marcuse

Jürgen Habermas

Glasgow University Media Group

T.S. Eliot and F.R. Leavis

Birmingham Centre for
Contemporary Cultural Studies

Anthony Giddens

Peter Kellner

John Tomlinson

Elihu Katz and Paul Lazarsfeld

Denis McQuail

Ivor Crewe

Greg Philo

As the main exams approach, get students to re-read these booklets, re-evaluate their strengths and weaknesses as part of their revision planning and complete any gaps. This can lead into a formularised planning session.

Planning revision

As the exams near, students will probably want to be set less directed work in order to focus on their strengths and weaknesses. Although this suggestion is so clichéd, well used and straightforward that you may be questioning why I am stating it, it is also so useful that it merits inclusion; *get students to plan their time in a revision timetable* (for example, see Table 11.4). Of course, this means we are, in a way, still scaffolding their learning away from class and this brings into doubt how 'independent' the students really are, but many will appreciate the help in doing so.

Table 11.4 Student revision timetable

James' Revision Timetable

	Monday	Tuesday	Wednesday	Thursday	Friday	Saturday	Sunday
Period 1	Sociology (Mr. Jones)	History (Mr. Marks)	Free (Revise Sociology)	Sociology (Mr. Cahill)	History (Mr. Marks)	Revise English	Football
Period 2	Sociology (Mr. Jones)	Sociology (Mr. Cahill)	History (Miss Smith)	English lit. (Mrs. Ash)	History (Mr. Marks)	Revise History	Football
BREAK	BREAK	BREAK	BREAK	BREAK	BREAK	BREAK	BREAK
Period 3	History (Miss Smith)	Free (Revise History)	Free (Revise History)	Free (Revise History)	Free (Revise Sociology)	Revise Sociology	Football
Period 4	Free (Revise English lit.)	Free (Revise Sociology)	History (Mr. Marks)	English lit. (Mr. Roberts)	History (Miss Smith)	Revise English	Revise English
LUNCH	LUNCH	LUNCH	LUNCH	LUNCH	LUNCH	LUNCH	LUNCH
Period 5	English lit. (Mrs. Ash)	Free (Revise English lit.)	Football Coaching	Free (Revise English lit.)	English lit. (Mr. Roberts)	Revise Sociology	Revise History
BREAK	BREAK	BREAK	BREAK	BREAK	BREAK	BREAK	BREAK
Before dinner	Revise Sociology	Revise Sociology	Revise History	Revise Sociology	Revise History	Relax	Relax
After dinner	Revise English	Revise History	Revise English	Revise English	Revise English	Relax	Relax

Set up study groups or study buddies

Another idea is to set up study groups or even study buddies. Choose students who get on or are friends and encourage them to meet up and discuss their work. This is a hard one as you might not completely comprehend which students get on with each other, but it is worth trying. If the students are sixth formers, suggest they meet up in their 'frees' in the school library or quiet study room as well as at home in order to revise together, share ideas and test each other.

ICT and social networking

Many sociology departments, or more specifically, sociology teachers, use blogs or create simple websites to promote independent learning. Again, you could question how independent this really is if teachers are writing loads of text for students to access 24/7, but to be fair students really appreciate these sites and teachers can adapt the text for the students they know. These blogs and websites will be discussed in more depth in the next chapter.

Another way to combine students love of all things technological (let us accept that when we teach about new media and neophiliacs, we are really teaching about our students), is to use social networking websites/apps. Of course, this is mildly controversial and some senior leaders without much knowledge of how social networking works will panic as they will assume you will be 'friends' with the students online. However, most social networks can be used without you being 'friends' with students or 'following' them etc. Although I would avoid Facebook, Twitter is well used by teachers as you can tweet or retweet revision ideas or useful links without following or befriending your students online. So long as your twitter account is clearly professional and labelled as something sociological, it will be perceived as above board; let your line manager know what you are doing though. In addition to this, get students to social network with each other. Messenger services like WhatsApp, Snapchat and Facebook Messenger allow students to create groups where they can help each other with homework and revision etc. Although you should not get involved with these groups personally, you can encourage the students to use them amongst themselves; there is more on this in the next chapter.

Further reading

Meyer, B., Haywood, N., Sachdev, D. & Faraday, S. (2008). *What is independent learning and what are the benefits for students?* London: Department for Children, Schools and Families.
> The authors of this report give an overview of independent learning. It includes a discussion on its importance, how it can be promoted, a few ideas for getting students to be more independent and what schools can do to promote it. It is, essentially, a literature review, but it is a concise introduction nonetheless.

Cottrell, S. (2012). *The study skills handbook*. London: Palgrave Macmillan.
> This is not really written for trainee teachers or teachers' CPD, but it does contain ideas that can be applied in secondary schools and promoted by teachers for their students' benefit.

Bibliography

Cottrell, S. (2012). *The study skills handbook.* London: Palgrave Macmillan.

Meyer, B., Haywood, N., Sachdev, D. & Faraday, S. (2008). *What is independent learning and what are the benefits for students?* London: Department for Children, Schools and Families.

12 ICT, social networking and the media

This chapter includes:

- A discussion on the advantages and disadvantages of using Wikipedia to find sociological information.
- Some ideas on where to find good websites to help students with revision and research.
- Some basic guidelines for creating your own blogs and websites.
- Using Google Classroom as an effective virtual learning environment.
- How to use YouTube and podcasts to help students learn, especially away from the classroom.
- The benefits of using social networking sites to communicate with students and contact colleagues.
- The importance of the media for demonstrating the reach and importance of sociological issues.
- An explanation of how to use pop culture to engage your students.

In 2013, Ofsted issued subject specific guidance for a number of key subjects, including ICT. Here, schools were encouraged to get pupils to:

> show exceptional independence in their use of ICT across all areas of the curriculum and exhibit very positive attitudes towards ICT. They take the initiative, for example, by asking questions, carrying out their own investigations, and working constructively with others.
>
> *(Ofsted, 2013, p. 3)*

It goes without saying that if schools fulfil this guidance, students should be able to use their ICT skills to further their knowledge and understanding of sociology. In fact, unlike my own studies of sociology at A Level in the 1990s, today's GCSE and AS/A Level sociology students have a world of sociological information at their fingertips. Therefore, you should consider ways of harnessing this information as part of your students' learning, especially their directed learning, and encourage them to use the internet, social networking websites or apps and the media to further develop their understanding of the subject.

Using the internet for sociology

The internet has opened up sociological research so much that it is silly to bypass it, even at GCSE and AS/A Level. It allows students to not only access basic information on sociology through websites such as Wikipedia, but it also allows them to access academic journals and research that used to only be available in university libraries. However, despite this wealth of information, students need to be aware of the pitfalls of using the internet, particularly the possibility of accessing dubious and incorrect material as well as being warned not to plagiarise and copy material from it.

Wikipedia

Perhaps a good place to start this discussion is in relation to the most used source of information on the internet: the online encyclopaedia Wikipedia. Wikipedia has an abundance of information on sociology, such as web pages about theoretical perspectives and about key sociologists. Although some people look down their noses at Wikipedia, it is often a good source of information; for example, studies have suggested that between 47% and 70% of doctors and medical students use it in their everyday practice (Dillner, 2014) and researchers have found that the accuracy of drug information in the German version of Wikipedia was 99.7% accurate when compared to textbook data (Kräenbring et al., 2014). So, yes, it can have inaccuracies, but the bulk of its content is correct. Thus, you should be aware and not naive to the fact that your students will probably be using it as their first port of call when looking for information. In this case, it is best to let them use it for general information, but at the same time teach them how to use it effectively, especially understanding Wikipedia's own system for checking the quality of its articles. Importantly, Wikipedia makes clear that their best articles are labelled '*featured articles*', which display a small star in the upper right corner of the web page, and they also label sound and thoroughly edited pages as '*good articles*'. For example, Wikipedia's page on Karl Marx is deemed a good article whereas its entry on ethnomethodology states it has '*multiple issues*'.

Sociology and social science websites for students

Aside from the inevitability that students will be using Wikipedia to find things out, it is essential that you give students some guidance on how to use the internet for research purposes. Here, it may be worth teaching them to be aware of the credibility, reliability and possible biases of things they find. In order to do this, you can teach them to assess the credibility of a website by checking the credentials of the authors of its content, if available, as well as the site hosting the information. For instance, if it is a well-known university's website, then the information is probably worth reading and citing. The same could be said for organisations such as the BBC or 'quality' newspapers such as *The Times, Guardian* or *Economist*. Students can then ascertain the quality of the information and arguments by checking whether they have references and sources to back up any claims made. And, lastly, students need to look out for any value-laden language, assumptions that are mere conjecture and one-sidedness to ensure they are not just reading someone's biased and unsubstantiated opinion. Of course, some of the newspapers in the second point can be guilty of this, so it is worth teaching them the differences between peer-reviewed academic journals, newspapers and information websites so they are aware of their reliability.

Furthermore, there are many websites that are set up for sociology revision, but can also be useful for general study. Although I am not responsible for any content in these and they may change their access over time, my students have used these:

- BBC Bitesize GCSE Sociology: www.bbc.co.uk/education/subjects/zbbw2hv
- Revise Sociology: www.revisesociology.wordpress.com
- Bennett and Kiefer's Sociology BOOM: www.sociologyboom.tumblr.com
- Twynham School Sociology: www.sociologytwynham.com
- Sociology Central: www.sociology.org.uk

For students interested in reading further afield or attempting research, it is worth pointing them in the direction of Oxford Brookes University's web pages on sociology as there is a good list of links as well as the University of Colorado's sociology department's website. For example, see:

- Oxford Brookes: www.brookes.ac.uk/library/sociol/socioint.html
- University of Colorado: www.sociology.colorado.edu/

Although it is unlikely that your school will have access to academic journals or digital repositories like JSTOR, the UK Data Service's online data catalogue, which was discussed in Chapter 9, is helpful to those students with a real thirst for knowledge.

Task 12.1 Book a computer room

Although students can access the websites mentioned above on their phones, it is a good idea to book a computer room so that they can visit the websites via a better connection speed and larger screen.

   Prior to teaching in the computer room, visit some sociology websites and put together a quiz based on the sociological trivia students can find on them. Bring in a prize and get the students to complete the quiz. If they finish early, then they can write their own quizzes for their friends. This will allow them to become familiar with the revision and research websites out there.

Sociology and social science websites for teachers

There are a lot of websites out there offering free resources for teachers. It is best to just find some time and have a search. Many schools now share their PowerPoint slides, revision books and worksheets on their websites and these will come up if you simply put, for example, 'family and households revision' in a search engine. Nonetheless, it is well worth signing up to the *TES Online* website as it offers a whole host of shared resources for teachers. These resources are also ranked and reviewed by teachers so you get a sense of whether they are worth using. There are also sociology resources to be found on the *Guardian Teacher Network* and *Resourcd*, which was formerly called *Sociology Exchange*. Both require you to sign up. Please, please share your own resources if you join these communities as you may be surprised just how grateful colleagues in other schools will be. These sites are available at:

- www.tes.com
- www.theguardian.com/teacher-network
- www.resourcd.com

Additionally, the BSA has a sociology Teaching Group and a magazine called *The Sociology Teacher*, which can be downloaded from their website. The Teaching Group also has a resources page. Lastly, have a look at TED Talks (www.ted.com) for educational lectures and inspirational talks as well as iTunes University, which includes lectures and talks from academics at institutions such as the Open, Cambridge and Stanford Universities.

Creating your own blog or website

As you can see from the websites listed earlier, many teachers have set up their own or departmental sociology websites. In fact, many of these are actually blogs that are presented like websites, but there is a slight difference between the two. A blog is website or web page that is regularly updated with *posts*, which are written in a chatty or informal way. A website, on the other hand, is a web page or collection of web pages that share a common theme. Both blogs and websites used in education are essential as students can easily access them and, by and large, use them more than books, magazines and newspapers.

Creating blogs and websites has never been easier (see, for example, Cottrell & Morris, 2012, Chapter 5). Moreover, they are also good for networking and sharing ideas with other departments as your blog or website will eventually get recognised and used by students from other schools; so long as the content is useful to them. If you are tempted to blog or create a webpage, it is worth considering:

- **Who will host your blog or website:** some sociology departments blog or have web pages on their school's website, but you could also consider using free blogging sites, such as:
  ○ Tumblr: www.tumblr.com
  ○ Blogger: www.blogger.com
  ○ Wordpress: www.wordpress.com
- If you want to create a website, you can use the above, but also consider:
  ○ Wix: www.wix.com
  ○ Weebly: www.weebly.com
  ○ Squarespace: www.squarespace.com
  Most of these sites offer a free service and fee based upgrades. There are loads of other hosting sites out there, too.
- **What you will call your blog or website:** you might want to use a name that can also be your blog or website's web address or domain name. For example, the domain name of the BBC website is www.bbc.co.uk. However, if you want a common name for your blog or website, such as *A Level Sociology*, you will find that www.alevelsociology.com is already taken (interestingly, as I write www.gcsesociology.com is still available). Despite this, you can check to see whether your chosen name is available on other domains, such as .org or .net (as I write there is no www.alevelsociology.org). As a rule of thumb, web addresses or domain names ending in .com tend to be commercial; those ending in .org tend to be non-profit organisations;

and those ending in .net tend to focus on communications or social networking. If you want to secure a domain name, your hosting site may charge you to register your domain name.

- **The design of your blog or website:** many blogging websites and web page hosting sites may be free, but they may charge you for their more flamboyant styles or formats. Nonetheless, if you are simply putting information on there for revision, homework tasks and interesting topics, you can always keep it simple and free.
- **Publicising and promoting your blog or website:** do not be too afraid to do this. If you spend time on your blog or website and feel it will benefit people, it is worth getting as many people to read it as possible to make it all worthwhile. When I started blogging, I did feel a bit uneasy at seeming self-important and egotistical, but I know students use my posts. I also hide behind my department by avoiding any reference to myself. Therefore, tell your students to use your blog or website for homework and tweet your posts or web pages; even put them on Facebook and use other social networking tools to get them out there.

Task 12.2 Write a blog

Using the websites suggested above, set up a sociology blog. Simply choose the blogging service that seems the easiest to use and write about something that could be useful to your students. This could include:

- additional notes on the homework task you set;
- a weekly biography on a sociologist;
- a review of what was discussed in class;
- some comments on an issue in the news that relates to sociology.

Google Classroom

Although Google has its critics and many sociology teachers may be predisposed to question its *hegemony* in terms of dominating information technology (aside from Microsoft and its Office programs, Google is everywhere in education from its all-powerful search engine and Chrome web browser to YouTube and Google Scholar), it does have – quite simply – some excellent tools for bringing technology into the classroom.

First and foremost is Google Classroom, which is basically a virtual learning environment that is very easy to use. It allows teachers to post lesson materials, such as PowerPoints and worksheets, on a web page that is only available to the students the teacher has invited. Moreover, it also allows teachers to create, collect, mark and return assignments electronically. Therefore, it is useful to teachers of sociology who have vast amounts of information to share with students and plenty of essays and other assignments to set and collect in. In addition to these practical applications for teachers, Google Classroom allows students to comment on resources the teacher posts and allows the students themselves to share pieces of work, which can be moderated by the teacher. Students can also respond to sociological issues more generally as the virtual classroom can facilitate discussion on topics addressed in actual class. Furthermore, it can allow online collaboration if you use Google Docs, Slides and other Google products available through Google Drive, which is Google's online storage and synchronisation service.

However, Google Classroom does require you to sign up to its G Suit for Education, which is free, but you may need to pass this by your senior leadership team or network manager before using it with your students. Of course, there are other platforms out there, such as Doddle Learn and Show My Homework, but the benefit of using Google Classroom is that it combines so many of its other products so easily, including YouTube (discussed below). To find out more visit: www. classroom.google.com.

YouTube and podcasts

In addition to virtual classrooms, blogs and websites, both you and your students can use YouTube and podcasts to research information, revise and even upload videos. As everybody now knows, YouTube gives you access to millions of homemade videos, archived video footage, TV clips, music videos and movie trailers as well as thousands of educational videos, school projects and video blogs that often centre on sociological issues. Like anything on the internet, some of this is useful and a lot is not, but your students will be using it regardless. Nevertheless, I use YouTube to engage students, often using seemingly random comedy clips, TV clips or music videos that have some mild link or connection to what we are studying. I have also found lots of interviews with sociologists discussing ideas as well as useful documentaries. Moreover, many teachers are now uploading homemade revision videos onto YouTube and some students are putting useful project work on there. A good example for A-Level sociology is a YouTube channel set up by Steve Barrett, which has plenty of lessons on topics from various units; to find this simply search 'Steve Barrett sociology' on YouTube. There are plenty of similar channels, too.

Podcasts are audio files or video files you share through the internet. The idea originates with a 'playable on demand' (Pod) 'broadcast' (cast) and is often associated with the development of Apple's iPod. However, although you can download podcasts from Apple's iTunes, you can now make them yourself with the simple recording equipment on any standard laptop, smartphone or even an audio recorder with a USB cable. After saving your recording as an MP3 or MP4 file, you simply upload it to your blog, website or even a social networking site. A sociological podcast could include an audio description of a concept or even a recording of a lesson. If you use a video file instead, you can also upload your file to YouTube.

There are a couple of negatives here, especially if your students know you are using podcasts of lessons. For instance, some negatives could include students not bothering to find the information themselves as well as your lessons becoming a correspondence course. Also, it is important to be aware of copyright if you are posting audio recordings or videos. Any text you read out, music you use in the background, images you use or video clips you use may be copyrighted material.

Social networking

As highlighted in the previous section, many sociology departments and sociology teachers now use social networking websites or smartphone apps to communicate ideas to students and to connect and share best practice with other departments and colleagues. There are dangers with the appropriation of social networking to communicate with students, especially as you could be seen to be too friendly and too informal in your approach to student-teacher interactions. Nonetheless, most social networks can be used purely to send out information without you becoming 'friends' with students or 'following' them. You can, however, become friends and follow other departments, fellow teachers and textbook writers as well as a fair number of sociologists. Good social networking websites and apps for teachers include *Twitter*, which allows you to 'tweet' snappy 140-character messages that are especially useful for students during the revision period, or *LinkedIn*, which is arguably better for professional networking. Some educationalists have used *Instagram* to send pictures of mind maps, graphs and charts, but I would be wary of connecting with students through this network as it focuses on pictures and videos. Accounts for these can be set up at:

- *Twitter*: www.twitter.com
- *LinkedIn*: www.linkedin.com
- *Instagram*: www.instagram.com

There are other ways to network through chatrooms on *TES Online* as well as other educational websites. There are also education specific social networking websites and apps out there, but too often students bypass these in favour of the networks they prefer.

You could also encourage your students to use social networking to revise together and set up revision groups. Social networking websites and apps that can be used for this purpose include:

- *Whatsapp*: www.whatsapp.com
- *Snapchat*: www.snapchat.com
- *Facebook Messenger*: www.messenger.com

As stated in the last chapter, you should not get involved with these student groups personally as you will put yourself at risk. Also, you should remind students of the dangers of cyberbullying and how to be safe on the internet – even if they are sixth-formers. Another precaution is limiting these ideas to older students, informing parents of what you are doing and flagging up any use of the above social networking ideas with your line manager. Lastly, double check your school's child protection policies to ensure you are fully aware of any guidance they offer on the use of ICT and social networking in relation to your responsibilities as a teacher.

The media

Even if you choose not to use the media as an area of study, you should use it as a teaching resource. In addition to newspapers, magazines and journals, there is so much content out there on the radio, TV and internet that address sociological issues. In the mainstream media there are news channels and current affairs programmes that address the social and political issues studied in sociology. Some of the best current affairs programmes include the BBC's *Panorama*, *Question Time* and *Daily Politics*. There are, of course, good equivalents on other channels. From time to time it is worth recording documentaries or seeing if they are available on the channels streaming websites or YouTube. Good examples include BBC3's *Poor Kids* and Channel 4's *Children on the Breadline*. I have used these in lessons on child poverty.

Another great, if underestimated, asset for sociology teachers is BBC Radio. BBC Radio 4 and 5 have plenty of news and current affairs programmes that are useful, but some stand out. For example, BBC Radio 4's *Thinking Allowed* is dedicated to sociological issues and is presented by the sociologist turned broadcaster Laurie Taylor. The same station's *In Our Time* has included programmes on Marx, Weber and the Frankfurt School. These are really good for dedicated students with a deep interest in the subject.

Pop culture

The biggest obstacle you will face when encouraging your students to watch *Question Time* or listen to *Thinking Allowed* is their possible lack of interest. Many students will see these programmes as dry and alien. They may well prefer to listen to music and watch films in their spare time. Perhaps they should, they are – after all – still children. However, it is a really good idea to use *pop culture* in your lessons to engage students. Pop culture is defined as popular culture that is particularly used by the young. I have mentioned this before, but my colleagues and I often use music videos to engage students, especially if there are social issues addressed in them. Although you must be wary of explicit lyrics, songs such as *Common People* by Pulp could be used to introduce lessons on class stereotypes whereas songs like *Julie* by The Levellers can be used to introduce issues surrounding child poverty. Be clever here – find out what your students like so that you can engage them. Also, be brave – be prepared to listen to things you may not initially like. Other good uses of pop culture can include comedy clips, interviews with famous people, such as Russell Brand, and soap operas and films that address social issues. For more on this, see Jones (2013).

Further reading

Cottrell, S. & Morris, N. (2012). *Study skills connected: Using technology to support your studies*. London: Palgrave Macmillan.

Although this book is designed for university students, it is a really useful primer for teachers unsure of using ICT and internet based technology. It covers everything from using virtual learning environments to voting handsets as well as elaborating on the sort of ideas touched on in this chapter, such as setting up blogs and producing podcasts.

Bibliography

Cottrell, S. & Morris, N. (2012). *Study skills connected: Using technology to support your studies*. London: Palgrave Macmillan.

Dillner, L. (2014, June 1). Is Wikipedia a reliable source for medical advice? *The Guardian*. Retrieved from www. theguardian.com/lifeandstyle/2014/jun/01/is-wikipedia-reliable-for-medical-advice

Jones, A. (2013, February 20). High culture versus pop culture: which is best for engaging students? *The Guardian*. Retrieved from www.theguardian.com/teacher-network/teacher-blog/2013/feb/20/pop-culture-teaching-learning-engaging-students

Kräenbring, J., Monzon Penza, T., Gutmann, J., Muehlich, S., Zolk, O., Wojnowski, L., Maas, R., Engelhardt, S. & Sarikas, A. (2014). Accuracy and completeness of drug information in Wikipedia: A comparison with standard textbooks of pharmacology. *PLoS ONE, 9*(9), e106930. doi:10.137/journal.pone.0106930

Ofsted. (2013). *Information and communication technology (ICT) survey visits*. Manchester: Ofsted.

13 Political bias and controversial issues

This chapter includes:

- The 1996 Education Act
- The importance of being aware of your own biases and balancing competing political views
- Some ground rules for debating controversial issues
- A brief word on prevent duty and safeguarding
- Some teaching methods that can be used for teaching controversial issues

One problem we face as sociology teachers is maintaining an objective view of the competing perspectives we teach and discuss in class. This can be hard on two counts: firstly, we may simply find one theoretical perspective more convincing than another and feel there is more empirical evidence to back up the theoretical arguments. Secondly, we may have certain political views that make us more sympathetic to a particular theory. For example, a member of the Labour Party may feel ideologically aligned to neo-Marxist or social democratic views, whereas a Conservative may feel more sympathetic to the arguments of functionalists or the new right.

Rules on the political views of teachers

It is important to remember that the 1996 Education Act forbids the promotion of partisan political views in schools. Although this does not completely prevent you from giving your political view, school governors, head teachers and local education authorities have a responsibility to ensure that teachers offer a balanced presentation of opposing political views. Therefore, sociology teachers need to be aware of their own biases whilst teaching theoretical perspectives and social policy to ensure they do not regularly promote one over the other. This includes considering the extent to which we air our political views, voting intentions and views of politicians in class. Students are interested to know our views and many will see us as a source of authority. In this sense, our views can be more pervasive than we may give ourselves credit for. Subsequently, Huddleston (2003) offers some practical advice for teaching about political issues, including:

- giving equal importance to conflicting views;
- presenting these views as open to interpretation, qualification and contradiction;
- to make sure we do not present our views as if they are facts;
- not giving our own accounts of the views of others, but letting others' opinions speak for themselves;
- avoiding facial expressions, gestures and tones of voice that may prejudice a point of view;
- establishing a classroom climate in which students are free to express their own views without fear.

Nevertheless, you will have to balance this with the need to be honest and open about your views, especially if asked. I would suggest telling students what you believe, but then emphasising that it is a personal view and that they must make up their own minds. You should then acknowledge that others' views have their strengths and that your views have their weaknesses. Also, avoid getting bogged down with these discussions and move the subject on as soon as possible. Alternatively, there is nothing wrong with keeping your views to yourself and sticking to the content. Your reaction depends on your relationship with students; do you discuss your life and opinions or remain a mystery?

Contrary to what many assume, students are allowed to be politically active in school so long as they are over 12 years old. This means students can set up Amnesty International groups and campaign on political issues, such as lowering the voting age to 16. However, as a teacher it is best to simply facilitate this and offer them support with rooming or slots in assemblies as opposed to leading and organising the campaigns yourself; even if you feel as strongly as they do.

In many ways sociology fulfils many of the requirements of the government's *British Values* policy (DfE, 2014), especially if students are engaged in political, social and moral debates on key issues such as welfare reform, immigration and the future of the NHS. The values of democracy, rule of law, individual liberty, mutual respect and tolerance are all exhibited if students participate in sociological discussions in a responsible and respectful manner. Moreover, this also aids students' spiritual, moral, social and cultural (SMSC) development as they learn to understand, listen to and respect each other's different views on these issues.

Teaching controversial issues

The government's Advisory Group on Citizenship (1998) defined a controversial issue as '...an issue about which there is no one fixed or universally held point of view. Such issues are those which commonly divide society and for which significant groups offer conflicting explanations and solutions' (p. 56). Although the Advisory Group advocated teaching these issues, some commentators have suggested that students should not be exposed to controversial issues at all. For example, Scruton, Ellis-Jones and O'Keefe (1985) have argued that political and social issues should not be taught to children under 16 years old, which would rule out much of the content in sociology at GCSE (as cited in Cowan & Maitles, 2012, p. 2). Despite disagreeing with this point of view, I would stress the importance of a thoughtful approach to these sensitive issues.

As evident in the GCSE and AS/A Level syllabuses, sociology is full of controversial issues. From issues such as mental health and immigration to domestic violence and alcoholism, it is chock-a-block with emotive issues that can really get debate going and feelings running high. Although this has its benefits for engaging students in debate, it also needs to be facilitated with sensitivity and care. There will be students in your class that have been affected by the issues we teach. In my own career, I have taught students with family members in prison, who had committed suicide or were going through difficult divorces; I am sure you have or will, too. It is important to also remember that these social issues are not only related to students from more difficult backgrounds, but can potentially affect students from any background. However, it is absolutely essential that we do not shy away from these subjects as they are part of the social world we are teaching. The Advisory Group on Citizenship (1998) summed this up nicely by stating that, 'Education should not attempt to shelter our nation's children from even the harsher controversies of adult life, but should prepare them to deal with controversies knowledgably, sensibly, tolerantly and morally' (p. 56). This can be applied to sociology as it covers a lot of similar ground to citizenship education.

Some ground rules for teaching controversial issues

It is important, then, that we endeavour to teach controversial issues whilst maintaining some ground rules for both ourselves and our students.

Firstly, teachers should be aware of their students' home life as far as is possible. Of course, child protection issues are dealt with through school policies and may not necessarily be shared with you, but it is important to liaise with heads of year or sixth form so that you are aware of any issues at home that may upset certain students or lead to issues in class. If there are controversial issues coming up, it may be sensible to:

- send a letter home at the start of the unit;
- notify heads of year or sixth form;
- discuss any students that may be affected with form tutors, heads of year and sixth form;
- delicately let potentially affected students know of the topics coming up;
- offer an alternative place to learn if they feel uneasy with the content;
- calling home to discuss the situation with parents (this point may be very sensitive and must be done in consultation with the school's pastoral staff to avoid making matters worse);
- familiarise yourself with the students social, cultural and religious backgrounds to ensure that any issues involving race or religious beliefs take these students into account.

Secondly, we should set clear ground rules for discussion and debate on these issues. These apply to us as much as they do the students. Ground rules for dealing with controversial issues include:

- no calling out;
- no interrupting others;
- no name-calling;
- no crude stereotyping;
- no personal attacks;
- avoidance of value-laden language;
- no sarcasm.

Moreover, it is then worth emphasising some other general rules, such as encouraging:

- thinking before speaking (perhaps facilitate this);
- active listening;
- a focus on empirical facts or theoretical ideas, not emotions;
- an avoidance of over-simplifications of complex issues;
- a student-teacher agreement that when you end the discussion, it must end.

You could also facilitate time out for students who get too emotionally charged in debate. This could be a whole class period of reflection or a written exercise to calm them down. You should also give space to students, especially sixth formers, who are clearly upset. Perhaps let your student support centre or lead teachers know so that the student can sit out the rest of the lesson if they find the topic too much; some schools have rooms set aside for this.

Prevent duty and safeguarding

Since July 2015 all schools and colleges must adhere to the statutory guidance on preventing radicalisation and extremism in schools. This is a duty under section 26 of the Counter-Terrorism and Security Act 2015. Better known as the *prevent duty*, many teachers have undergone training to spot potential radicalisation and extremist sympathies in schools. This could include extreme religious, political or prejudiced points of view. It is essentially a safeguarding framework and I would advise you to follow your school's policy guidelines if you are concerned by any extreme views held by your students.

It is also important that you read and follow your schools more general safeguarding and child protection policies so that you act straight away if any issues crop up in class. This protects both yourself and, more importantly, your students. Another document worth reading is the equality policy as it may contain guidelines for dealing with racist, sexist or homophobic incidents.

Teaching methods

As these issues will inevitability be tackled through discussion, it is useful to use some of the discussion techniques mentioned in Chapter 6. More specifically, if you wanted to add your view, you could use the *committed participant model* where the teacher will act the part of a committed participant if needed. However, Hayward (2011) suggests that you should ensure students have time to think about and then challenge your opinion. If this is done, then you must be able to take criticism and not become overly defensive. Also, it is important that students are in a 'suitable intellectual and psychological position to be able to do this' (p. 1), which suggests that your involvement depends on the maturity of the class.

On the other hand, if you want to avoid giving your opinions, you can use the *neutral judge model*, where the teacher is the objective manager of the discussion or overtly play *devil's advocate*. In the latter model you would be acknowledging your role and emphasising that any opinions are not your own. For more on facilitating discussion, please see Chapter 6.

Further reading

Cowan, P. & Maitles, H. (Eds.). (2012). *Teaching controversial issues in the classroom: Key issues and debates.* **London: Continuum.**

> This book gives theoretical insights and practical guidance on the complexities of teaching controversial issues. Although not aimed at sociology teachers *per se*, it covers key issues and topic areas relevant to most sociological syllabuses, including racism, discrimination and globalisation.

Huddleston, T. (2003). *Teaching about controversial issues: Guidance for schools,* **London: Citizenship Foundation. Retrieved from www.citizenshipfoundation.org.uk/lib_ res_pdf/0118.pdf**

> A short, but useful guide on teaching controversial issues that covers issues related to the 1996 Education Act. Despite being written for citizenship teachers, the advice can easily be applied to sociology as the syllabuses are often similar.

Department for Education. (2015). *The prevent duty: Departmental advice for schools and childcare providers.* **London: Department of Education.**

> If you are unsure about the prevent strategy in schools, it is worth reading the government's statutory guidelines. Yes, the strategy is controversial, but it is best seen as part of wider safeguarding policy and you should be aware of what it means for teachers.

Bibliography

Advisory Group on Citizenship. (1998). *Education for citizenship and the teaching of democracy in schools.* London: Department for Education.

Cowan, P. & Maitles, H. (Eds.). (2012). *Teaching controversial issues in the classroom: Key issues and* debates. London: Continuum.

Department for Education. (2014). *Guidance on promoting British values in schools* [Press release]. Retrieved from www.gov.uk/government/news/guidance-on-promoting-british-values-in-schools-published

Department for Education. (2015). *The prevent duty: Departmental advice for schools and childcare providers.* London: Department of Education.

Hayward, J. (2011). *Teaching controversial issues.* Retrieved from www.amnesty.org.uk/sites/default/files/teaching_controversial_issues_2.pdf

Huddleston, T. (2003). *Teaching about controversial issues: Guidance for schools.* Retrieved from www.citizenshipfoundation.org.uk/lib_res_pdf/0118.pdf

Scruton, R., Ellis-Jones, A. & O'Keefe, D. (1985). *Education and indoctrination.* Harrow: Education Research Centre.

Last words

I hope that you have found the suggestions in this book useful. Sociology is such an important subject that it needs to be taught by outstanding practitioners who can really inspire and motivate students to take an interest and become active in the society around them.

At the start of the book, I suggested that Durkheim's writings on education can be used as a *modus operandi* for teaching sociology. As we have now reached the end of the book, I would like to briefly revisit his ideas to justify their inclusion.

Firstly, Durkheim said that education should provide students with *specialist skills*. Although all subjects do this to some degree, sociology thoroughly equips students with the skills of selection, interpretation, analysis and evaluation amongst others. This was highlighted in both Chapters 2 and 6 and echoed throughout the book. Moreover, the theoretical depth of the subject, as emphasised in both Chapters 3 and 7, means that these skills are applied to complex abstract arguments. Applying them in this way will deepen students' higher order thinking skills, which has positive knock-on effects for other subjects. Furthermore, the central role of research methods in the subject extends students' specialist skills by giving them a comprehensive overview of how to design, conduct and analyse research on the social world they live in. This was discussed at length in Chapter 8.

Secondly, Durkheim also argued that one of the key functions of education was to create *social solidarity*. Undoubtedly, the topics taught in sociology, which were listed in Chapter 2, affect us all and any discussion on them can lead to students being better informed about others' personal troubles and how these become public issues; in turn, studying these troubles and issues can develop students sociological imagination, as championed by Mills (1959). Subsequently, Chapter 3 gave an account of possible sociological pedagogies that could develop the sociological imagination in varying ways. The connecting theme amongst these pedagogies was an overriding concern with understanding other people as well as their and our place in society as a whole. Although sociology contains conflicting perspectives, it is this concern with others in relation to ourselves that can lead to a better understanding of our shared norms and values and, of course, some element of social solidarity when it comes to acknowledging society's problems and why these should concern us all.

Thirdly, Durkheim saw school as a *mini-society* as it prepares children for adulthood through the processes of secondary socialisation. This is no more evident than in the sociology classroom. Despite the need for solidarity in recognising that a healthy society is important to us all, sociology exposes students to the different theoretical perspectives on how to do this. Therefore, sociological debates in the classroom will mirror the social and political debates adults have in living rooms, pubs, council chambers and parliament. Importantly, Chapter 7 aimed to give you the skills to help students better understand the different theoretical and ideological approaches to solving society's problems. Chapters 11, 12 and 13 gave advice on how you can widen this debate and be wary of how you influence the students.

Lastly, Chapters 9 and 10 were designed to further your own skills as a practitioner so that you can plan outstanding lessons and inspire the next generation of budding sociologists and active citizens. This is essential as the subject you teach is so important that without it we would all be worse off. To finish on a quote from Mills (1959), we should do this because:

> It is the political task of the social scientist – as of any liberal educator – continually to translate personal troubles into public issues, and public issues into the terms of their human meaning for a variety of individuals. It is his task to display in his work – and, as an educator, in his life as well – this kind of *sociological imagination*. And it is his purpose to cultivate such habits of mind among the men and women who are publicly exposed to him. To secure these ends is to secure reason and individuality, and to make these the predominant values of a democratic society.
>
> *Mills*, The Sociological Imagination *(1959, p. 187)*

Index

Locators for figures are in *italics* and those for tables in **bold.**